This photograph shows Exeter Corporation 47 (BFJ 157) undergoing the obligatory tilt-test, in the end bay of Brislington tram depot – a tram car can be seen to the right. Very often a pendulum device was carried to record the degree of tilt for the photographer, but there is no such device in this case. However, in a contemporary press report using a photograph from in front of the bus, the angle of the base platform from the horizontal was shown as 28 degrees.

# COACHWORK
## BY
# BRISTOL TRAMWAYS

## ALLAN MACFARLANE

## MILLSTREAM BOOKS

WORKS
BRISLINGTON
BRISTOL

4 TON 31-SEATER OMNIBUS.

2 TON 20-SEATER OMNIBUS.

4 TON LORRY

First published in 1999 by Millstream Books, 18 The Tyning, Bath BA2 6AL

Set in Times New Roman and printed in Great Britain by The Amadeus Press, Huddersfield, West Yorkshire

© Allan Macfarlane 1999

ISBN 0948975520

British Library Cataloguing-in-Publication Data: a catalogue record for this book is available from The British Library

# Contents

The photographs which appear in this book are, I believe, credited correctly in the captions. Some, however, I have bought during the past 40 years, so I have credited these as best I can. I am very grateful to the photographers for enabling their work to be made available. Where no credit is shown beneath the caption, these are prints made directly from the Bristol Tramways & Carriage Company negatives. The illustrations on pages 161, 162 and 169 were drawn by Phil Sposito.

# Preface

It seems I have always been mad about buses – indeed, when I was only three, my father acknowledged my passion by making me a wooden model of a green Bristol bus for Christmas! That was in 1948. My interest was probably germinated by the fact that single-deckers owned by the Bristol Tramways & Carriage Company passed our front gate, going up our road on the hour and back down at twenty-past. They were working the 25D, a town service in Clevedon, which is on the north Somerset coast about twelve miles from Bristol.

I would hardly ever miss watching a bus pass the house and soon I began to appreciate the differences in detail between each bus. There were two basic categories. The more old-fashioned had tiny windscreens, a shallow destination box showing just one name, and steps up to a hinged door at the front. The other, more modern, buses had much more cream paintwork encircling the side windows and advertisement panels, much larger destination boxes, and a rear entrance. Besides that, there were all sorts of differences among the latter buses, especially relating to the shape of their sliding ventilators ... and make no mistake, these shapes were vital in enabling me to identify the bus! Some of the vents had rounded upper corners (which I used to call 'round bits') while others had square upper corners ('square bits'). It didn't end there because there were different shapes of 'round bits' and different depths of 'square bits'! And then some with 'square bits' had round corners to the fixed window beneath the vents – unending variety! What I was in fact looking at every day was a mixture of 1946- to 1950-vintage Bristol L-Types bodied by Eastern Coach Works and pre-war Bristol J-Types with post-war bodies built by BBW ... the 1947- to 1951-Style bodies referred to elsewhere in this book.

The 25D had just the one bus allocated, on a daily basis, but along the bottom of our road there was also the 25C, so as I got a little older I would have to find out what bus was working that route. At the age of five, in 1950, I started using the buses almost daily to get to school. Inside the buses I detected other differences between the types, despite their standardised layout, such as the shapes of the seats, the position and pattern of the bells, and the material or paint finish to the underside of the parcel shelves and ceiling. I can just recall Bristol B-Types built in the early 1930s, certainly recalling rearward-facing seats alongside the front door.

Even with such variety the BBW bodies were the objects of greater fascination for me. I do not know how old I was when I first read the plate above the rear doorway, 'Coachwork by The Bristol Tramways & Carriage Company',

but many, many of my questions were answered in about 1953 when I bought a copy of the 1949 Ian Allan booklet, *ABC of Bristol Tramways*.

In 1958 our family moved to the Westbury-on-Trym area of Bristol, a city where modern double-deckers dominated. I attended Cotham Grammar School and here, for the first time, I met others with an interest in buses. Before long we started to visit the depots of Bristol Omnibus Company (as it had just become) and organised our first conducted tour of the main works at Lawrence Hill depot, in April 1959. This was a memorable occasion. I had already become only too well aware that the BBW-bodied J- and L-Types on which I had been brought up were fast disappearing. Here, at Lawrence Hill, were some of the last few, laid up, forlorn and dejected and I felt quite saddened, as if losing some old friends. But other things were going on inside the works. The memory is clear of the 1950-Style BBW body from J-Type 2060 freshly re-mounted on the post-war L-Type chassis of 2188. Furthermore it was undergoing reconfiguration as a front-entrance bus, being adapted for the latest type of fare-collection ... 'one-man-operation'.

Having written to the editor of the Ian Allan magazine *Buses Illustrated* in 1958 with questions about some of the more unusual Bristol buses that I was beginning to see, such as the prototype Lodekka, my reply actually came from Michael Tozer, to whom my letter had been passed. Mike evidently appreciated I already had a sound knowledge of Bristol buses and, after more correspondence, he invited me to go round for a chat one evening and to look through his collection of photographs. I could hardly believe what I saw! Mike possessed hundreds of photos and his records of BT&CC's buses had me totally amazed!

Mike became a source of great encouragement and during our 40 years of friendship he has always been a tremendous help when I have carried out historical research. He has more recently concentrated his interest on the earliest Bristol buses and has amassed a remarkably comprehensive collection of photographs. For this book, Mike willingly devoted a lot of his time to helping my detailed researches; we spent several enjoyable hours over my draft, having fun proving that a certain bus was what it was alleged to be – or otherwise, or course! – or ascertaining how many of such-and-such a type of bus were actually built. Mike also read my draft and I have happily incorporated his suggested revisions. So, first of all, I would like to record a big thank-you to Michael Tozer.

As time went on, I got to know others dedicated to researching Bristol-built vehicles, such as George Vowles, the late Peter Hulin, Peter Davey, Dave Withers, Phil Sposito and the late Roy Gingell. Geoff Bruce and I spent many an evening with the late Dennis Howell, and I made extensive copies of his records of BT&CC buses, paying particular attention to the dates he showed the buses as being rebodied by BBW.

In 1965 I was working in the Sales Office of Bristol Commercial Vehicles Ltd, the builders of the Bristol chassis I had admired for so long. One day, the telephone rang in my office. It was someone from one of the other departments, who knew I was a bit of a 'bus freak', to tell me that on clearing out an old store cupboard they had found a wooden case full of old glass-plate negatives; would I like to have a quick look, see if there's anything worth keeping, otherwise throw them out? What I looked upon was unbelievable! Here were the negatives of a host of official photographs of Bristol-built buses – and consequently bodied by BBW – ranging from the early 1900s to the middle of the 1930s. One or two were familiar to me, but BCV had not kept a collection of the prints. It was agreed, therefore, to get the negatives reprinted and for me to be custodian. There were so many that the process was nowhere near complete by the time I changed employers and eventually, in 1983, the factory closed down. Thankfully, someone had succeeded in rescuing the negatives!

Back in 1938, George Vowles had founded The Bristol Interest Circle with Peter Hulin, to provide an organisation for recording details of Bristol buses at work throughout the country. From 1949, George, Michael Tozer and Mike Mogridge took turns to edit the B.I.C.'s *West Country Transport Bulletin*, until pressures on their free time caused the magazine to cease in 1953. Twenty years later, I started a magazine dedicated to recording the events of the last few Bristol KSW-Type buses left at work around the country, under the auspices of The KSW Club. It was with great pride that I welcomed several members of the former B.I.C. into the ranks. Once the KSWs had run their last, however, it was agreed that our new magazine, *Bristol Passenger*, should be devoted to all models of Bristol. The name KSW Club was no longer relevant, so in 1984, with the willing encouragement of the founders and editors of the B.I.C., I resurrected the name The Bristol Interest Circle. In 1998 we have been celebrating the B.I.C.'s Silver Jubilee!

I have made many friends through the B.I.C. One of special significance in the context of this book is Maurice Doggett, the leading authority on Eastern Coach Works and whose photographic history of the company has been published in three volumes; because of the strong similarity between BBW and ECW bodies since 1947, it will be seen that I recommend readers of this book to refer to Maurice's excellent ECW histories.

Another valued friend is Mike Colson. I launched an appeal through *Bristol Passenger* for any information readers had about BBW and found Mike was a man after my own heart, as it were – he has also had a special interest in BBW bodywork! Mike, though, had first-hand knowledge of the bodies built since the 1920s. Mike is also blessed with an artistic talent and had made detailed, coloured drawings of BBW-bodied BT&CC buses – a valuable insight from the days before colour photography became established. While many members of the original B.I.C. visited BT&CC's sites and made hand-written copies of their records, Mike specialised in the BBW aspect and even found bodyworks records that, possibly, no-one else studied. From one or two old catalogues in my possession I had been aware that BBW had issued code-letters or designations to some body styles, but I had no idea of the extent. Mike had it all written out! I consider that the codes are a vital part of the BBW story and special thanks go to Mike for sharing with me his detailed records, as well as his affection for BBW bodies.

Allen Janes is another with a specialist interest, though in Allen's case it is the earliest Bristol buses, dating from 1907-1915. He has made studies of old photographs in minute detail, to discover the intricacies of the workings of the chassis as much as body construction. He has also made selective copies of the Trade Press of the day that carried descriptive articles about Bristol's products. These reports appeared quite frequently and were seldom short of praise for Bristol. In contrast, Allen has also devoted much time to studying Bristol's lorries of (in particular) the 1950/60s, being joined in this by Phil Sposito; the culmination of this study was their publication of a book, which has been a valuable reference work for me. Many thanks go to Allen for his assistance and especially for checking the draft of my captions covering the period up to 1915.

Beside the friends acknowledged above, there are several people I wish to thank for their willingness to lend photographs from their collections and to spare me the time to delve into their records. These include Dave Withers and Phil Sposito (who deserve special thanks for reprinting hosts of negatives, often at short notice), Peter Davey (who also reprinted some of the photos taken by his late father, S. Miles Davey), Bob Crawley (an acknowledged expert on Western/Southern National buses) and Chris Taylor (an expert on the south Wales operators), together with Gavin Booth, Graham Brooks, Geoff Bruce, Geoff Green, Martin Curtis, Paul Lacey, Dilwyn Rees, George Robbins and Alan Townsin. I must acknowledge the PSV Circle, who have published various listings of Bristol chassis, together with Fleet Histories of BT&CC and others, to which I have referred frequently during my research. Another word of thanks goes to those who have bought old buses for preservation and, in so doing, have restored some BBW bodies for present and future generations to admire.

My final word of thanks is reserved for my wife Anne, and our three teenage children, for being so tolerant of the long hours I have spent working on this book in my study.

Allan Macfarlane,
Westbury-on-Trym, Bristol, April 1999

# Introduction

In the later decades of the nineteenth century, it would appear that the Western World was in the grip of 'tramway fever'. In busy towns and cities across the continents entrepreneurs or groups of businessmen were investigating the potential of this new form of street travel. In the British Isles, the first street tram ran in 1860, in Birkenhead. It was operated by George Francis Train (of all names!) and received much publicity, due in no small part to the flamboyant Mr Train himself.

It was only a matter of time before Bristol City Council was asked to look into the possibilities of running trams in that city. This proposal was raised in 1871 by a group of London businessmen, acting through a firm of Bristol solicitors, Stanley & Wasbrough. The council opposed the application, preferring to consider running trams on their own account. They even got as far as laying tracks along Whiteladies Road in 1873/74, but faced with rapidly increasing prices in the materials, they concluded that the cost of operating a tramway themselves would seem unjustifiably high in the eyes of their ratepayers.

Bristol City Council therefore enquired of local businessmen whether the tramway could be taken over as a private venture. It was the firm of solicitors Stanley & Wasbrough that received instructions to form a syndicate and the responsibility for organisation was entrusted to their very young yet promising Bankruptcy Clerk, George White. Accordingly, in December 1874, The Bristol Tramways Company Ltd was set up, George White being the Company Secretary, duties which doubled as Managing Director.

At the official opening of the Whiteladies Road line in August 1875, the leading car was conducted by Charles Challenger, who was later to rise to Traffic Manager, a position he was to hold for 37 years. Even after retirement Challenger was appointed a director. In both George White and Charles Challenger, together with James Clifton Robinson who was engineer and one-time General Manager, the Tramways Company was blessed with three visionary, progressive and enterprising businessmen. George White, in particular, became a highly respected and talented financier and a successful Stockbroker; he had his own financial interests (often in a controlling capacity) in several railway companies in the Bristol and South Wales area.

**1.** Rhondda Transport's five 1928 L1-Type Bristol Bs (see Plate 103) are lined up here in Brislington Tram Depot. The company's commercial artist would skilfully eliminate the background for publicity photographs, but the sight of the overhead wiring, traction poles and ornate lamp standards adds immensely to the flavour of this view.

White and Clifton Robinson held the posts of Chairman and Managing Director of other tramway companies, including Imperial Tramways (with systems at Reading, Middlesbrough and Dublin, together with the Corris Railway at Machynlleth) and they also launched London United Tramways, which was to grow to great prominence.

In 1886, the Bristol Cab Company was formed, three of the four Directors being also on the Board of the Bristol Tramways Company. The Bristol Cab Company aimed to bring organisation to the miscellany of poorly conducted carriage and cab services in Bristol; as it happened, all the city's funeral undertakings came under their control as well! The Bristol Cab Company rapidly brought much improved standards and quality, with a fine fleet of carriages in a dignified blue livery and driven by uniformed drivers. On 1st October 1887 the two firms, the Bristol Cab Company and the Bristol Tramways Company, merged to create the Bristol Tramways & Carriage Company Limited.

George White continued to steer the BT&CC and in 1900 was appointed Chairman. Of greater tribute was the bestowing of a Baronetcy by King Edward VII in His Majesty's 1904 Birthday Honours; henceforth the company's Chairman was titled Sir George White.

Significantly, in keeping with the progressive attitude of the company's directors, Bristol's tram system had been one of the first in the country to commence conversion from horse to overhead electric power, in 1895. Similarly, in 1904, Bristol Tramways took the bold step of agreeing to introduce motor buses to the city, despite the internal combustion engine still being in its infancy at the time. A fleet of one dozen Thornycroft motor buses duly took to the road from January 1906.

The motor buses were initially housed in part of the spacious and specially built electric tram depot at Brislington, which had been opened in 1900. The administrative building fronting Bath Road was designed to be imposing in typical BT&CC manner. It included a high central archway through which all trams and buses were to pass. Beyond was a long but narrow yard, with the running sheds along one side (Bloomfield Road was built beyond the wall on the other side). The further sheds were the overhaul works and it was also in here that new electric trams had been assembled, having been delivered as sets of parts. Body sections made in Birkenhead and Shrewsbury had been transported by train to Bristol, then taken to be built up – and married to the trucks – in Brislington depot.

2. Through a complex switch of share ownership, Western National gained a controlling interest in Bristol Tramways & Carriage Company, but did place some work in the hands of BBW. Seen here are three of their first nine Bristols, new in 1933. They have AM3 bodies on H-Type chassis (see Plate 154) and were photographed in Hengrove, with the fledgling Knowle West housing estate visible in the distance.

The Thornycroft motor buses had bodies built in Preston by the United Electric Car Company. They were built as double-deckers, but it was soon found that the swaying of double-deck motor buses on uneven country roads alarmed several of their passengers. Besides that, tree-lopping was not carried out with much care or consistency and, even at a maximum speed of 12 mph, injury could be occasioned by overhanging branches. Consequently, most ran as single-deckers on country routes starting at the trams' outer termini, but those operating on inner city services remained as double-deckers.

BT&CC also placed in service a number of Fiat double-deckers during 1906/07. Before long, however, it was disclosed that all was not well with the motor buses.

Both makes failed to come up to the level of reliability the company had stipulated when agreeing to their purchase. Serious negotiations were then entered into with their suppliers before BT&CC received satisfactory settlements. Modifications had to be carried out to the chassis before they were capable of undertaking their duties efficiently.

It was while this was going on that Charles Challenger, the Traffic Manager, saw a new potential market to tap – the operation of char-à-bancs for pleasure traffic. In the spring of 1907, three of the Thornycrofts had their bus bodies removed and, to take their place, the Bristol Tramways & Carriage Company's own Brislington tramcar works built and fitted new open char-à-banc bodies – the first 'Bristol' bus bodies!

3. Following the trial of a Bristol G-Type demonstrator, Exeter Corporation ordered four G05Gs with BBW AM9 bodies (as described in Plate 169). The four were placed in line astern for this shot at Bristol's Lawrence Hill bus depot before delivery in October 1935.

# Chapter 1

The spring of 1907 saw the emergence of the first three motor bus bodies built by Bristol Tramways & Carriage Company Ltd. The bodies, which were mounted on one-year-old Thornycroft chassis from the company's own fleet, were designed by Charles Challenger, the company's charismatic Traffic Manager. The design was well thought out, while the styling followed the tastes of fashion prevalent at a time when elegant horse-drawn carriages still dominated the streets. As the vehicles were expected to be used on local stage-carriage services when not undertaking excursions, they were carefully laid out to meet both requirements. They featured a sloping floor-line, to provide all passengers with good forward vision.

The success of these three new char-à-bancs during the summer of 1907 cannot be doubted, but the vagaries of the British weather soon led Challenger to design a modified version. This would be suitable for use in all weathers and at all times of the year. It was indeed named by Challenger as the 'All-Seasons Char-à-banc'. The basis of the new design was much the same as the original, but the major difference was that the passenger saloon was now enclosed, with large glazed windows. In order to perpetuate the char-à-banc element in good weather, these windows were fully removable. Two 'All-Seasons' char-à-banc bodies were built, in August and October 1907, again on 1906 Thornycroft chassis.

Meanwhile, the reliability of the current motor bus chassis was still open to question. Significantly, on 18th July 1907, at the company's Directors' Meeting, a decision was made that was to have a profound effect. The Managing Director approved the construction, in the company's own works, of both the bodies and *chassis* of six light single-deck buses, with about 16 seats each. It was recorded that "the cost of these if built throughout in the company's own works, with engines of 24HP company's pattern, would be £3,270, or £545 each". It was suggested that "six chassis and three bodies should be built at Brislington and the other three bodies at Leek Lane Works". Leek Lane was located in central Bristol as a turning off Milk Street, in an area which, since the 1950s, has been redeveloped within the Broadmead shopping complex. Leek Lane accommodated the company's carriage works, where the horse-drawn vehicles were bodied and repaired; there was not space (nor was the doorway big enough!) to build any large bodywork there.

The six all-Bristol 16-seat single-deckers were duly built in 1908 and were designated Type C40. They were registered AE 770-775, marks which evidently were transferred from the short-lived Fiats. The first entered traffic in May 1908 on the service between the Victoria Rooms and Clifton Suspension Bridge. They took the place of the earlier motor buses. The service was extended two years later to start at the Tramways Centre and to run by way of the long and steep Park Street. The term 'Tramways Centre' was applied to the area which, as might be expected, was the hub of the tramway system, located where a spur of the city's harbour projected into the shopping and commercial heartland, at St Augustine's Parade and Broad Quay. The name has remained ever since, although abbreviated to 'The Centre'.

The company had not ruled out the operation of buses of other manufacture and placed in service a small number of double-deckers on Berliet chassis. In general terms of new motor buses, though, there was now a curious hiatus of a few years between the initial activity and the addition of any further new stock being made to the fleet.

In 1909, though, the body shops started work on building some Large Closed Saloons, as they were termed. These had seating for 28 and the first were mounted on the five 1906 Thornycroft chassis which, up till now, had retained 'top-seat' bodies.

The year 1910 was another important one for the business interests of Sir George White, as in that year he decided to proceed with his latest transportation venture ... the building of aircraft, or Flying Machines as they tended to be described. Open countryside just to the north of Bristol, at the village of Filton, on a site where a new bus depot had recently been opened, provided the base for his manufacturing facility; the first outcome, however, was that the buses had to move out. Sir George established the British & Colonial Aeroplane Company at Filton, while also registering other names, including the Bristol Aeroplane Company, which was to be brought into use at a later date. The aircraft which were built at Filton were marketed as 'Bristols', of course!

Sir George was joined at the Aeroplane Company by his nephew, Sidney Smith (whose own nephew, Reginald Verdon Smith, was to achieve notable status at Filton), and by George Challenger, son of the Tramways Company's Traffic Manager Charles Challenger. George had been a foreman at Brislington, but very soon was to become responsible for the first Bristol-designed aeroplane, which became known as the Bristol 'Boxkite'. It is recorded that the finest 10% of the Tramway Company's timber stocks were commandeered by the Aeroplane Company, leaving the remainder to the coach-builders – only Sir George White could have got away with such a demand!

In 1911 some more new all-Bristol passenger vehicles were built. Again classified C40, four were 16-seaters just like the initial 1908 sextet, while the other three were covered char-à-bancs. These had entirely open sides, rather like the original 1907 Bristol bodies, although the new examples were somewhat smaller, had level saloon floors and full-width bench seats, without a centre gangway.

It was not until 1912 that the building of chassis by Bristol started to be undertaken in significant numbers, with 21 entering service in that year. Naturally, all had bodies built by the company. Moreover, there was remarkable variety among the vehicles built, including Small and Large Bus bodies, covered char-à-bancs and the first open 'Torpedo' char-à-bancs, and 'Composite' saloons. Beyond this, the company also built on some bought-in chassis; the Leek Lane works built small bodies on Dennis and Lacre chassis, these buses being supplied on contract to major local hotels to operate for the benefit of their guests.

Considerable publicity surrounded the Composite bodies. They were claimed as being designed by Charles Challenger, although vehicles of similar layout could be found elsewhere in the country. Their composite nature was to blend covered char-à-banc seating at the front, with an enclosed saloon at the rear.

The company now had its sights firmly set on the manufacture of chassis and bodies and, to cope with the increase in production, they were fortunate in 1912 in being able to acquire premises just a short distance up Bath Road from Brislington depot; these would be developed as the 'Motor Constructional Works'. The previous owners had been scale and weighbridge manufacturers and the premises fronted the tracks of the Bristol & North Somerset Railway (of which Sir George White had been a board member, by the way, and for which Charles Challenger had once been a Messenger Boy!). The factory was laid out either side of a central administrative building. The chassis Erecting Shop was located on one side of the offices and the Body Building Shop on the other. BT&CC took occupation in October 1912; the Motor Constructional Works were formally opened through a visit by shareholders on 30th June and 1st July 1913.

Just how much bodybuilding was undertaken here is uncertain, as from 1920 and for many years hence bodybuilding was carried out back at the Tram Depot at Brislington. The furthest bays from the entrance archway were progressively improved as a coachworks. In early records, bodies were simply stated as being built at or by 'The Tram Depot'; the term Body Building Works (BBW) is a later one, used to distinguish it from the Motor Constructional Works and also the Motor Maintenance Department established at Lawrence Hill, Bristol, from 1924 to provide engineering and body repair facilities for the operational fleet of BT&CC motor buses (and later termed the Central Repair Works). For this history, the term BBW will be used henceforth.

Production of buses increased once the new MCW came into use, to approaching 40 vehicles in 1913. Body styles ranged from the last Small Bus – to much the same design as the 1908 examples – through covered char-à-bancs, Torpedoes and Medium Closed Buses to Large Buses. During this period there were also cases of bodies being transferred from one chassis to another and, although records are incomplete, it would appear that some or all of the 1909/10 Large Bus bodies were transferred from the 1906 Thornycroft chassis to new Bristol chassis.

The years 1912-14 also saw the first examples of Bristol chassis and bodywork enter the fleets of operators elsewhere in the country. In both instances, the recipients were associated with Bristol Tramways through the business interests of Sir George White. The Corris Railway at Machynlleth received some covered char-à-bancs on loan, but more significantly, all but one of the nine C65 model buses (Bristol's largest to date), built in late 1913, were transferred in the early weeks of the next year to the Middlesbrough branch of Imperial Tramways. Here they were re-registered with local DC number-plates, although one is known to have worked in neighbouring Stockton-on-Tees, for which it received a County Durham J registration.

Output of bodies in 1914 was at a similar level to 1913, but concentrated on Composite and Large Buses, and Torpedoes, one of which was supplied new to Imperial Tramways of Middlesbrough. The distribution of the other char-à-bancs reflected the growing sphere of BT&CC's own operation in the counties around Bristol.

The Bristol Tramways company had something very exciting up its sleeve when the Great War broke out on 4th August 1914. Plans were well advanced, however, and construction of an all new single-decker was duly completed in March 1915; it was the only new bus to be built in that year. The bus was a 29-seater, designated Type W. It incorporated the latest technical developments, but it was in terms of styling that the Type W was remarkable. It was a huge leap forward from the buses of the previous year, as it had a deep roof, well-rounded contours and all-in-one side windows. On the other hand, previous buses had showed little advance since 1908. The continuation of the Great War allowed long, in-service trials to be made with the Type W, with the aim of introducing a production version once peace had returned. Later this prototype vehicle became affectionally known as 'Old Mother Bristol'!

The coming of the Great War had a profound and sudden effect on BBW and the MCW. In common with motor vehicle manufacturing plants throughout the country, the factories were turned over to the production of items of military hardware. The close association of BT&CC with the British & Colonial Aeroplane Company, who were now well established in building 'Bristol' aeroplanes at Filton, led to the Brislington works becoming a natural extension of the B&CAC's production facility. During the closing months of 1914, BBW built six Bristol Boxkites (in fact, the last six of all Boxkites to be made ... until three replicas were constructed for the film *Those Magnificent Men in their*

*Flying Machines*). In February 1915, BBW turned over to production of the Bristol Scout C, this being joined in the September by the Coanda TB8. Numbers of these two had reached 161 and 24, respectively, when the production at Brislington ended in 1916. These were penny numbers, however, when compared to the output of Bristol Fighter aircraft from 1916, as a total of 1,045 was completed there. The first 50 were F2A versions, but the remainder were of the improved F2B model. Although the end of the Great War was marked with the signing of the Armistice on 11th November 1918, production of the F2B at Brislington continued at the command of the Government until September 1919.

**4.** The Bristol Tramways & Carriage Company undertook the construction of the first bodies of its own design at its Brislington works in the spring of 1907. These first three bodies were char-à-bancs. They were mounted on Thornycroft chassis that had originally been supplied with bus bodywork to initiate motor-bus operation in Bristol in January 1906. The new char-à-banc bodies were designed by BT&CC's traffic manager, Charles Challenger. The front and sides were open, but there was a brougham-shaped back equipped with a large window. The top of the window rose gently to a central point. The back was said to give protection from dust and adverse weather, as well as supporting the roof which was very slightly curved in cross-section and extended beyond the driver and the passengers seated alongside him. To quote Challenger's report in *Tramway & Railway World* of 6th April 1907: "As the name char-à-banc implies the seats are across the vehicle with the faces of the passengers towards the driver, and the seats are sufficiently high from the ground to bring the view of the passengers above the walls and hedges, and from front to back, the floor slopes somewhat, so that the view of the hindmost passengers is not obscured by those on the front seats". There was a central gangway and in this form, in which it was suitable for operation on local stage carriage work, the vehicle would seat 27. However, the five rows of seats behind the driver's bench could be fitted with additional seats in the gangway, thereby increasing the capacity to 32 for outings. The first char-à-banc was placed in service on Saturday 30th March 1907. The photograph here, featuring AE 727, was taken at the top of Westbury Hill, Westbury-on-Trym.

**5.** The three original char-à-bancs featured an entrance close to the rear on the nearside. This required no fewer than five steps in order to reach the elevated floor. For operation after dark, the char-à-bancs benefited from the installation of electric lighting; just five lamps were used, each of 5½ candle power, and some can be seen suspended below the ceiling, near the tops of the roof supports. The completed vehicles were painted a royal blue, with gold line decorations. They were virtually identical, although there were slight detail differences in the finish and decoration around the rear corners of the bodywork. *(M J Tozer Collection)*

**6.** On 28th August 1907, the first of two improved char-à-bancs, named by Charles Challenger as the '**All-Seasons Char-à-banc**', took up service in Bristol. Again mounted on 1906 Thornycroft chassis, these two bodies featured fully-removable side and front windows. The side windows were large, and the side panels quite shallow, to produce a spacious aspect. Additionally, hinged top-lights were installed above the main windows to provide ventilation when the bodies were fully enclosed. The finishing touch was the use of curved glass for the windows in the front corners, which were also removable. In other respects, the layout was similar to the

original open char-à-bancs, with 27 or 32 seats and five-step rear entrance. This photograph shows AE 725 when newly in service. The style of dress of the passengers matches the elegance of the new bus! It will be seen that the windows are removed (also that curtains were featured); Charles Challenger kept a diary of company events and on 12th September he wrote: "Char-à-banc on Thornbury service. Front windows up. Fine summer weather set in - ordered windows to be taken down". Then, on 1st October: "Today put in front windows". 10th October: "Cold and rain set in; put in side windows". Was the weather so much more stable in those days? On 27th October 1907 the second All-Seasons Char-à-banc was turned out, on the Ashton service. *(M J Tozer Collection)*

14

**7.** In May 1908 the Bristol Tramways & Carriage Company placed in service the first of six 16-seater buses in which both the bodies and the chassis were built in the company's own works. The body styling was clearly influenced by the 1907 All-Seasons Char-à-bancs, in the use of large, fully-removable side windows, surmounted by top-lights hinged along their lower edge. The top-lights in this case used patterned glass. The floor-line, however, was level, as befitted their use on local stage-carriage work; they were built for the tramway feeder service into Clifton. This view of Bristol Type C40 AE 773, although taken later in its life, serves to demonstrate how the first window has been removed in fine weather, as well as showing the curtains and tipping top-lights. Entrance was made by three steps to a platform alongside the driver. From there, the passenger would enter the saloon through an opening in the front partition. This was slightly off-set to the nearside, due to the driving position, and was fitted with a sliding door which ran along the outside of the partition to rest behind the driver when open. It was fitted with an ARCHed window. The body sides continued forward of the partition to produce the one-third length fly-screens at either side of the front platform. *(M J Tozer Collection)*

**8.** This enlargement of a photograph of Bristol's Tramway Centre taken from the foot of College Green shows by chance two of the 1908 C40 Bristols passing each other. On the left is AE 773 again and this shows that the rear window was a simple rectangular shape, with slotted ventilation grilles above. Approaching the photographer is AE 772, which shows that at a later date an additional passenger was allowed on a seat on the front platform, between the door and the fly-screen. The gangway was offset in line with the door, with double seats to the offside and single to the nearside. Three of the bodies on these C40s were built at the Brislington Car Works, while the other three came from the Leek Lane Carriage Works; there were very slight differences between the products of the two body shops. *(M J Tozer Collection)*

**9.** In the closing years of the first decade of the 20th Century, the Leek Lane Works assumed the responsibility for the production and upkeep of BT&CC's large fleet of cabs (known as Blue Taxis) and contract-hire fleet of lorries and vans. A typical Blue Taxi built there in 1909 is AE 1420, a landaulette on Charron chassis (French makes dominated the cab fleet), which remained in service until 1930. *(M J Tozer Collection)*

**10.** In 1909/10, more 1906 Thornycrofts, including the last of the double-deckers, were fitted with new Bristol single-deck bodies. These were described as **Large Closed Saloons** and were 28-seaters with a rear entrance. A sloping floor was featured, possibly with a view to their use on char-à-banc outings. This time, five windows were used along the offside, although the size of the trailing window was narrower to match the width of the nearside doorway; on both sides, though, the top-lights were uniform throughout. The front corners featured angled, *flat* glass windows. The front partition was very similar to the 1907 bodies, with a wide central window and arches to the tops of all three windows. Again, all windows were removable. The rear window also matched the 1907 bodies in rising to a central peak. AE 726 is seen here on the Horfield to the Tramways Centre route. *(M J Tozer Collection)*

**11.** The 1907 **All-Seasons Char-à-bancs**, as shown in Plate 6, were later modified by the substitution of flat glass for the extravagant curved glazing at the front corners. Appropriate changes were made to the corner panelling and canopy supports. This is demonstrated by Thornycroft AE 735, working the Old Market, Whitehall and Fishponds service in Bristol. The body has gained patterned glass to the top-lights. *(M J Tozer Collection)*

**12.** 1911 saw the building of seven more Bristol C40 chassis. Four of them received 16-seat Small Bus bodies very similar to the 1908 examples as seen in Plate 7, while the other three received 22-seat covered **char-à-banc** bodywork as illustrated here by AE 1156 alongside one of the gateways to Ashton Park. In these vehicles, the floor was level. There was no central gangway, therefore restricting their use to excursions and outings. Access to the full-width bench seats was by way of a small door at the end of each row, on which a small BT&CC monogram was applied. Five rows of seats accommodated 20 passengers, while two more persons were allowed alongside the driver. Weather-resistant side curtains were tethered to the roof supports, but the driver had the benefit of a large glass windscreen for the first time. This, though, did not extend to the roof, as that would interfere with the flow of fresh air! The rear window was rectangular. *(M J Tozer Collection)*

**13.** 1912 saw a major increase in the production of vehicles by BT&CC, with new types of chassis and several new styles of body being introduced. One of the new chassis was the C60, which was capable of carrying bodywork of similar capacity to that mounted on the Thornycrofts. Photographed outside Clifton College in January 1912 is AE 2551, with covered **char-à-banc** bodywork. The legal lettering on the side, below the driver, reads: "To carry 27 passengers; with centre seats, 32". Like the 1907 bodies of this size, it had a sloping floor and a rear window with a peaked top. The C60, however, had a three-step entrance near the front, behind the driving position, *on each side*. It can be imagined that when these vehicles were used on bus services, the offside

egress must have presented a particular danger. Note the driver's divided windscreen and the quarter-length windows, including top-lights, towards the rear. The side panel, which carried the Bristol city crest above the wheel arch, was a one-piece item. *(M J Tozer Collection)*

17

**14**. A C40 service bus which had entered service in 1911 with re-issued registration AE 779 was rebodied in 1912 with a revised **Small Bus** body. This had the doorway relocated in the side, just behind the front partition. The seating capacity was 17, two places being situated alongside the driver. Wide steps were provided to assist entry to this seat and to the doorway, the lower step being neatly combined with the vehicle's mudguards. The front vestibule again had fly-screens at either side. The top-lights above the windows were in this case hinged on their trailing ends and projected outwards when open. The bus is seen here posed on Bristol's Downs. *(Allen Janes Collection)*

**15**. A great deal of publicity for BT&CC came from the trade press in 1912, with articles written by Charles Challenger about the progress he had made with the design of motor buses. His latest idea was to combine the pleasures of open char-à-banc travel with the practicalities of town or city bus operation in what he called the **Composite Char-à-banc**. This vehicle is portrayed here by Y 1584, intended for the Weston-super-Mare town service between Uphill and Ashcombe Park and mounted on another new chassis type,

the C45. It will be seen that the rear part of the body was an enclosed saloon, with a doorway at its forward end, while ahead of that were two full-width seats which were entirely open, save for the protection that the roof and driver's windscreen afforded. For safety reasons, a decorative wrought-iron screen was positioned at the outside end of the second seat. Fourteen passengers could be seated in the rear saloon, with a further four on the bench ahead of the partition and two alongside the driver – 20 in all. In the event of a private hiring, two more seats could be installed in the gangway of the rear saloon. The vehicle was completed in August 1912. *(M J Tozer Collection)*

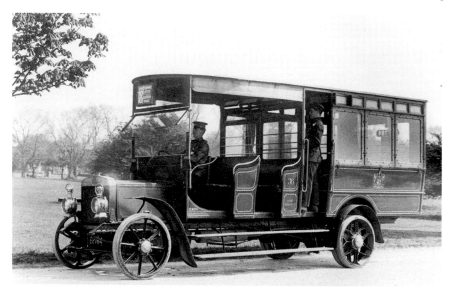

**16**. Slight changes were made to the design of the **Composite** body on the C45 chassis of AE 2784, seen here on The Downs in Bristol. Entry was eased by the addition of an extra step, although that necessitated narrowing the body floor at the doorway and beneath the ends of the benches. The legal lettering states the capacity was only 18 and it is believed that the seat on the benches closest to the steps was forsaken due to the narrower floor. Note the side curtain that could be pulled down in wet weather. *(Allen Janes Collection)*

**17**. Further Bristol C60 chassis built in 1912 were completed with **Large Bus** bodies that continued the theme set by the rebodied Thornycrofts, in having a sloping floor, 28 seats and a rear entrance. This view of AE 2554, in service at *The Engineer's Arms* in St John's Lane, Bedminster, Bristol, shows the '5½-bay' version of this body; the main side windows are thought to be slightly shorter than in the body shown on Thornycroft AE 726 above (Plate 10), resulting in a half-size window appearing at the front of the saloon. The top-lights above the windows, furthermore, were all single panels. *(M J Tozer Collection)*

**18**. A development aimed at emulating the comfort of the burgeoning private motor-car was the **Torpedo Char-à-banc**. In this design, plushly upholstered seats extended the full width of the vehicle, each row having doors at both ends. The total capacity was 22. There was no permanent roof, but for weather protection there was a collapsible cape hood. The first Bristol Torpedo was another C45, AE 2773, seen here in August 1912. In this, the hood was of a patented Bristol design for operation by one man. It used a system of cables and winding gear and could be raised while the operator stood alongside the front wing. *(M J Tozer Collection)*

**19**. In 1912 BT&CC's Leek Lane Carriage Works built a scaled-down **Torpedo** body, on a Dennis 18hp chassis. The outcome was registered in Somerset as Y 1583, for operation from Weston-super-Mare or Wells. The deep, soft seats carried only 14 passengers.
*(M J Tozer Collection)*

**20 & 21**.  Other products of the Leek Lane works in 1912 were two small buses for operation by major hotels in the BT&CC's area. They provided transport for the guests between hotel and railway station. Shown here is AE 2424, a 14-seater mounted on Dennis 30cwt chassis. The body had a lot in common with that mounted on Bristol C40 chassis since 1908, except that the vents above the windows were of a slatted design. Furthermore, there was a roof-mounted luggage pen, access to which was by a ladder attached to the rear. The seats were upholstered in red leather and there were curtains to match. Two drop windows were incorporated for lowering in hot weather. AE 2424 was contract-hired to the Lansdown Hotel in Bath, while an 8-seater on 1-Ton Lacre chassis (AE 2774) ran on contract to the Grand Hotel in Bristol. In the latter vehicle, the rear of the body was devoted to the accommodation of luggage. Note the plaque alongside this vehicle - 'B.T & C.Cº. Lᵈ., Builders, Leek Lane Works, Bristol'. *(Both photographs, M J Tozer Collection)*

**22**. Leek Lane continued its usual output of van and lorry bodies for BT&CC's contract operation, which, in 1912, included a fleet of Royal Mail vans on Dennis 18hp chassis. Pierce Arrow, though, provided the basis of this canvas-topped lorry built at Leek Lane in 1912. It was supplied to Rogers' Brewery of Bristol. Similar bodywork was built for the contract fleet on other chassis of equivalent carrying capacity. (*M J Tozer Collection*)

**23**. Also built at Leek Lane was AE 2571, a small Clermont Bayard (a make also favoured for the company's Blue Taxi fleet), seen on completion in May 1912 with a van body featuring an additional roof carrier. It was beautifully sign-written for James Fortt of Bath. (*M J Tozer Collection*)

**24**. With the maker's plate reading 'Bristol Tramways & Carriage C$^{o}$ L$^{d}$, Builders, Bristol' placed beside it as it stands across the tram track in Brislington depot yard is this van on Dennis 30cwt chassis. It was supplied on contract to Cerebos Salt of London and remained on hire until about 1917. (*M J Tozer Collection*)

21

**25**. In March 1913, Leek Lane built this neat little 8-seat hotel bus on a Lacre 1-Ton chassis, for a group of hotels to operate in the popular spa town of Cheltenham, to and from the town's Midland Station. The bus was registered in Gloucestershire, appropriately, as AD 2789. Interestingly, the shape of the side windows, including the smaller version in the door, is strongly reminiscent of railway carriage practice of the time. The front partition was staggered, with the nearside part being set well forward of the back of the driver's seat. The rear of the body was devoted to the carriage of luggage, for which safety rails were placed vertically across the last two side windows. Luggage space was also provided on the roof. Note yet another style of maker's plate is placed alongside the vehicle. *(M J Tozer Collection)*

**26**. Cheltenham's neighbouring city of Gloucester was 'invaded' by BT&CC in May 1913, with the opening of a branch there. Char-à-bancs and taxis were provided, including this 22-seat **Torpedo** on C45 chassis. A practice common within BT&CC's operating area was that the company's vehicles were registered (or even re-registered) with the local council; in this case, Gloucester supplied the number FH 629. The body styling has been modified since the first Torpedo of 1912, seen in Plate 18. The beading along the top of the doors was now curved up to meet the windscreen pillar, while the rear wheel arches were reduced in size, this in turn enabling a deeper door to be used at this point. *(M J Tozer Collection)*

**27.** This is a picture taken inside the Brislington body shops around 1913. Seen under construction are **Torpedo** char-à-banc bodies and, to the left, two **Composite** bodies. Across the other side of the shop **Large Bus** bodywork was in the process of being built. It is recorded that by 1913, nearly 500 bodies for cabs, buses and commercial vehicles had been constructed by BT&CC. *(Allen Janes Collection)*

**28.** A common practice in the early decades of this century was to change the role of a vehicle to suit the occasion. Many of BT&CC's large fleet of char-à-bancs were soon transformed – often permanently with the onset of war – to service buses. This C45 of 1913,

AE 3183, is seen in Clifton now carrying a **Composite** body, for the bus service to The Tramways Centre. The styling was revised so that there were only two main windows to the rear saloon, instead of three. Also, rounded corners were given to the top of the doorway and the canopy. In this body, it is possible to see that full panelling and a window were placed at the offside end of the 'outside' seats. *(M J Tozer Collection)*

**29**. An offside view of a 'two-window' **Composite** body, but in this case mounted on an example of the new C50, introduced in 1914, AE 3799. Here the ends of the outside seats were open above the waist. On this design of body, the front canopy had a gentle downward curve. Note the top-lights above the partition; these are hinged outwards along their top edge, anticipating the idea that was to become popular in front-facing windows of buses from the late 1940s! In March 1914, the London General Omnibus Company requested plans and permission to build Charles Challenger-designed Composite bodies. Nothing seems to have come of this venture, however. *(M J Tozer Collection)*

**30**. AE 3196 was another Type C50, but with a very different body from that on AE 3799 above, in being a **Large Closed** 28-seater. This was a '5½-bay' body similar to that shown previously on C60 model AE 2554 in Plate 17, but of note in having a level saloon floor. As a result, the entrance only required four steps, rather than five. Note the mother and two very small children seated alongside the driver. The bus was new in February 1914. Torpedo char-à-banc bodywork when mounted on the C50 chassis was also able to accommodate 28 passengers. *(M J Tozer Collection)*

**31**. The largest Bristol chassis to appear so far was the C65, which totalled just nine examples built at the end of 1913. Both documentary and photographic evidence is inconclusive, but it is likely that some of the C65s received the 1909/10 28-seat **Large Closed Bus** bodies from 1906 Thornycroft chassis – certainly, this example had received the registration transferred from one of those Thornycrofts, in being AE 731. This body was of '5-bay' construction, with double top-lights, so is identical to that shown on Thornycroft AE 726 in

Plate 10; note, also, the gap between the wheel arch in the body side and the rear wing of the chassis. It is possible that the C65 chassis featuring '5½-bay' bodies carried new coachwork. This AE 731 was photographed in December 1913, but in February 1914 it was transferred to Imperial Tramways of Middlesbrough where it was re-registered. *(M J Tozer Collection)*

**32**. New coachwork was given to some existing Bristol chassis as the need arose. Depicted here is 1911 C40 AE 1156, already shown in Plate 12 with a covered char-à-banc body. In 1914 it received a new saloon body, with a seating capacity believed to have been 22. Interestingly, entry was effected in the same manner as in the 1908 C40 saloons, by steps to the front platform and access to the saloon through the front partition. There were even half-bay fly-screens at each side of the front platform. The devices suspended from the wheel-hubs were splash guards – judging from the marks towards the rear of the bodywork, their success was limited! *(M J Tozer Collection)*

**33.** A huge leap forward in terms of styling was achieved with the experimental Type W of 1915. The roof was deepened and the profile rounded, the side panels were curved under and included a styled waistband in place of the tram-derived moulding at wheel arch level, the windows were lengthened, with the end window receiving a curved trailing edge, and a new form of easily-controlled ventilation provided through hinged apertures in the sides of the roof, in place of top-lights to the windows. The three windows in the front partition could be lowered just enough to supply fresh air, without causing a draught. As before, however, the side windows could be removed entirely in warm weather, although the design was greatly improved, to give very slender pillars. This broadside photograph of the Type W is enhanced by the manufacturers' plaque being placed alongside. It reads: 'Bristol Tramways & Carriage Co Ld., Builders, Motor Constructional Works, Bristol'. *(M J Tozer Collection)*

**34.** The Type W was registered as AE 4973 and entered service on 12th March 1915. This photograph of it working on the Clifton Suspension Bridge route, now numbered 18, shows the middle of the three front windows lowered. It also shows that the partition was aligned with the pillar at the rear of the half-bay, but the solid panelling in the faring ahead of this window must have somewhat obstructed the driver's vision. The Type W was the first vehicle to have the Bristol scroll emblazoned across the top of the radiator! A few years later, the ventilators in the sides of the roof were removed.

27 seats could be reached through a rear entrance, while a further two passengers could sit alongside the driver. *(M J Tozer Collection)*

**35.** In recognition of their involvement in building Bristol aeroplanes during the Great War, this group portrait was taken in the yard of Brislington depot against a background of a Bristol Fighter F2B and a banner reading: 'Bristol Tramways Aircraft Workers 1914-1918'. *(M J Tozer Collection)*

# Chapter 2

By the time the material and labour position had settled down following the end of the Great War, it was 1920 before Bristol Tramways was able to consider returning to full production of buses. At a Shareholders' Meeting held in May of that year consent was given to proceed with motor bus chassis production. The intervening years had been taken up partly by analysing the Type W bus built in 1915, with a view to introducing a new model. From its chassis was developed the new 4-Tonner and from its body was developed the saloon coachwork for the new chassis. This bus formed a platform for a new beginning for Bristol.

The company was no longer to make buses solely for the use of themselves or associated operators but, instead, the manufacturing departments were to offer their products to all-comers. As an initial move, Bristol reserved a stand at the 1920 Commercial Motor Exhibition at London's Olympia, on which to display their new 4-Tonner.

The design team at the Body Building Works at this stage initiated the use of sequential letters of the alphabet to distinguish their various designs. This was five years before the company's Motor Constructional Works took up the same method of designation. The new 4-Ton chassis was made available with a choice of two bodies – the A-Type body was a 29-seat 'Torpedo' char-à-banc, while the B-Type body was a 29-seat saloon. The A-Type Torpedo body was very much like that built in 1914, while the B-Type saloon was obviously derived from the experimental 1915 Type W bus.

Although initial production of A-Type char-à-bancs was undertaken at the tram depot at Brislington, considerable spare capacity of skilled aircraft builders at the associated Bristol Aeroplane Company plant at Filton resulted in all but a few early B-Type saloon bodies being constructed by BAC. (Restructuring of the British & Colonial Aeroplane Company earlier in 1920 had seen the title Bristol Aeroplane Company brought into use.)

An interesting order was placed with BT&CC in 1920 by London General Omnibus Company. They required eight 1919 AEC YC emergency lorry-buses to be fitted with new Torpedo char-à-banc bodywork. These bodies seated 27. The first four entered service at Dalston (D) Garage in late May 1920, with the other four following from Nunhead (AH) Garage early in June. The chassis which received these Bristol bodies were registered LU 8067/86/9/91/7, 8144/94 & 8206 and the LGOC allocated their own body numbers 8481/3/5/0/78/9/84/2, respectively.

A novel deviation for Brislington's bodybuilding staff came in 1920 with the decision to build six new tramcars for the city's fleet. The existing fleet had been constructed in 1900/01, assembly taking place at Brislington, as already recorded. Interestingly, the new cars were to be built to almost exactly the same pattern as the 20-year-old cars, which had never been modernised. So they had open tops and open vestibules, with seating for 29 'outside' and 24 (on longitudinal benches) 'inside'. Subsequently, most of the existing fleet of over 200 trams was to be reconstructed at Brislington, amounting in most cases to new bodywork.

Production of the Bristol 4-Tonner soon got under way in large numbers for renewing the BT&CC fleet. However, despite glowing press reports about the 4-Tonner displayed at the 1920 Show, sales to other customers were slow to pick up. Some of the first to be sold elsewhere, in 1921, were supplied to neighbouring (and still unrelated) Bath Tramways Motor Company, with B-Type saloon bodies. They were followed by examples for Devon Motor Transport and, interestingly, Middlesbrough Corporation, who, during the same year, acquired the Middlesbrough operations of Imperial Tramways, complete with their Bristols.

In 1922, following the completion of more than 110 B-Type saloon bodies, BBW introduced the C-Type saloon. This was also built at Filton by BAC. In terms of styling, the C-Type seemed to be a bit of a step backwards, by reverting to tipping top-lights above its side windows and beneath a relatively flat roof. Customers for the C-Type body included West Riding Automobile Company, Sunderland District Electric Tramways, Doncaster Corporation, Rhondda Tramways, Devon Motor Transport again, plus an associate, Jersey Motor Transport ... the first exported Bristols? One other was built for a small but valued customer who was to return to Bristol consistently for several years, this being A & R Graham of Kirkintilloch, near Glasgow.

In 1923, the wheelbase of the 4-Tonner was increased and for the new version BBW produced a revised body. The designation for this broke away from the alphabetical sequence and, despite several options on doorway and seating layouts now being made available, all were termed the HA-Type. The body differed in appearance essentially by dispensing with the curved-down front canopy derived from the Type W and repositioning the rear doorway further towards the rear. Besides continuing to supply the needs of their own fleet, Bristol produced 4-Tonners with HA bodies for West Riding, Doncaster Corporation, Rhondda Transport and Devon Motor Transport/ Cornwall Motor Transport, and for more new customers – Aberdare Urban District Council and the Corporations of Manchester, Chesterfield and West Hartlepool.

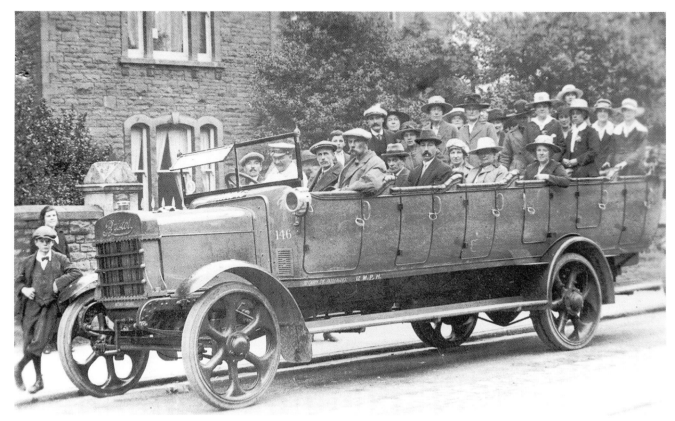

**36** (above). Bristol's decision to sell its products on the open market was based on the new 4-Tonner. This was promoted as equally suitable for passenger or goods applications and the body building works offered a choice of products to match the chassis. Alphabetical sequence letters were introduced to distinguish the passenger body variations, starting with the **A-Type** body, which was a Torpedo char-à-banc. Seen here is BT&CC's HT 1046, an early 4-Tonner. The body was similar to the 1914 Torpedoes on C50 chassis, in featuring a two-part, upright windscreen and door handles in the form of rings, with elliptical grab handles alongside. The capacity was again 28 and, as before and clearly seen here, one passenger was permitted to sit on the driver's *right*-hand side. The rearmost seat was connected to the row in front by way of a movable seat; this slid forward, then hinged over to one side to permit clear access. Interestingly, the production of aircraft during the Great War had its effect on the method of construction of these new bodies. For example, bolsters were not solid wood but two shallow strips, between which was a thin steel plate. This made the complete unit many times stronger than a solid wood bolster of the same size. The seat cushions were horse-hair stuffed, while on the back of the seats (which were covered in hard-wearing Bedford cord) a brass coat rail could be folded down to hold coats in position. The lower panel of each door was covered in cork linoleum, to avoid scratching. *(M J Tozer Collection)*

**37** (right). Prior to being displayed at the 1921 Commercial Motor Exhibition, this 4-Tonner with **A-Type** Torpedo coachwork, HT 4602, was used to demonstrate the Bristol patented one-man hood. These three views show, firstly, the operator in position and just starting to raise the hood from its resting place, the hood partially erected, with the control cord, attached to the centre of the hood's leading spur, deliberately slackened, and, finally, the hood fully erected and taught. The body styling has been amended, with a simplification of the front dash and the elimination of the curved line of beading rising to the windscreen pillar. Gone, too, are the external door handle rings. At an early stage of this version, the rearmost door was dispensed with, relying on the movable seat to reach the back row, but the sixth door was soon reinstated. *(M J Tozer Collection)*

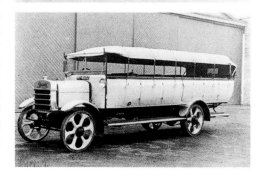

**38**. The saloon bodywork for the 4-Ton chassis was designated **B-Type** and it was clearly derived from the body designed for the 1915 Type W, shown in Plates 33 & 34. The B-Type body accommodated 29. Two of the seats were alongside the driver and accessible through a door in the cab, while otherwise there was a rear entrance which now only required three steps. The Brislington bodyshops were in full production of A-Type char-à-banc bodies at this stage, to meet the demand for post-war fleet renewal and the public's appetite for outings, so it was decided to use spare capacity at the Bristol Aeroplane Company's works at Filton and to construct the B-Type

saloons there (with one or two early exceptions). This bus, registered HT 1524, carried the first BAC body and appeared in the Trade Press in September 1920. The B-Type bodies also used the steel sandwich method of construction and the body weight was kept down to 23cwt (1.17 tonnes). The panels were beaten from lead-coated plate. The windows had separate frames and were inserted after the rest of the body was completed. Every part was made from template so accurately that units were merely drawn from stores and erected with no need for further adjustment or tooling. *(M J Tozer Collection)*

**39**. The rear panelling of the **B-Type** body curved under quite markedly, as shown here. This was one of the first Bristols to be sold to an operator with no connections with BT&CC, the customer being Powell & Gough, trading as The Knowbury Bus Company of Ludlow. It was registered in Shropshire as NT 546, being delivered in August 1921. As the sign-writing on the rear panel proclaims, it was known as The Green Parrot! Note the upward curve of the waistband at the rear corner and the rectangular rear window. This had three safety bars placed across the glass on the inside and was surmounted by slotted ventilation grilles. *(M J Tozer Collection)*

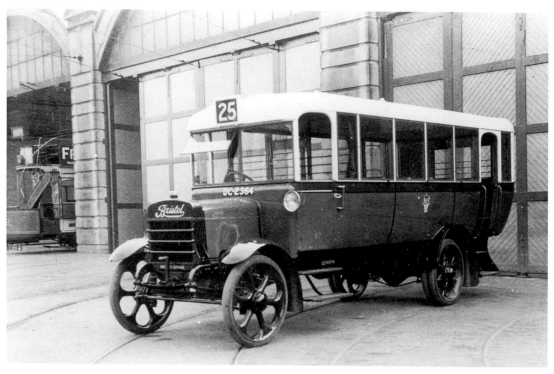

**40**. The distinction of being the first municipal operator to take delivery of Bristols went to Middlesbrough Corporation. They received two 4-Tonners with BAC-built **B-Type** bodies in April 1921, about the same time that the Middlesbrough operations of Imperial Tramways, with their Bristols, were taken over. No.87 (DC 2364) is seen here posed outside the tram sheds in Brislington depot yard. A significant improvement over the Type W was the adoption of windscreens for the driver and front seat passengers. It was standard practice to carry a route-number box in the leading edge of the curved front dome, while the destination display took the form of a slip-board in the windscreen. *(M J Tozer Collection)*

**41 & 42**. When manufacture of the 4-Tonner initially got under way in 1920, chassis production outstripped bodybuilding, besides which the Brislington shops were concentrating on A-Type char-à-bancs. As a result and probably in order to commence in-service trials in Bristol with bus versions of the 4-Tonner, one dozen assorted chassis received secondhand Bristol bodies from pre-Great War chassis. Shown here are two interesting examples. Firstly, HT 1508, which received one of the four-window bodies dating from *1907!* This All-Seasons Char-à-banc body was originally mounted on a Thornycroft chassis. (Note that although it has received flat glass front corner windows, the panelling above and below retains its original rounded shape.) Even in 1923, when new coachwork was built for HT 1508, the 1907 body was sold to Tresillian Motors in Cardiff for further use! The second photograph is an enlargement of a general view of the Tramways Centre and just happens to capture, working the 33 to Bath, HT 1516, which had received the distinctive 1915 body from the Type W. Comparing this with Plate 34 it will be seen the ventilators had been removed from above the side windows, although the three hinged ventilators remained along the centre of the roof. After displacement by a new body in 1922, this structure was sold to become a static caravan. *(Both photographs, M J Tozer Collection)*

**43**. The Brislington bodyshops built six trams in 1920 for the Bristol fleet. Numbered 86 and 233-7, they were mounted on Peckham trucks, No.86 having an experimental 7ft (2133mm) wheelbase instead of 6ft 6in (1981mm). All six were for increasing the fleet strength. The bodies were specifically styled so as to be virtually identical to the company's 1900 intake of trams, which had never been modernised. So the top deck, staircase and vestibule were still open to the elements! Subsequently, the existing fleet was reconstructed at Brislington, in many cases receiving new bodies, which were again of this 1900 design. *(S Miles Davey)*

**44**. The 4-Ton chassis received considerable custom over the years from goods transport operators. One of the earliest supplied was this van, exhibited at the 1920 Commercial Motor Show. The body was built at the Tram Depot and the cab was styled in the fashion of the era, with shaped valance above the windscreens. When finished for display at Olympia, the wooden body was varnished but not painted, revealing the attractive wood grain. The van is shown here in the depot yard after it had been sold to Fletcher Hardware of Birmingham (with registration OH 8164). The wooden body has now been stained and revarnished, allowing the grain to remain visible. The van was handed over on 16th July 1921. *(M J Tozer Collection)*

**45**. A 4-Ton tipping lorry was completed by BBW for exhibition at the 1921 Show. The cab in this case featured elliptical windows in the sides and rear. The lorry was subsequently registered HT 4600.

**46**. The photograph above, taken at Filton on 19th September 1921, shows a 4-Tonner with an experimental body of a new design. Although furnished with seats, it is unpainted and, indeed, its identity has not been established. The design showed a step backwards from the B-Type body in terms of styling flare, in that the roof was once again rather flat and the side windows were surmounted by tipping top-lights. These windows were longer than before and the rear doorway was relocated at the extreme rear of the saloon. The front of the roof did not curve down so sharply, leaving solid panelling visible above the windscreens. *(Allen Janes Collection)*

**47**. This advertisement for 'Bristol Motor Bodies' appeared in the trade press in 1921. It was placed by the Bristol Aeroplane Company and it will be noticed that the Bristol scroll differed slightly from that used by BT&CC, in that the upright in the letter B was not extended above the top of the letter. The advertisement illustrated a **B-Type** 4-Tonner and a broadside view of the experimental body shown in the previous plate. The other two vehicles were Armstong Siddeley cars, for which BAC built a number of enclosed or open bodies for well-to-do customers. *(M J Tozer Collection)*

**48**. In 1922 a new design of body was introduced in place of the B-Type and was classified **C-Type**. Some of the features of its styling had appeared in the experimental 1921 body shown in Plate 46, most noticeably the flat roof and windows with top-lights. The front portion of the roof curved down to a similar degree, but now there were slatted permanent vents above the wind-screen. The C-type body was especially designed with two doorways, to speed up loading and unloading on busy city services. The rear door reverted

to the customary position just behind the rear wheels and was designated as the entrance. The front door was located within the front partition or bulkhead and was specifically the exit. This positioning resulted in the elimination of the seats alongside the driver, who would no longer be distracted by passengers. From his seat, though, the driver could reach to open the exit door for alighting passengers. This retouched photograph of one of the first batch of C-Types, HT 5328, was used in Bristol's press advertisements through to 1925.

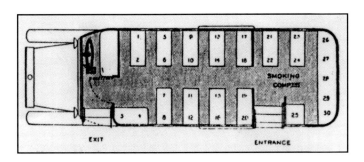

**49**. This is a plan of the seating layout of the **C-Type** body as it appeared in *Motor Transport* for 14th August 1922. It shows that 30 seats were provided, even with the additional doorway. Note that three seats faced inwards. The rear of the saloon was designated as a smoking area and a full-height partition was installed on each side, level with the left-hand side of the entrance steps. The accompanying report stressed that ventilation, as a result, had been carefully considered. The number of opening windows and vent panels was mentioned and it went on to say that, with the front door open, "a good draught is secured"!

**50**. The interior of the **C-Type** body on HT 5328 is shown here, from the very back of the bus, so as to include the partition of the smoking compartment. The exit door can be seen to be entirely left of the centre-line and that the front bulkhead was staggered at this point, with this half being set further forward than the section behind the driver. The roof was tongued and grooved boarding and enamelled white inside, while covered on the outside with canvas. The panels below the windows were in three-ply walnut. The body pillars were made of ash, with the steel reinforcing plates, and ash was used for the hoopsticks as well. There was claimed to be only a slight increase in weight over the B-Type body.

**51**. This photograph shows **C-Type** bodies under construction at the Bristol Aeroplane Company's plant at Filton. All the bodies are being built on trestles and the basic material in use is revealed by the amount of wood shaving covering the floor! Other photographs taken in this shop show that the Armstong Siddeley motor cars were built under the same roof. The 4-Ton bus chassis to receive these bodies were stock-piled in the open nearby, in Patchway, and were extracted in a some-what random order (they had gained chassis numbers in strict building order at the MCW). *(M J Tozer Collection)*

**52**. Shown here from the rear is a 4-Tonner with **C-Type** bodywork in service at the Victoria Rooms in Clifton, when the roadway was still paved with stone setts. It shows that the waistline was straight all round and that two rear windows, surmounted by ventilation slats, were featured. It therefore contrasts quite strongly with the bus in front, HT 4498, one of the last with **B-Type** bodies.

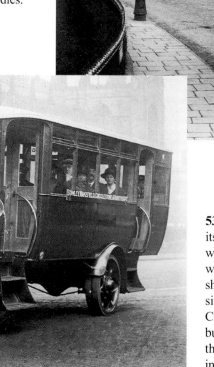

**53**. The West Riding Automobile Company began its lengthy association with Bristol in July 1922, with the start of the delivery of nineteen 4-Tonners with **C-Type** bodywork. Here, 110 (HL 1376) is shown in front of Wakefield Cathedral, with its side route board reading: 'Stanley, Wakefield, Crigglestone and Painthorpe'. As first built, the buses carried the standard route-number box at the front, but this example has a destination indicator in that position.

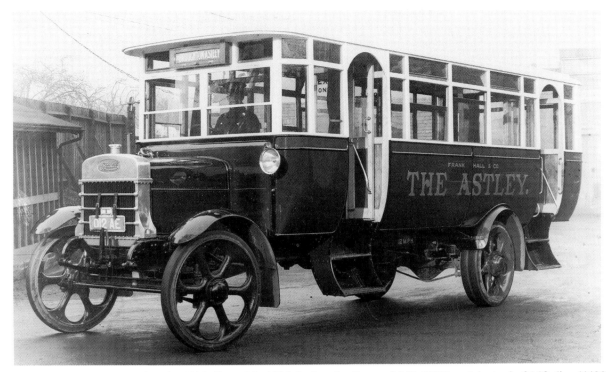

**54**. The 4-Ton chassis displayed at the 1922 Show, No.1534, had a wheelbase of 16ft (4876mm) instead of 14ft 6ins (4420mm). During 1923 a two-doorway body was built for it, but of a revised design. This was the first of a family to be known as the **HA-type** body. The rear doorway was moved slightly aft, with a half-bay ahead of it, and the roof at the front was levelled out, with a re-siting of the destination indicator below the peak. In the event, there were to be several variations of entrance and seating layouts and this first example was duplicated only once. In this bus, the front exit was located in the side, immediately behind the front bulkhead, and fitted with twin doors at the top of the steps. There were therefore two short windows between the door arch and the windscreen pillar and one short window to its rear. Later, the bus was painted for Frank Hall & Company, trading as 'The Astley', of Broughton Astley, Leicestershire, and was sold to them on 1st January 1924 for £550. It was then registered NR 3534.

**55**. The building of 14ft 6in wheelbase 4-Ton chassis continued for a short while, until the 16ft version was put into production in 1923 at chassis number 1556. The first batch with **HA-Type** bodywork comprised 12 more buses for West Riding, including 142 (HL 1803), shown here. On these buses there was just a single doorway, at the front, and 32 seats. The rather wide doorway was directly alongside the driver, the bulkhead being at right angles to the first pillar. An emergency exit was provided, located in the centre of the rear wall and flanked by matching windows. Note the lowering side windows and hinged top-lights. *(M J Tozer Collection)*

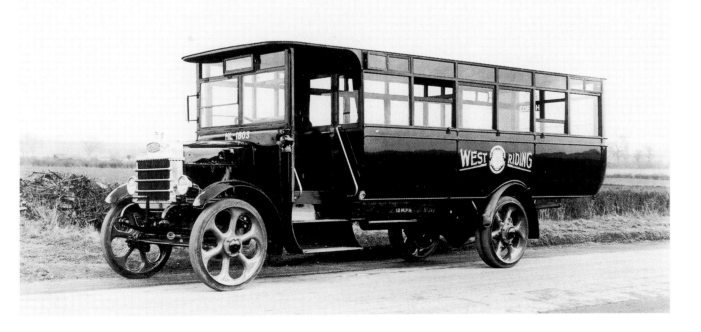

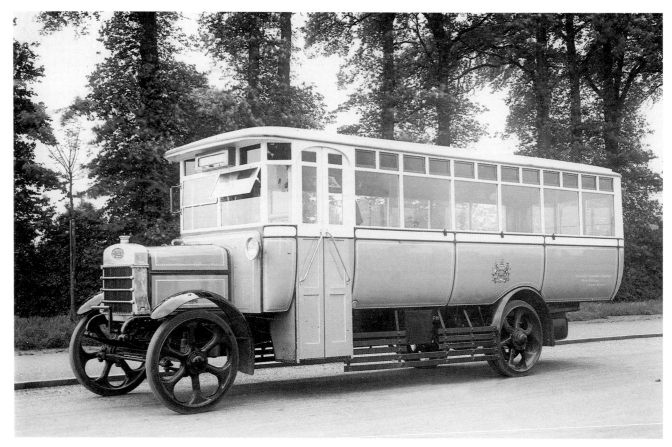

56. The 12 single-door West Riding buses were followed by six for Manchester Corporation, also with single-door **HA-Type** bodies. These, however, had yet another type of front door layout. This had a narrow opening, protected by two leaves that closed across the bottom of the steps. There was one short window ahead of the door and the rear featured the central emergency exit again. The main side windows were fixed, with a compensation being made in the quantity of opening top-lights. This batch, which carried smartly lined-out red and white livery, was registered ND 6234-7, 8183 and 8201.

57. Although the 16ft wheelbase had become the standard for 4-Ton passenger models, a further twelve 14ft 6in chassis were built in 1924, complete with **C-Type** bodywork! These had chassis numbers 1581-7/9-93 and were distinguished by the radiator which had been introduced with the 16ft wheelbase chassis, featuring a small Bristol scroll within an oval surround. Shown here is one of a pair that was supplied to Sunderland District Tramways, namely 51 (PT 2956); others went to Doncaster Corporation and Devon Motor Transport.

**58**. Typifying the most numerous variant of the **HA-Type** body are these two buses with two doorways and thirty seats. They were delivered in 1924 to Cornwall Motor Transport, which was allied to Devon Motor Transport and Jersey Motor Transport, all of whom received 4-Tonners. They were registered in Cornwall as AF 8752/3. In this version, the front exit was by way of a door within the front partition, this partition meeting the sides through curved panels, so making the steps a little narrower than on the West Riding bus shown in Plate 55. Inside, there was another partition, in this case attached to the pillar at the after end of the third main window.

**59**. The offside aspect of the **HA-Type** body on 4-Ton chassis is depicted here on Rhondda Tramways 143 (NY 8871). Note the short window between the driver's door and the first main side window. With the exception of Imperial Tramways subsidiary Corris Railway of Machynlleth, Rhondda owned the first Bristol bus to work in Wales, in the form of a 1923 4-Tonner with C-Type bodywork. This was followed by five bodied more locally by William Lewis, before the arrival of the three with HA-Type bodies in 1925. 'Cardiff' is displayed in both destination box and slip-board for the service from Pontypridd, via Taffswell. *(Chris Taylor Collection)*

60. Doncaster Corporation standardised on Bristol chassis for its first motor buses in 1922-24 and added thirteen 4-Tonners with C-Type bodies to the fleet, before taking this odd-one-out in 1925. No.20 (WU 2851) alone had an **HA-Type** body and this was of particular interest in being all-but identical to the body built in 1923 and supplied to Frank Hall, as shown in Plate 54. This pattern featured the front exit located behind a full-width cab. It is believed that only the two bodies of this style were built. The Doncaster livery was crimson lake and white. *(M J Tozer Collection)*

61. The first Welsh municipal customer for Bristol was Aberdare Urban District Council. One of the two 4-Tonners with **HA-Type** bodies delivered in 1925 is shown here. Its registration was NY 9777, issued, as on the Rhondda examples, by Glamorganshire County Council. These two had single-doorway bodies of the Manchester Corporation pattern, as shown in Plate 56, except that the side windows were of the conventional lowering type, with tilting top-lights. Note that this bus had pneumatic tyres instead of solids.

62. Chesterfield Corporation became an enthusiastic customer for Bristol vehicles. The operator placed in service no fewer than 17 **HA-Type** 4-Tonners in 1924-26. One of the 1926 delivery, with pneumatic tyres, was No.65 (NU 7907). The body was an example of the most numerous version of the two-door model and is similar to the Cornwall Motor Transport bus shown in Plate 58. On earlier Chesterfield 4-Tonners, the white relief to the green livery had been limited to the roof.

63. Yet another variation of the single-doorway **HA-Type** body was supplied on two 4-Ton chassis in 1926 to West Hartlepool Corporation. On these buses, the features of the doorway and steps were the same as in the most numerous version of the two-door bodies, such as that shown in the previous plate by the Chesterfield Corporation vehicle. Only just visible here is evidence that between the second and third side windows there was an extra window pillar; it would seem that this supported the internal partition, which was set further forward than normal and needed the special frame due to the positioning of the seats. The only opening side windows were ahead of this partition, curiously, although there were several double top-lights.

# Chapter 3

Bristol introduced an additional model in 1923. This was a somewhat smaller vehicle, to accommodate about 20 seats, and was called the 2-Tonner. The driver was seated alongside the engine – over the front axle – for the first time on a Bristol and, from the outset, it was designed to have fully-fronted bodywork to surround a smaller version of the Bristol radiator. The first chassis (numbered 0100) was fitted with a van body (both 2-Tonner and 4-Tonner Bristols were advertised as being equally suitable for goods or passenger applications), but the second chassis (0101) received a char-à-banc body and underwent extensive testing around Bristol before acting as a demonstrator. The saloon body that first appeared on 0102 had features similar to the 4-Tonner's HA body, but had a single doorway located at the front of the saloon. The body designation was FB, which might or might not have any connection with its being a full-front bus.

Early customers of FB-bodied 2-Tonners were Doncaster Corporation, St Helens Corporation and Devon Motor Transport. Interestingly, the latter then had second thoughts about running 20-seaters and soon traded in their six back to Bristol, against more 30-seat 4-Tonners! Those 2-Tonners were thereafter added to a rapidly growing stock of new examples in the Bristol company's operating fleet. The second 2-Tonner to have been built, which, as mentioned, had carried a char-à-banc body as a demonstrator, was soon rebodied with an FB saloon body and sold to West Riding, as one of the first of many 2-Tonners for this customer. Other early examples became the first of many Bristols supplied to Rotherham Corporation; on these the bodywork was built by Charles H Roe of Leeds, but the styling was very similar indeed to the Bristol FB body. Lancashire United, West Hartlepool Corporation and the Llandudno Coaching Company (trading as Royal Blue) were further customers of the FB body, as was A & R Graham of Kirkintilloch. The last FB bodies were built on 2-Tonners in 1926.

With new passenger models being launched in 1925/26, production of the 4-Tonner as a passenger chassis was drawing to a close, although it continued to win orders for goods applications. The last twelve 4-Ton passenger versions entered service in the winter of 1926/27 with BT&CC's operating fleet. Curiously, rather than carrying HA bodies, these twelve had a body of revised layout, designated the J-Type. This was slightly shorter in the tail section and accommodated only 29, rather than 31.

**64**. The first Bristol 2-Tonner to be registered following the model's introduction in 1923 was the second chassis built, 0101, which became HT 6520. This received a char-à-banc body, seating 20 in five rows of four. Each row had its own door, of course, and there were two continuous steps along the side, interrupted only by the rear wheel. The fourth door was shallower, due to the wheel arch, but an extra tip-up step was provided at the foot of the door. This door was hinged at the rear, while all others were hinged at the front. The completed vehicle, as seen here, was painted in a new shade of light blue and the finishing touch to the beautifully rounded rear panel was a splendid Bristol scroll, in gold! HT 6520 underwent stringent road testing in the west country and its ascent and descent of the infamous Porlock Hill was closely monitored by the trade press. In the event, this vehicle was to be short-lived in this form, besides which it turned out to be the last true char-à-banc – that is, with full-width seats and access to each row from outside – to be built by Bristol.

**65**. The 2-Tonner soon started to be built in large numbers and a high proportion for BT&CC's own fleet were again canvas-hooded 20-seaters, aimed at excursions and tours. Although looking similar to HT 6520 in the previous plate, the production vehicles had only the one doorway, at the front, and a central gangway. This is exemplified by HT 9977, with 20 adults – and a few toddlers! – out to enjoy the summer sunshine. Note that the two steps below the door could be folded flat against the body. The 2-Tonner was designed from the outset to carry fully-fronted coachwork. *(M J Tozer Collection)*

**66**. The first 2-Tonner to receive bus bodywork was HT 6524, with chassis number 0102. It accommodated 24 and had a single, front, entrance. There was a two-part door that closed across the foot of the steps. An emergency exit was provided centrally in the rear wall. The body design received the code of **FB-Type**, but it is not recorded whether FB stood for Full-fronted Bus! This vehicle acted as a demonstrator before entering BT&CC's own fleet.

**67 & 68.** Interior rearward and forward views of the **FB-Type** body on 2-Tonner HT 6524 show the light and spacious aspect of this model, for all its 24-seat capacity. It is notable that one seat was permitted across the rear emergency door; a notice painted on the door panel read, 'Emergency door – lift up seat and pull up lever'. Also visible is the method of lowering and raising the side windows. These used leather straps at the bottom in the same manner as used for many years in railway carriages and when the window was opened to the desired amount, a hole in the leather strap could be pushed over a brass stud. Bell push buttons were located at each juncture of window pillar and top-light, with an additional bell cord along the ceiling. The rearward view was taken through the opened driver's windscreen, so as to include the top of his seat. *(Both photographs – M J Tozer Collection)*

**69**. In October 1923 Doncaster Corporation received two **FB-Type** 2-Tonners as numbers 21 and 22 (WT 982/1), to join nine C-Type 4-Tonners already in the fleet. Unlike HT 6524, these FB bodies featured a full-width bulkhead behind the cab and a hinged door at the top of the steps, with an arch effect given to the door aperture. This became the most common style of body and in this form the FB-Type could be seen to resemble the HA-Type bodies on the 4-Tonners, particularly those for Frank Hall and Doncaster and shown in Plates 54 & 60. The FB-Type featured a pronounced waistrail, however.

**70**. Doncaster Corporation's immediate neighbour, Rotherham Corporation, also became a devotee of Bristol chassis. Rotherham, however, did not go in for Bristol bodywork, generally favouring Yorkshire builders. It was of interest, though, that for Rotherham's first two Bristols, 2-Tonners of December 1923, the styling of the bodywork built in Leeds by **Charles H Roe** was very similar indeed to that of the Bristol FB-Type body, particularly on HT 6524 in Plate 66. The only differences of any significance were that the two windows between the doorway and the windscreen were not of equal widths and all the windows around the front were deeper than the side windows. There was no raised waistrail but, curiously, a raised waistrail later became regarded as a Roe trade-mark! *(B.V.B.G. Collection)*

**71**. This offside view of an **FB-Type** 2-Tonner shows the last of a batch of six 20-seaters delivered to Devon Motor Transport in October 1923, but which remained there for only a short time. The bus, with Devon registration TA 8119, is seen at Crownhill while on a short-working of a service that in later years would be run by Plymouth Corporation buses. As early as April 1924, these six 2-Tonners were returned to Bristol, but in part-exchange for more 4-Tonners. BT&CC added the 2-Tonners to their own stock, but most spent a few years firstly on hire to the Corris Railway around Machynlleth. *(Allan Macfarlane Collection)*

**72**. In November 1923, the unique char-à-banc body on chassis 0101, illustrated in Plate 64, was removed and in its place an **FB-Type** 20-seat saloon body was fitted. The bus was painted for West Riding and was sold to them on 9th January 1924 as one of 50 similar vehicles. The original Bristol registration was cancelled and West Riding obtained a new mark, HL 1778, from Wakefield Borough Council. *(M J Tozer Collection)*

**73**. Bristol Tramways' own fleet, besides receiving a considerable stock of 2-Tonners with coach bodies, also received several with **FB-Type** saloon bodies. Some of these even worked services in the outer suburbs of Bristol, as shown here by HU 3516, rostered to run between Fishponds and Kingswood. The MCW offered a longer wheelbase version of the 2-Tonner, measuring 12ft 6ins (3810mm) instead of 11ft 6ins (3505mm). This bus is the second of two early chassis that were not initially bodied and were rebuilt in 1925 to the long wheelbase form and also re-numbered to 0251/2. The white-coated driver in this photograph was 'Skipper' Hooper, while the young conductor, Arthur Thorne, was the brother of the then district engineer at Lawrence Hill depot, Bert Thorne. *(M J Tozer Collection)*

**74**. The idea of the 'hotel bus' was still present in 1926 when this 2-Tonner was hired to the Grand Hotel in Bristol. Registered HU 6124, it carried a considerably modified **FB-Type** body, containing seats for only 16 passengers, together with the customary rear luggage compartment. The side windows were shorter and totalled five instead of four, while the twin doors at the entrance closed across the foot of the steps. The interior was trimmed rather more luxuriously than the conventional bus and the windows were fitted with curtains. It operated for the

Grand Hotel until 1933, after which it became firstly a road-test vehicle, then a ticket van and remained in use until 1947.

**75**. Both the 2-Ton and 4-Ton models of Bristol chassis were always made available for goods vehicle applications. Indeed, after new passenger models were introduced from 1925, the 2-Tonner and 4-Tonner were kept in production primarily for goods work. 2-Ton chassis 0259 was completed in 1926 with a Bristol van body of attractive styling, with a curve through the length of the roof. It was supplied to the Stroud Piano Company of Stroud in Gloucestershire, with registration DD 8905.

**76.** This 1925 4-Tonner with standard two-doorway, **HA-Type** 31-seat body, registered HU 1972, was one of the first of the sort to be built entirely at Brislington, following the termination of the arrangement with the Bristol Aeroplane Company earlier in 1925. The appearance was indistinguishable from those of the same pattern built at Filton. This photograph, with the background retouched by the commercial artist, was used in Bristol's trade advertisements of the period.

**77.** The last 4-Tonners to be built for passenger work were delivered to BT&CC's own fleet in 1926/27. Remarkably, these 12 buses had a new pattern of body! This was designated the **J-Type** and was slightly shorter in the tail section than the HA-Type. The half-window ahead of the rear door was eliminated, thereby bringing the door close to the wheel arch. Furthermore, the windows were shortened slightly, in order to accommodate the extra pillar – needed to support the internal partition – between equal-sized windows (the partition was located against the rearward of the two closely-pitched pillars). The seating capacity was reduced to 29. HU 6630 was photographed working service 84 from the Tramway Centre to Fishponds (Cassell Road), which was by this time operated jointly by BT&CC and Greyhound of Bristol. *(M J Tozer Collection)*

**78.** The 4-Tonner chassis remained in production for goods vehicle operators until 1931; most were completed as tankers for the major petrol companies. On 5th February 1929, however, chassis 1830 was completed with a Bristol van body for Fletcher Hardware of Birmingham, bearing registration VP 5414. Apart from having a fully-enclosed cab and being on pneumatic tyres, comparison with the van illustrated in Plate 44 will show the general outline; the shape of the valance over the windscreen and the signwriting on the body sides were the same, even though the two vans were built eight years apart. *(M J Tozer Collection)*

# Chapter 4

The highlight of 1925 was the launch of a new Bristol heavy chassis, in which the floor level of the bodied vehicle was appreciably reduced in height. This was achieved by lowering the frame, basically through the simple expedient of cranking the longitudinal members over the axles. Three steps were still required to reach the interior, however, even if shallower. The new model had the driver seated alongside the engine, as in the 2-Tonner. At this point, Bristol's MCW commenced the alphabetical designation system for chassis as already started by BBW and care should be taken not to confuse the two. (Care should also be taken not to confuse the term MCW, as used in this book, with the post-1932 bodybuilding organisation, Metropolitan-Cammell Weymann.) The new lower chassis was the Bristol A-Type and BBW built a fully-fronted, two-doorway, 32-seat body for the first example (A.101). In styling, it was very much a scaled-up FB body, with a good amount gleaned from the HA as well. No designation code is on record for this body, but the bus was universally known by the nick-name 'The Crab'!

The A-Type chassis was designed to be bodied either as a single-decker or as a double-decker and, indeed, A.102 to A.108 were constructed with double-deck bodies, of other makes, over the next two years, for Doncaster and Kingston-upon-Hull Corporations. In 1927, though, BBW came to build its own double-deck bus bodies for the first time, to the order of Manchester Corporation. These elegant buses had a total seating capacity of 52. Three equally elegant single-deck versions were to follow, for Bath Tramways Motor Company, with seating for no fewer than 36.

Even before the A-Type had entered production, Bristol Tramways was able to launch, in 1926, an improved low-loading light passenger chassis, the B-Type. This took the technology of the A-Type one step further and the completed prototype, B.101, was still lower and sleeker in appearance ... and gone were the top lights over the side windows for ever! Interestingly, the body for B.101, built in December 1926, was actually made by the MCW rather than BBW. Obviously the full co-operation of BBW was gained, but the policy of constructing experimental bodies by the MCW rather than BBW was to be repeated. Looking at it from a practical point of view, it would be logical for the MCW to take on the financial and technical responsibility, though the actual construction work was probably undertaken by skilled BBW staff.

The body built on B.101 was a two-doorway 30-seater, classified as the AB-Type. Interestingly, the completed body was initially left unpainted, but with a burnished finish to the metal panelling, as later became a popular feature for the bonnets of Bristol vehicles.

A great deal was made in the trade press of the method employed to bring the floor of the bodied B-Type down to only 26 inches (66 cm) above ground level, which was four inches (10.2 cm) lower than even the A-Type. The decision, quite unconventional at the time, was to do away with the body-bearing timber underframe, which was laid upon the chassis members. Instead, the body floor, made up of boards placed transversely, was laid directly on to the chassis, with a layer of felt as insulation. The body pillars were then bolted through the floor and attached to outriggers which were themselves secured to the chassis frame. The pillar joints were encompassed in steel brackets, which were bolted in place, giving a much stronger structure than the mortise and tenon wood joinery.

The B-Type turned out to be Bristol's most successful chassis yet and during its seven-year production run, BBW offered several good-looking body styles, progressively improving their appearance. The introduction of further new construction methods also occurred while producing coachwork for the B-Type chassis.

While the drawing office was styling the coachwork for the first B-Type chassis, it also restyled the 2-Tonner body in the same fashion. In so doing, the 2-Tonner became a half-cab model for the first time. The first examples appeared in mid-1927, when production resumed after nearly a year's break. This new body style was classified BB and was obviously related to the new AB body.

Construction of the B-Type chassis soon got under way in significant numbers, particularly for municipalities. These early customers, however, ordered their bodywork from other builders, like Roe and Reeve & Kenning. It is interesting to relate, though, that the batches of Roe bodies for West Hartlepool Corporation and Northern Counties bodies for Wigan Corporation were both built very much to the BBW styling! Even more flatteringly, Wigan Corporation shortly afterwards took delivery of some Northern Counties-bodied Pagefield chassis – a very uncommon make – and these bodies, too, closely resembled the Bristol body.

The first BBW bus to follow the prototype B-Type chassis was as late as B.158, new in September 1927 and the first of three for Aberdare Urban District Council. The body was very similar to that on B.101, but BBW introduced new codings for the three variants of entrance position and equipment available on production bodies; these were L1, L2 and L3. The first was the dual-doorway model, the second similar but convertible for driver-only operation, while the third was a front-entrance body. Another variation, however, a rear-entrance body built on 15 consecutive chassis for Manchester Corporation, was coded as the EB, while the EB4 was a major variation – with central entrance – for Chesterfield Corporation.

A canvas-hooded coach was also made available for the B-Type chassis. Unlike previous specimens, this style of coach had permanent side windows (albeit with slender, metal frames). Plush seating was provided for 26 or so, with a central gangway. Interestingly, the driver's cab had its own canvas hood. On these coaches there was the option of the main hood folding down behind the rear seats, or, as on the coach displayed at the 1927 Commercial Show (B.148 for Richard Baxter's Manor Motor Coaches of Clapham, London), there was a solid rear dome and roof section. The rear wall contained a new item of high fashion – an oval rear window! This item was later to be incorporated into Bristol saloon bodies and remained in fashion until the mid-1930s.

The original location of the front destination box on L1, L2 and L3 saloon bodies for B-Type chassis, as well as on the concurrent BB bodies for the 2-Tonner, was suspended under the front canopy. From May 1928, though, the box was resited in the leading edge of the roof, which was thereafter the customary position. No 2-Tonner saloons were built in 1928, but when they next appeared, in 1929, these carried the revised destination box location; they also carried a revised body classification, of CB.

Meanwhile and to revert to bodywork for the B-Type chassis, more new variations in 1928/29 saw resumed use of alphabetical sequence letters for their designations. Given that the current saloons were classified in an L-series, the newcomers were the M-Type, an open-rear-platform saloon for Manchester; the MA, a rear-entrance body for Bradford; and the N-Type, a high-waisted body furnished with coach seats and curtains. After those came the P1 in 1930, a central-entrance bus for Pontypridd U.D.C., yet very similar to Chesterfield's EB4.

**79**. Bristol took a major step forward in 1925 with a new model featuring a lower chassis frame than hitherto and designed specifically for passenger carrying. The MCW now followed BBW's lead in allocating designation letters in alphabetical sequence, so the new chassis was the Bristol A-Type. The first example, A.101, was bodied by BBW as a 32-seater, with two doors and a full-front. The body styling was clearly derived from both the FB-Type body on 2-Tonner chassis and the HA-Type body on 4-Tonners – particularly of the Frank Hall pattern seen in Plate 54. The entrance was at the rear, with a two-leaf door at the top of the steps, while the exit was at the front, directly behind the bulkhead of the spacious cab, and had a single door. It will be seen the panelling of the door and porch was in polished wood. The front profile was very upright, but the appearance was eased by the clever finish to the radiator. This was designed so that the body panels were set almost flush with its face. The headlights, as previously, were situated just below windscreen level. The three side windows ahead of the internal partition were able to be lowered. When first completed, the bus was painted in a light colour, with a contrasting shade to the waistband and window surrounds. In this picture, the bus is in standard BT&CC dark-blue and white and is registered HU 4325. A body designation code has not been revealed, but the bus earned the nickname of **'The Crab'**!

Most N-Type coaches were supplied to a well-known operator, Greyhound Motors of Bristol. This company's claim to fame is that when they established their coach service between Bristol and London in 1925, it was the world's first long-distance express service with scheduled boarding and alighting points *en route*, yet requiring no pre-booking arrangements. Greyhound also ran stage services in and around Bristol, in competition with Bristol Tramways, but in 1928 BT&CC had gained control of Greyhound. For the next eight years, Greyhound functioned as a subsidiary of BT&CC and was now furnished with new buses and coaches of Bristol manufacture ... naturally!

Quite clearly, BBW's draughtsmen and designers were being kept very active during this period and besides the special patterns of bodies mentioned in the preceding paragraphs, they were designing bodies of an experimental nature – one of particular significance –

as well as preparing a major styling update for the conventional range of saloon bodies!

The updating of the saloon's styling was well in hand under designations commencing at L4 and production of the L1 to L3 range was planned for phasing out by early 1930. The last were delivered to BT&CC's operating fleet early in the spring, but then some experimental subjects appeared, adapted from the L1 pattern. A solitary body was classified L8 and mounted on B.378 as BT&CC's HW 8366. The only visible difference from an L1 was that the front doorway was made wider. The L8 was immediately followed by just five L9s, the last of which went on five weeks' demonstration to Rhondda. No official portraits were taken of the L8 or of any L9, but it is known that they all resembled the L1 and were the last vestiges of that pioneering design. Already a good-looking successor was emerging from the Body Building Works!

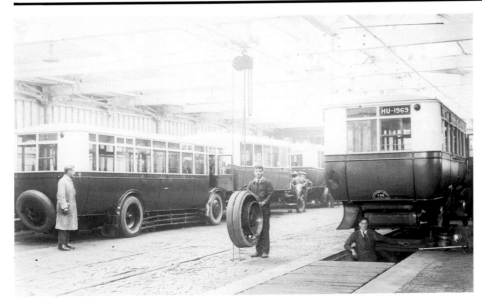

**80**. This shot taken inside the Motor Maintenance Department at Bristol's Lawrence Hill depot shows a variety of buses. On the left is HU 4325, the 1925 A-Type known as '**The Crab**'. This clearly shows the bus was considerably lower than the 4-Tonners around it. Those standing ahead are 1920/21 examples with **B-Type** bodies, while on the right is HU 1969, a 1925 specimen with **HA-Type** body. It will be seen that the A-Type bus has the spare wheel suspended rather awkwardly on the tucked-under rear panel, almost as if it was an afterthought!

**81**. BBW built its first double-deck bus bodies in 1927, to the requirements of Manchester Corporation. Chassis A.109-114 were fitted with these bodies and this photograph shows there was adequate head-room in the bodyshops to accommodate double-deckers. As can be seen by the painters at the left of the picture, external work on double-deckers required tall trestle ladders, although they would have been necessary during the assembly or painting of tramcars. All six buses here are in a similar stage of completion. They have been painted in red and white, but have not received the elaborate lining out, the bonnet and wings are detached and they have no seats: it is believed that 26 seats were installed in both the lower and upper saloons.

**82**. The completed double-deck A-Types for Manchester Corporation presented an elegant sight. The paintwork was tastefully lined out, the hinged top-lights contained patterned, coloured glass and there was a decorative fairing between the canopy and the bulkhead. Whereas the single-deck body on A.101, seen in Plate 79, was fully-fronted, these 1927 double-deckers were the first BBW bodies to feature a half-width cab! The dash was again set nearly flush to the front of the radiator, but the windscreen was inclined and set well back, with a considerable lip to the top of the dash. This is most evident in the elevated view in Plate 81. There were three windows

across the front of the upper deck, each with slotted, metal, permanent vents above, and small angled windows at the front corners. The roof contours were well rounded and the front dome overhung the front bulkhead, which was sited directly above the lower bulkhead, as it was still not the practice to continue the upper saloon over the cab. This nearside view shows the base of the curved external staircase, rising from a high rear platform. The access to the upper saloon was through a simple arched aperture; neither saloon had closing doors.

**83**. All six Manchester Corporation double-deck Bristol A-Types (which were later registered NF 4078-80 and 4143-5) are seen here posed in Brislington depot yard, below tramway overhead and beside ornate lighting and traction poles. It will be seen that the bodywork featured a top-light of plain, fixed glass over the windscreen and the destination box was suspended beneath the canopy. Side-lights – a new item – were also suspended here, while headlights were now level with the foot of the radiator. Although the major characteristics of the body were derived from the HA- and FB-Type bodies of the earlier single-deck models, the general layout is influenced by the Short Bros double-decker built on A.103, which had spent some time at Bristol in 1926. All the double-deck A-Types were soon to be rendered old-fashioned, though, with the launch later in 1927 of Leyland's trend-setting new Titan double-decker of an altogether lower build.

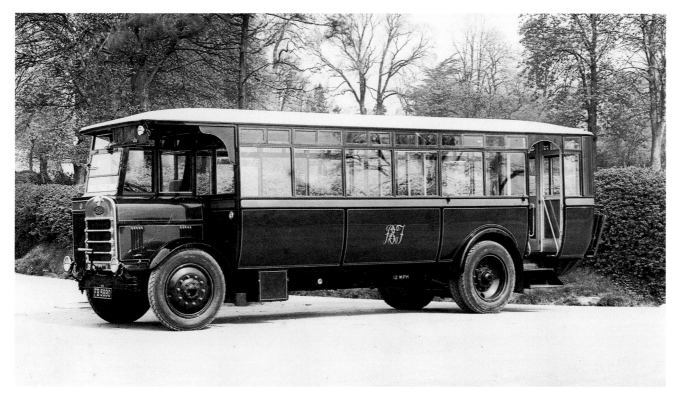

**84**. Delivered around the same time as the above Manchester A-Types, in April 1927, was a single-decker for the Bath Tramways Motor Company Ltd. It was painted in the company's livery of dark-green, with a white roof, but the monogram on the body sides comprised the letters BET of the parent company, Bath Electric Tramways Ltd. Registered FB 5890, it was the first of three for the operator that was a neighbour to BT&CC, but as yet was not under BT&CC administration. The body contained a single doorway at the rear and as such had the creditable seating capacity of 36, a figure not to be exceeded in BBW single-deckers until the dark days of World War II. The treatment of the cab and canopy styling is clearly derived from the double-deck version. The side window pillars, though, were slightly closer pitched than in the double-decker, as the rear doorway was up against the rear wheel arch.

**85**. Even before the Manchester and Bath A-Type buses had been bodied by BBW, the MCW had launched a lighter low-loading chassis, the B-Type. The body on the first chassis was even built in the MCW's works. The new bus was lower still than the A-Type and as the roof level was brought down, the side window arrangement dispensed with the top-lights ... for ever! (Taking their place were vertical ventilation slots.) Longer side windows further enhanced the low, sleek look. The body on chassis B.101 was designated **AB-Type** and was a dual-doorway 30-seater. The arrangement of the cab was similar to the Manchester and Bath buses, but as the

radiator of the B-Type was not designed to be partially enclosed by the bodywork, the front dash was not projected forward so much. The windscreen had a wide ventilation slot above it, rather than a top-light. The canopy fairing was gently curved, as were the tops of the door archways. There was a feature rail around the entire edge of the roof. Interestingly, the body panels were not painted; instead they were given a burnished finish to the sheet steel, while the deep waistrail was of polished wood. B.101 is posed here in Kings Road, a turning off Bath Road near to the works.

**86**. B-Type buses started entering service from 1927 and became a popular choice with municipalities. Early customers, however, did not receive their bodywork from BBW. Nevertheless, it is of some significance that the styling of the bodies built by Roe for West Hartlepool Corporation and by Northern Counties for Wigan Corporation had more than just a passing resemblance to the BBW design, whilst having almost nothing in common with the appearance of other products from those builders! Shown here is West Hartlepool 13 (EF 3473), whose **Roe** body emulated the Bristol AB-Type on B.101 even to the extent of having burnished steel panelling! The treatment of the roof edge, windscreen and dash, canopy fairing, general side-window arrangement and waistband closely followed the AB-Type. The side windows were slightly longer, though (with a rearward repositioning of the rear door) and there was an extra set of ventilation slots just aft of the front doorway. *(M J Tozer Collection)*

**87**. **Northern Counties** built the bodies on early B-Type chassis for Wigan Corporation and again these had strong similarities to the BBW design. This picture was part of an advertisement that Northern Counties placed in the trade press in November 1927, featuring Wigan Corporation 26 (EK 4999), although the lettering on the side was changed for anonymity. These bodies possessed a single, front doorway, and like the West Hartlepool buses, twin leaves closed across the foot of the steps. The windscreen appears to have been slightly more upright than on the BBW or Roe bodies. It was commonplace in this era for coachworks to build to styles specifically requested by customers, but in the case of

these two batches, it suggests that BT&CC supplied body drawings to go with the chassis ordered from their works. *(Allen Janes Collection)*

**88**. In June 1927, the first of 11 more small 2-Tonners was built for BT&CC's own operations. The buses carried a new design of 20-seat body, the **BB-Type**, which was clearly derived from the AB-Type built for B.101. HU 8170, seen here at Lawrence Hill bus depot, was the first example. It was on chassis 0297 and this was the first 2-Tonner to carry half-cab coachwork.

**89**. September 1927 saw the delivery of the first BBW-built saloon bodies on B-Type chassis since the prototype had appeared. Three buses were completed on chassis B.158/61/2 for Aberdare U.D.C. (respectively numbered 40, 32 and 39: TX 4105/9/7). For its production bodies, BBW introduced new model codes, namely L1, L2 and L3. This Aberdare bus had an **L2** body, which had the two-doorway layout, but was adaptable for operation by the driver only (known as one-man-operation). For this reason, it was equipped with an angled device between the cab nearside window and the bulkhead window, through which cash and tickets could be passed. When working in this mode, the rear door would be locked shut, while the front doorway was protected by a mechanically operated folding door that closed across the foot of the steps. Note that there was no ventilation slot above the windscreen.

**90**. The **L1-Type** body had the two-doorway layout, but the bus operated with a conductor on board in the manner then usual.

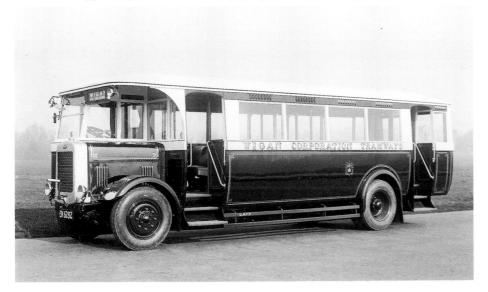

This picture shows that Wigan Corporation, having received the Northern Counties bodies in emulation of the BBW design, took delivery in March/April 1928 of genuine BBW-bodied B-Types, this being the first of three (31: EK 6282). The other two were delivered to Wigan with the exterior panels in primer, so the final painting could be applied by the Corporation. A small modification to the design from this point was that the height of the windscreen was increased, to eliminate the panel above. The opening upper part of the screen retained the same dimensions, resulting in deeper glass being used for the lower part.

**91**. This photograph shows that Wigan Corporation and Northern Counties had not finished with copying the BBW design yet. This time No.34 (EK 6284) illustrates that BBW styling was used for the **Northern Counties** bodies on *Pagefield* chassis – an uncommon make and a bizarre situation! The layout reverted to the single-doorway, 32-seat pattern. The front dash was sloped to match the rake of the radiator, while the trailing side window took on a shape that was never found on genuine BBW products.

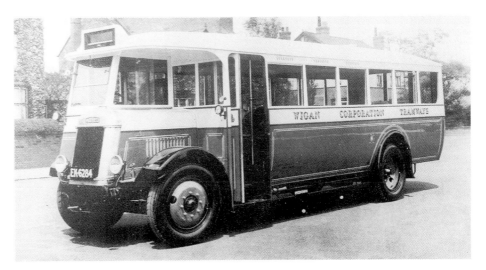

**92**. The trade press frequently used the highly developed skills of technical artists to illustrate features of chassis and bodywork that could not be captured by a camera. This combined drawing illustrates excellently the method adopted by BBW to enable the floor height of bodies on B-Type chassis to be only 26 inches (66cm) above the ground. The bodies did away with the traditional bulky (and heavy) underframing and passed the body pillars through the floor to be attached to chassis outriggers. The different parts of the body frame were secured by steel pieces, giving strong, rigid joints.

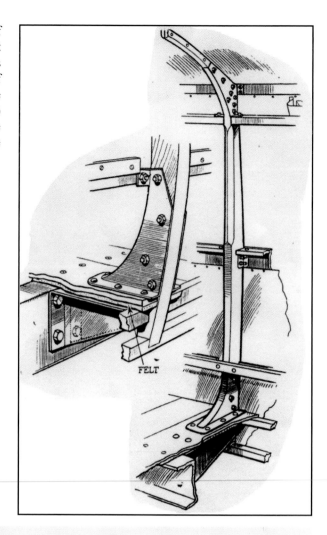

**93** (below). Although Devon Motor Transport and Cornwall Motor Transport had ceased buying Bristols before the 4-Tonner was dropped from the passenger range (the two companies were taken over in 1928 anyway, by the National Omnibus & Transport Company), their former relation Jersey Motor Transport did continue to support Bristol, with one batch of three B-Type chassis. They were delivered in March 1928 and carried **L1-Type** bodies. A luggage pen was installed in the space behind the rear doorway and this can be seen in No.16 (J 4326), which was photographed on Bristol's Durdham Downs, in an area known as the Sea Walls.

**94**. Although not under municipal control, Norwich possessed an urban transport network which was equal to many municipal systems. When the Norwich Electric Tramways Company started to develop local bus routes, the Bristol B-Type was regarded as a suitable choice. No.15 (VG 378) carried an **L1-Type** body, with the usual 30-seat capacity. This picture clearly shows the arrangement of the front door, set at an angle and hung from a short longitudinal partition attached to the bulkhead. A rearward-facing seat was placed beyond this, with its back to the driver's cab.

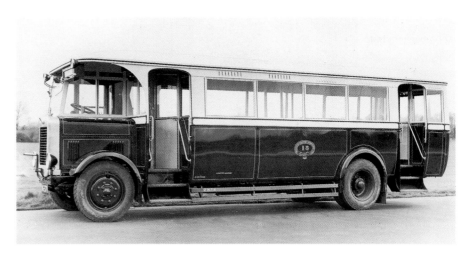

**95 & 96**. The first **L3-Type** bodies were built in May 1928, for St Helens Corporation. This model featured a single, front, doorway, with seating for 32. An emergency door was provided in the centre of the rear wall, as had become customary. The rear view of No.17 (DJ 3648) shows that the rear windows, as well as those in the front bulkhead, still featured top-lights. The right-hand one, though, would normally carry the registration number, permitting back-illumination to be obtained after dark from the saloon lighting – meagre though that arrangement was. From this stage, the frontal appearance of the bodywork was enhanced by resiting the destination box into the leading edge of the roof. St Helens was still perpetuating an elaborately lined out livery, with the lower sides in white, in the fashion of the tramcars. For this purpose, these BBW bodies were finished with an extra rubbing strip at wheel arch level. Kings Road is again the location for these photographs. *(Rear view – M J Tozer Collection)*

**97**. Returning to the autumn of 1927, the second batch of saloon bodies built by BBW on B-Type chassis were to a special 32-seat single-doorway layout to the order of Manchester Corporation. (They were delivered only about six months after the A-Type double-deckers shown in Plates 81-83.) In this case the entrance was at the rear and an unusual aspect was that the emergency door was located on the *nearside* of the bus at the front. This door was of regulation size, so was narrower than the width of the bay; a filler window was therefore inserted between the door and the first pillar. BBW gave this design of body a separate code and it was known as the **EB-Type**. Depicted here on the northern side of the Sea Walls area of Bristol's Downs is No.80 (NF 8258).

**98**. In contrast to the sunny conditions in which Manchester No.80 was photographed, No.83 (NF 8259) and two sisters were photographed in dismal autumn conditions, in the driveway of the MCW's main works; the railway line passed behind where the furthest bus was standing. This photograph shows the general aspect of the offside of the late-1920s Bristol bodywork on B-Type chassis.

**99**. This is an interior view of a Manchester Corporation **EB-Type** rear-entrance 32-seater. The location of the front nearside emergency door can be seen, together with the dividing screen between smoking and non-smoking areas. Careful study will reveal the metal brackets used to join the wooden roofsticks. More clearly seen, though, is a familiar item in the bodywork on B-Type chassis, and that is the split-level front bulkhead. The short bonnet allowed the nearside half of the bulkhead to be positioned further forward than the part behind the driver's seat. In this case, though, a short section to his right is again set forward, to give as much leg-room as possible to the passengers in the forward-facing offside seat. The bodybuilder's plate is attached to the wooden rail beneath the lettering 'Emergency Door'.

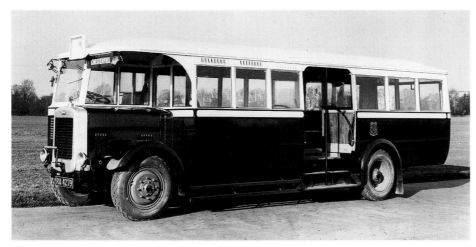

**100**. In February 1928, a solitary body was built for an established customer, Chesterfield Corporation. Their seventeen 4-Tonners, as illustrated in Plate 62, were followed by no fewer than 31 early B-Types. For the latter, however, Chesterfield contracted Reeve & Kenning of near-by Pilsley to build the bodywork, with central-entrances. One further chassis was then bodied by BBW. This also incorporated a central doorway and was given the type code of **EB4**. The entrance was very wide, but it was not furnished with doors. It can be seen that the windows ahead of the doorway were slightly narrower than those to its rear. The front destination box is in the underslung position of the time, but Chesterfield specified the addition of the route number box. The 30-seat bus was numbered 84 (RA 4279); note the pressed aluminium registration plate – this was another item specifically ordered by Chesterfield.

**101**. Around May 1928, Manchester Corporation received a second batch of rear-entrance Bristol B-Types. These, however, were to a different specification, in which Manchester required a wider access to the rear door. As a result, the rear nearside corner panelling was inset, to be level with the door, and the steps were widened in consequence. The size of the door aperture and the position of the grab-handles was not improved, so the flow of passengers into the saloon was unlikely to have been speeded up. BBW introduced a fresh code for these bodies, resuming an alphabetical sequence, and they were termed the **M-Type**. The batch comprised Manchester's 114-125, which bore VM registration letters.

**102**. In July/August 1928 Bradford Corporation, who, earlier in the year, had received two B-Types with L1 dual-door bodies, took delivery of a further twelve Bs. These had another variation on the rear-entrance theme and the body was coded the **MA-Type**. In these, the rear door was moved up close to the wheel arch, while the window pillars were set closer together, to accommodate the mountings for the internal partition in relation to a revised seating arrangement. A short window was inserted ahead of the door and repeated on the offside. The emergency exit was located at the front of the offside, but the door was narrower than the bay's width, leaving solid panelling between this and the driver's door. Unusually, the front bulkhead was not staggered (note the gap between the bulkhead and the front wing), yet with the other changes to the design, an increased seating capacity of 34 was achieved. Bradford 343 (KW 4362) was photographed at the Sea Walls, with the Avon Gorge beyond.

**103**. Following the construction of the MA-Type bodies for Bradford, the idea of siting the rear doorway close up to the rear wheel arch was adopted as standard for the L1 and L2 bodies. Shown here in Brislington depot is an **L1-Type** for Rhondda Tramways (51: TX 6379). Its seating capacity was 32. The moving forward of the rear door slightly upset the symmetry of the body, by eliminating the short blank panel between the door and the side window ahead of it, while leaving such a panel in place by the front door. This bus was one of five delivered on 28th November 1928.

**104**. A demonstrator with **L2-Type** 32-seat bodywork, suitable for one-man-operation, was built in September 1928 and registered HW 3107. The aperture between the bulkhead and driver's windows was fitted with curved glass. The side windows received sign-writing in the form of the Bristol scroll and lettering to indicate the 'Dual Purpose' nature of the bus – one-man or conductor operated. In the December, this bus was sold to Aberdare Urban District Council as number 33. *(M J Tozer Collection)*

**105**. The interior of the **L2-Type** body of demonstrator HW 3107 serves to illustrate the usual finish of a BBW body of the late 1920s. The tongue-and-groove roof, grab-rails along the ceiling, the smoking partition and leather-clad seats are captured in this view. *(M J Tozer Collection)*

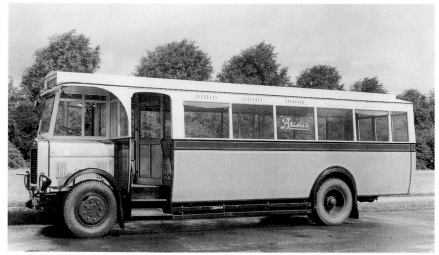

**106**. Another demonstrator, although built nearly a year later (August 1929), illustrates the **L3-Type** front entrance body which, until now, had only been built for St Helens Corporation (Plates 95 & 96) and West Riding. More emphasis was to be placed on the front-entrance version from this point onwards. The pillar spacing is as revised in 1928 and shown in Plates 103 & 104, resulting in a longer trailing side window than in the St Helens bodies. Additionally, the chassis was on a 16-foot wheelbase, rather than the earlier 15ft 7in. This L3 was registered HW 6638 and it was sold in January 1930 to the Merseyside Touring Company of Bootle, as number 74.

**107**. The styling of the six 1929 2-Ton Bristols for BT&CC's own fleet was updated to match the concurrent bodies on B-Type chassis, by featuring the destination box in the leading edge of the roof. The body code was accordingly changed from BB to **CB-Type**. When compared to the BB-Type in Plate 88, it will be noticed that the slight lip to the front dash has been dispensed with and the side windows have received glass louvres at the top. HW 5640, the first 2-Tonner with a CB body, is labelled for a Weston-super-Mare town service.

**108.** For B-Type chassis intended for operation on express services, a new body was designed, combining comfortable trim with a functional appearance. It was called the **N-Type**. The styling was based on the current saloon (compare with the L3 in Plate 106), but the waistline and window line were somewhat higher, leaving no room for the ventilation slots. The door was an outward-opening hinged item and the base of the windscreen was brought forward, eliminating the lip at the top of the dash as well as increasing its slope. There was a luggage carrier on the roof and route boards attached to the sides of the roof. The N-Type shown is the first of two delivered to West Riding (268: HL 4218) in March 1929 and which, despite the luxury of a plusher trim and curtains, still accommodated 32.

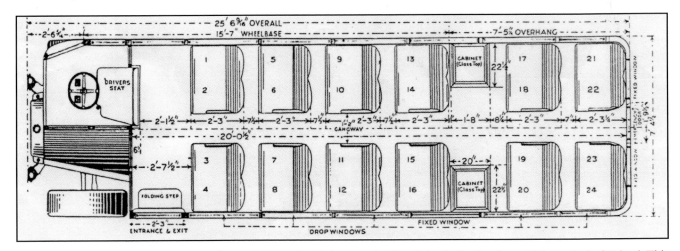

**109.** A further five **N-Type** express coaches on B-Type chassis became the first Bristols for Greyhound Motors Ltd of Bristol. This pioneer of long-distance services had come under BT&CC control in 1928 and subsequent new stock was, naturally, of Bristol manufacture. This plan, from *Tramway & Railway World* of 14th February 1929, shows that in these coaches, seating was provided for only 24. No seat faced sideways and the rear wheel arches were covered by glass-topped cabinets; in these were kept refreshments for passengers on the long journeys. Seats were spring-filled, overlaid with horse hair and upholstered in moquette. Some seat backs incorporated folding glass-topped tables. It was stated that ash was used for the body framework; the floor was made from ash and deal, $^7/_8$ inch thick, and covered in green linoleum, overlaid with grey Wilton carpet. The bent ash hoop-sticks of the roof were reinforced with steel flitch plates, the roof being of silver spruce, tongued and grooved. The roof was lined inside with Sundeala panels and lincrusta enrichments. Teak was used for the cant rail, while the interior side panels were birch plywood, carpeted to match the seats. Mouldings and cappings were in polished walnut. A clock was attached to the bulkhead and the finishing touch was the drapery with silk rep curtains.

60

**110.** Merthyr Tydfil Corporation joined the growing list of operators in South Wales which turned to Bristol for the supply of buses, with two B-Types in July 1929. These two, illustrated by No.21 (HB 3475), had **MA-Type** rear-entrance bodies as supplied in the previous year to Bradford Corporation (Plate 102). In Merthyr Tydfil's case, though, there were only 32 seats. The livery was deep-red and white, with a bright red waistband.

**111.** BBW 'look-alike' bodywork was built by Northern Counties, by Roe and ... by Rhondda Transport! In early 1930, in a very unusual move, Rhondda rebodied three of their Bristol 4-Tonner chassis that had been received initially in 1924/25 with bodies by William

Lewis. The new bodies are recorded as having been built by Rhondda themselves, but the strong similarity to the BBW product is very clear; it cannot be ruled out that BBW supplied parts, or at least drawings. Curiously, the new bodies were of rear entrance layout, unusual on 4-Tonners and not specified by Rhondda for its newer Bristols. The treatment of the rear corner, the door archway, and even the leading edge of the roof and destination box is unmistakably BBW in character. Seen here is NY 6731. *(Chris Taylor Collection)*

**112.** Another new customer for Bristol from South Wales was Pontypridd Urban District Council and again the operator was to feature in Bristol's order-books for a long while. Their first specimens were four B-Type chassis which were bodied by BBW to Pontypridd's specific requirements. These buses were of central entrance layout, with seating for only 26. The bodies were coded

**P1-Type**, although in fact they were very similar indeed to the EB4 body built for Chesterfield Corporation in 1928 and shown in Plate 100. In the P1 bodies, the seats in the rear half of the saloon, excepting those at the very back, were inward-facing and accommodated five on each side. The entrance vestibule was 4 feet wide, protected by two doors placed at the top of the steps, and a luggage pen was located opposite the doorway. Twelve forward-facing seats occupied the forward saloon. No.4 (TX 9545) and its consorts was completed in May 1930, by which time BBW bodies of conventional layout had a more rounded outline.

113. While the wide variety of saloon-type bodies was being built on Bristol B-Type chassis from 1927, a range of soft-topped luxury coaches appeared, albeit in small numbers. These coaches featured doorways front and rear and there was a central gangway. Moving further from the char-à-banc theme, there were now permanent windows to the sides, albeit with slender metal frames. The first B-Type to be registered by BT&CC received the mark HU 9646 on 22nd July 1927. The vehicle was a 26-seat coach on chassis B.147. This elevated view from the front shows the layout of the leather-covered seats, whereby there were three together behind the driver's cab, while at the rear, the seats were inclined from the transverse. Note the four rear seats benefited from arm-rests and that the hood was rolled into a space behind these seats. *(M J Tozer Collection)*

114. The hood on the canvas-topped B-Type coaches could be raised and lowered by one person and the winding handle and pulley wheel mounting can be seen attached to the front bulkhead. Note that the driver's cab had its own hood. This coach is lettered for Richard Baxter's Manor Motor Coaches of Clapham Common, London. However, none of the coaches actually delivered to Baxter quite resembled this vehicle, so, as the styling was virtually identical to the coach in the preceding plate, it is assumed to be one of BT&CC's ten examples specially painted in Baxter livery for demonstration. The photograph was taken at the Sea Walls in spring sunshine about April time, so probably in 1928.

**115**. The 1927 Commercial Motor Show had on display the coach shown here, mounted on chassis B.148. Again it was a 26-seat, two-doorway model, but in this case there was a solid rear dome and roof-section, on top of which was mounted a luggage carrier. The rear wall featured an 'oval' rear window, which was just coming to the height of fashion! The coach was painted for Richard Baxter's Manor Motor Coaches of Clapham Common, London, to whom it was not delivered until 4th April 1928, being registered YV 3659.

**116**. Following the construction of the 11 coaches described above in 1927/28, only one more canvas-topped B-Type coach was built, as the style was fast going out of fashion. B.407 was completed on 17th May 1929, again for Baxter's Manor Motor Coaches. Again the body featured a solid rear dome and roof section, but the window pillars were coarser and part of the main body framing. The capacity was increased to 30. Kings Road is the location of this photograph of what was to become UU 3129. Note the polished radiator shell.

**117**. The year 1929 saw Bristol Tramways take a renewed interest in the 2-Tonner, as beside the construction of the six CB-Type 20-seat service buses, as shown in Plate 107, they also built an equal number of 20-seat soft-top coaches around the same time. The bodywork had obvious similarities to that on B.407 in the plate above, although there was only a front door, while an emergency door was located in the rear wall. These coaches featured a new livery for BT&CC coaches, of deep and medium blue, with a white waistband.

# Chapter 5

The 1929 Commercial Motor Show was the occasion at which Bristol displayed a strikingly restyled and particularly handsome saloon body, on B.600. The roof was deepened and gently curved down to meet the body sides, instead of forming a sharp edge at cantrail level, and the whole rear end was attractively rounded. The finishing touch to the new rounded theme was found in the rear wall ... the oval back window! The new body was one of a series that was to go into production early in 1930 and, in its various forms, classified between L4 and L10.

Also on display at the 1929 Show were examples of no fewer than three new Bristol chassis types, although none was bodied for this occasion. The *six*-wheeled double-deck models – the C-Type motor bus and E-Type trolleybus variant – unfortunately never got beyond prototype stages. However, the new single-decker, which featured a six-cylinder engine for the first time and was designated D-Type, did go into production, albeit limited in comparison with the B-Type from which it was derived. Indeed, other than the need for a slightly higher bonnet line and the introduction of a sleek new pattern of radiator, the D-Type chassis was able to accept the same range of bodies as applied to the B.

The new range of 'rounded' BBW bodies initially comprised three variants, as successors to the L1 to L3. The L4 was a front-entrance bus (in which the emergency door was placed in the centre of the rear wall as usual, although this precluded the use of the stylish oval rear window); the L5 was a dual-door version convertible for use under driver-only operation; and the L10 was a dual-door body without the latter facility. When the D-Type chassis entered production later in 1930, D.101/2/4 were bodied with L10 coach-work for demonstration work. No rear-entrance bodies were built to this rounded design.

Of great interest, for their own operating fleet BT&CC contracted out the building of L10-type bodies to two other coachbuilders in 1930. Eighteen were built by Northern Counties of Wigan, whose involvement with BBW designs on B-Type chassis has already been noted, while six were built at Dartford in Kent by J C Beadle. All were successful copies of the Bristol L10.

During 1931, the front-entrance body was made available with a wider doorway. This was classified L6, but was sub-designated L6-1 when fitted to B-Type chassis and L6-2 when applied to the D.

Reverting to September 1930, a body that had been under development for more than a year emerged on chassis B.384, under the designation L7. Of considerable interest, this was Bristol's first 'all-metal' body. The use of steel for framework had long been employed in railway carriage manufacture and firms involved with both railway carriage and bus body construction had already adapted the technology to suit the road vehicles. Making the framework from steel enabled the same amount of strength and rigidity to be reached from an appreciably lighter and more slender structure.

Two other experimental bodies appeared the following month under code L10-1. One was on B.385, the next chassis to that which received the L7 body, while the other replaced the AB body on chassis B.101! Unfortunately, records no longer exist to indicate how the L10-1 body differed from others; what is known is that it was of dual-doorway layout, with the oval back window. It is said to have had taller side windows, eliminating the permanent vents above them, also a feature of the L7.

The AB body from B.101 was not wasted; it had already been transferred in April 1930 to the D-Type chassis that had appeared incomplete at the 1929 Show. This D-Type was now prepared for service, only to be re-engined in July 1930 with a four-cylinder engine and accordingly renumbered B.777. The latter, complete with the 1926 AB body, then entered BT&CC traffic registered HY 1969. As an aside, one of the requirements of receiving the 1926 body was that the D-Type had to be fitted with a chassis frame of the 15' 7" wheelbase variety, applicable to B-Types until 1929; from then on, a 16' wheelbase was used on B- and D-Type chassis.

A further experimental body appeared in June 1931. This was mounted on chassis D.110 and differed considerably from current BBW bodies. It had its own designation of XB and, interestingly, the body was hand-built at the MCW, rather than in the Tram Depot. The XB body was a 32-seat front-entrance saloon, which featured a rather heavy-looking, overhanging front dome and an upwardly-curved waistline at the rear. The bus entered service with BT&CC, but remained unique.

In April 1930 the designation Q was reached with a 30-seat 'Parlour Coach', as it was described. This body was based loosely on the L4, but had taller side windows (eliminating the permanent vents above them) and featured a sliding head to the roof. The first Q body was supplied on a B-Type chassis to A & R Graham of Kirkintilloch, already mentioned in connection with their purchase of Bristol-bodied 4-Tonner and 2-Tonner buses. A & R Graham received another Q-Type Parlour Coach in 1931, but this time mounted on a D-Type chassis.

An entirely fresh design of touring coach was completed in April 1931 on chassis D.103 and D.105. This was all-enclosed, except for the folding canvas head to the roof, so really marked the end of the fully-opening 'char-à-banc' era as far as BBW was concerned. The new body was designated Q1 and shortly after it appeared a batch of six was built on B-Type chassis which, like the D-Types, featured the slender new radiator. These six were supplied to BT&CC's subsidiary, Greyhound Motors of Bristol.

It was 1932 that saw the new style of coach being built, all on D-Type chassis and now under the designation of Q2.

**118**. A new generation of bodies for Bristol B-Type chassis was signalled by the display of B.600 as an exhibit at the 1929 Commercial Motor Show. BBW's design team had significantly improved the looks of the saloon bodywork by subtle changes to the roof and tail-end contours, to introduce a more rounded shape. Gone were the harsh edges where roof and sides met and in their place came gentle curves. Slight revision to the pillar spacing restored the symmetry to the body sides, with 'matching' solid panels alongside each doorway. The finishing touch was the incorporation of the fashionable 'oval' window to the rear wall. The outcome was an especially finely-balanced bus, with a most attractive appearance. The example here had the new-style coachwork in **L5-Type** format, equipped for one-man-operation, with a two-part front door which closed across the foot of the steps. Although the bus in this picture, taken in Kings Road, has not formally been identified, it can only be B.600, finished in show condition and painted in lined-out blue and white livery. As such, it was sold on 6th January 1930 to Merthyr Tydfil Corporation as No.25 (HB 3569), being delivered before completion of an order for three similar buses. Interestingly, it was not repainted in Merthyr Tydfil livery until March 1931, when it returned specially to Brislington for the purpose.

**119**. The **L4-Type** front-entrance version of the new style of body was featured on a batch of 15 buses for West Riding (293-307: HL 4536-4550), on chassis B.580-594. Low January sunshine in 1930 captured the detail of the window arrangement around the cab and bulkhead, while emphasising the rounded contours of the white roofs against the bare trees at the edge of The Downs in Bristol. The white rose of Yorkshire formed the basis of the emblem in the centre of the operator's fleetname, carried on the green lower panelling.

**120**. Stockton-on-Tees had been one of the first towns away from Bristol to witness the operation of buses built by Bristol Tramways, as a result of the near-by Middlesbrough branch of Imperial Tramways receiving some C65-Type buses in 1914. In 1930, Stockton-on-Tees Corporation bought two Bristol B-Types, complete with BBW **L4-Type** front-entrance bodies. These were unusual in three respects. They were fitted for one-man-operation, although this was usually coupled to a two-doorway layout; only 26 seats were installed; and the destination boxes, both front and rear, were somewhat taller than the usual pattern applied by BBW. No.9 (UP 3712) was completed on 27th February 1930.

**121**. February 1930 also saw the completion of the first two of the three buses ordered by Merthyr Tydfil Corporation, with **L5-Type** two-doorway bodywork for one-man-operation. Seating was installed for 32 in these bodies. In the livery of deep crimson and white, with a red waistband, these must have been among the best-looking buses of their day! The vehicle shown here was the first of the pair, No.22 (HB 3589); the last bus did not appear until April. Study of the trailing side window, to the rear of the door, shows that the top corner was of a smaller radius than the lower, whereas in L4-Type bodies the corners were of equal radius.

**122**. It was doubtless gratifying for Bristol Tramways when the owner of a small fleet of buses in a rural area returned with an order for a new bus, especially several years after the last order. A case in point was the request from Frank Hall & Co of Broughton Astley, Leicestershire, who traded as "The Astley" and who had last received a new Bristol, a 4-Tonner with HA-Type bodywork, in 1924, as shown in Plate 54. The new Bristol B, registered UT 7300, was completed on 29th May 1930 and was a very early example of the **L10-Type** dual-entrance body. From this stage, the radii of the corners of the trailing side window were revised to match the front-entrance L4 bodies.

**123**. Basking in late-afternoon sunlight in June 1930 is one of a pair of B-Type chassis carrying **L5-Type** coachwork suitable for one-man-operation, to the order of Aberdare U.D.C. (No.38: TX 9957). The photograph clearly shows the signwriting at the front entrance, which is identical on each leaf of the door, requesting passengers to 'Please Pay As You Enter' and warning that 'Passengers entering or leaving the bus whilst in motion, do so at their own risk' – presumably, should a bus have a conductor aboard, they would not entertain such behaviour!

**124**. The rounded outline of the new family of BBW bodies was at its most impressive when viewed from the rear; the bodywork even appeared to bulge at waist-level and the oval rear window only emphasised the features. This is all captured in this photograph from the contemporary press, of HY 734, with **L10-Type** bodywork. It had been completed in July 1930 as a demonstrator, but shortly passed into the BT&CC operating fleet. It is shown here at Temple Meads Station in Bristol, having just arrived from Clifton on what was an extension of the company's original motor-bus service, on which their original Bristol-built vehicles had been employed – see Plate 7, etc. The rear number-plate was now painted on a metal base, with the single tail light doubling as a device to illuminate the plate. A reflector disc was located on the upper rear panel. *(Peter Davey Collection)*

**125**. Greyhound Motors Ltd, BT&CC's subsidiary company, was most famous for its long-distance express services. In addition, however, it operated local bus services in and around Bristol. The first bus to be built by BT&CC for these routes is shown here, photographed on 13th November 1930 before receiving its registration HY 340. It had **L10-Type** 31-seat bodywork to the same specification as those for BT&CC.

126. Understandably, Bristol Tramways' own fleet contained a large number of B-Type buses carrying the latest style of bodywork. Initially, dual-doorway **L10-Type** coachwork was favoured, as seen here. This bus represents the initial batch of 11, built in May and June 1930 and registered between HW 9065 and HW 9579. Note that the company still favoured a roof-mounted luggage carrier. Some bodies in this batch, instead of featuring the oval rear window, are known to have had twin windows, in which an arc was prescribed through the top of the pair.

127. Delivered to BT&CC concurrently with the Bristol L10-Type buses shown in the previous plate were 18 buses bodied by **Northern Counties** of Wigan, yet constructed very much to the BBW L10 design. Comparison of the two photographs will show that, other than the strange covers added to the rear wheel arches, the only significant differences are that the white waistband is continued through both door porches and the door arches have the top valance of the shape applied to West Riding's L4-Type bodies (Plate 119). Also, the windscreen is set at a slighter greater degree of slope on the Northern Counties bodies. *(M J Tozer Collection)*

128. Once assembly of the new, six-cylinder D-Type Bristol chassis started later in 1930, the L4, L5 and L10 bodies were adapted to fit the newcomer, with its higher bonnet-line and more slender JV-Type radiator. The main changes, of course, were made in the area of the cab and front bulkhead, including the need to raise the base-line of the windows. This was achieved not by using a simple, straight, sloping edge, but by employing a base-line on the form of a shallow wave. The front dash was moved forward to meet the new radiator, so the

slope of the windscreen was increased. In other aspects, including the retention of horizontal waist-level beading across the bulkhead, the bodywork was not modified and illustrated here is an otherwise standard **L10-Type** body. It is mounted on chassis D.104 and was completed on 27th October 1930. The body weight was 1 ton, 16 cwt and 2 quarters. The bus was registered HY 1284 as a demonstrator – note the Bristol scroll applied to the saloon windows. It was painted bright-blue and yellow – rather garish colours for 1930 and maybe why it was repainted in April 1932 into red, white and blue.

**129**. On 10th September 1930, BBW completed a body that had been two years in the making and for which chassis B.384 had been set aside. The body was the solitary example of an **L7-Type** and, of greater importance, it was BBW's first body to feature all-metal framework, rather than timber with metal flitch plates. A considerable amount of interest was starting to be shown in the bus world over the use of metal for framing, where the necessary strength and rigidity could be achieved from a much more slender structure. Problems of corrosion were not fully appreciated by many builders at the time, but, after they had manifested themselves, several manufacturers resorted to timber framework, even if only temporarily. Such problems evidently did not affect the L7 body, as the bus remained in service with BT&CC (registered HY 325) right through to 1949 – later than many a B-Type – and it was not listed among those undergoing structural rebuilding later in their lives. Note the larger windows, that eliminate both the permanent ventilation slots above the glazing and the narrow solid panels alongside each doorway. The glazing on the nearside of the cab has been tidied up, but the faring below the canopy is perhaps a little pretentious.

**130**. Shown here is the interior of the L7-Type body on B.384 (BT&CC's HY 325). From the memory of one enthusiast who recalls

not only discovering the bus standing in Prince Street, Bristol, but moreover ready to work the service to take him home, the major impression was of a more spacious interior, given by the notably less bulky window frames and roof sticks. Note that the ceiling was now lined with a skin of wood, instead of tongue-and-groove boards, and that separate compartments for smokers and non-smokers had been dispensed with. The two leaves of the rear door are shown here in the open position and the track in the ribbed floor covering can just be seen. Above the oval rear window is the bodybuilder's plate: it reads, 'Bristol Tramways & Carriage Co Ltd, Manufacturers of *Bristol* Commercial Vehicles', the trade-name *Bristol* appearing in scroll form.

**131**. A new designation was introduced for front-entrance bodies in the spring of 1931, of **L6-Type**. Identification was made possible by the fact that the entrance was widened and eliminated the solid panel ahead of the first window. To differentiate between bodies for B-Type and D-Type chassis, with their differing cab structures, the body codes received suffix designations. Shown here, on chassis B.719, is an **L6-1** body. Seating remained at 32. The bus was completed on 16th May 1931 and was supplied through the National Electric Construction Company to the Musselburgh & District Electric Light & Traction Company, who traded as Coast Line – the coast in question being that of the Firth of Forth, eastwards from Edinburgh. The Coast Line livery was bright red, with ivory or pale cream relief. This bus was subsequently registered with Midlothian County Council as SY 4507. In 1937, Coast Line was taken over by its large neighbour, SMT.

**132**. When mounted on the D-Type chassis, the new front-entrance body was termed **L6-2**. This example, mounted on D.115 and seating only 30, was completed on 22nd May 1931, for Greyhound Motors Ltd of Bristol. The roof luggage rack had solid sides and there are brackets for mounting route boards along the edges of the roof.

**133**. Buses with only one passenger doorway were required to have an emergency exit in a different area of the body. BBW standardised on fitting this exit in the centre of the rear wall on front-entrance bodies, although that meant that one of the main design features of the current range, the oval rear window, had to be excluded. Nevertheless, the two windows flanking the door had well-rounded outer corners, as shown here on an **L6-2** body on a D-Type chassis for Bristol Tramways, later registered HY 3620. A small route board was inserted into a side window for service 66, from Swindon to Cricklade, and it will be seen that stencils were used in front and rear windows for the service number.

**134**. Chassis B.705 was built to receive an **L6-1** body, but before completion, the chassis was used for some development work. It was decided subsequently to place the body on a new chassis. Doncaster Corporation had expressed a desire to order more B-Types and, although they were to order Roe bodywork for three of the chassis, evidently their interest was gained for the L6-1 body for the fourth chassis, doubtless on favourable terms and with a quick delivery date. The chassis chosen to receive the body was B.790. By this stage in the production of the B-Type, however,

a slightly shallower version of the tall and slender radiator of the D-Type had been introduced, designated the EV radiator. The cab of the L6-1 body therefore had to be rebuilt to suit. It emerged looking almost identical to an L6-2 body on a D-Type chassis, although the lack of any change to the bulkhead windows only confirmed that the bonnet was actually no higher than before. B.790, now seating only 30, was delivered to Doncaster on 4th September 1931, becoming No.39 (DT 3296).

**135**. An experimental body was constructed in the MCW in 1931, on chassis D.110. It received the designation of **XB-Type** and had little in common with contemporary BBW bodies. It was a 32-seat, front-entrance body, but featured a prominent, raised, waistrail that curved upwards across the back. The rear destination box was attractively blended into the rear profile. Slightly taller windows were used, with a fall-away at the top of the rear-most window. The bus was completed on 3rd June 1931 for BT&CC and was registered HY 3449.

**136**. The **XB-Type** body was significantly different at the front, where there was a deep extension of the front canopy, which incorporated the destination box in its front face. The side-lights, often suspended below the canopy, were relocated, the nearside unit being placed on top of the front wing, in the fashion of private cars. Note the hooded mask to the nearside headlamp. The passenger door was now located against the front bulkhead and the door was unusual, in being a folding affair, hinged on its centre-line.

**137**. A new type of body designed for long-distance work, and called 'Parlour Coach' in company publicity, received the designation **Q-Type**. It made its first appearance in April 1930. The example shown here was mounted on chassis B.633, to the order of A & R Graham of Kirkintilloch, being registered SN 5014. There were 30 seats and the front doorway was enclosed by a folding door at the foot of the steps. The side windows were taller than on the bus, while the roof was shallower and slightly more square-shouldered, as the overall height, excluding the luggage rack, was reduced by about four inches.

**138**. The 'Parlour Coach', or **Q-Type** body, when mounted on D-Type chassis, underwent the same modifications in the cab and front bulkhead region as were applied to saloon bodies. This is exemplified by D.118, also for Graham of Kirkintilloch. This coach was completed just a year after the B-Type shown above and was registered SN 5304.

**139**. The interior of the **Q-Type** Parlour Coach on D-Type chassis for Graham of Kirkintilloch shows that, despite the coaching application of the vehicle, the seats were no taller than bus seats, although they were more sumptuously padded. The inward-facing seats over the rear wheel arches, however, suffered from very shallow backs and cannot even be seen in this photograph! The parcel racks were meagre by any standard. The Q-Type had a Walman sliding head to the saloon roof. The front bulkhead was embellished with mirrors above the window line.

**140**. A restyled coach body, termed the **Q1-Type**, made its appearance in April 1931 as a demonstrator on chassis D.103 (the second chassis of that number, replacing that exhibited at the 1929 Show with Northern Counties coach bodywork). This Q1 was registered HY 1952 and had 26 very deep and attractively upholstered seats, all of which were forward-facing. The roof again had a sliding head and, as no destination equipment was installed, the front canopy was open in the middle. The front door was hinged and outward-opening, while a very interesting touch was the fitting of curved glass on the front corner, between the door and the bulkhead. The side windows possessed radiused corners.

**141**. A production run of six coaches based on the **Q1-Type** design were delivered to BT&CC's Greyhound Motors subsidiary in June 1931, registered HY 2701-4/8/9. To maintain the modern appearance, the chassis were chosen to be the first to receive the new EV-Type slender radiator. The top of the bonnet retained its customary position and length and the coachworks filled in the area between the bonnet and the bulkhead with special curved panelling. To suit Greyhound's needs, the bodies carried a conventional destination box, a larger roof luggage carrier (so, presumably, no sliding head) and side route-board brackets. The corner window at the front used flat glass, while, as this photograph of HY 2709 shows, there was a curve through the top of the three windows in the rear wall. Not so clear is the pronounced lip between the windscreen and the front dash. *(M J Tozer Collection)*

**142**. 12 similar coach bodies, but designated **Q2-Type**, were built in May and June 1932, all mounted on D-Type chassis; all but one were destined for BT&CC's coaching fleet, the exception being allocated to subsidiary Greyhound Motors. This photograph of HY 6034, taken while on an outing to a local beauty spot, shows that BT&CC's coaches lacked destination equipment, had folding roofs and the windows were of the half-drop variety. Interior lighting, mounted on the window pillars, featured diffusers of the Olympic Torch shape that were then popular.

**143**. All dressed up and ready to go to Lynmouth ... yet captured by the photographer in the grounds of Brislington depot. Maybe it was the start of a Works Outing, but the photograph clearly aims to show the features of the **Q2-Type** coach, with its canvas roof folded back, as conveniently demonstrated by the two gentlemen, who must have been standing on the seats! HY 6225 was based on chassis D.139.

# Chapter 6

The 1931 Commercial Motor Show was the second in succession that saw Bristol publicising three new chassis models! The first of the latest trio was the G-Type, which was the first Bristol designed specifically for double-deck bodywork. The H-Type was a four-cylinder single-decker built to take advantage of an increase in the permitted overall length from 26 feet to 27 feet 6 inches. Thirdly there was the J-Type, which shared its chassis frame with the H-Type, but was powered by a six-cylinder engine.

No examples of the G, H or J at the 1931 Show carried BBW bodywork and the first to be completed was H.102, in February 1932. For this new range of chassis it is significant that Bristol had decided to adopt 'all-metal' bodywork, indicating that the prototype of 1930, the L7 body, had returned encouraging results. The steelwork for the metal frames was fabricated to Bristol design by Metal Sections Ltd of Birmingham, a division of Accles & Pollock who used photographs of BBW bodies in their subsequent press advertisements. The coachwork was assembled and completed at the Tram Depot. The styling of the body on H.102 was new, yet distinctly BBW in origin. This bus accommodated 36 seats (reflecting the increase in overall length) and featured a rear entrance.

The first J-Type, J.101, was licensed in July 1932, as a demonstrator. The body was a rear-entrance saloon, designated L11, which indicates metal framework was not used. For some reason this bus seems to have escaped the attention of the official photographer, so its original appearance is not recorded.

The new range of all-metal bodies constructed from 1932 was recognised with new designations, using the letters AM to signify All-Metal. Firstly there was the AM1, for mounting on B- and D-Type chassis, which were still being marketed, and this was a dual-doorway saloon with 30 or 31 seats. It followed the style of the L7 prototype in having the larger side windows, with no permanent vents above them. The first AM1 bodies were mounted on the last series of B-Type chassis to feature the 'square' radiator design, before the adoption of the slender pattern already introduced to the D-Type.

The 36-seat rear-entrance body mounted on H.102 was classified AM3 and apart from the greater length to suit the new chassis range, it had obvious visual similarities to the AM1. The AM3 was to be suitable for both H and J chassis and to have optional entrance positions. In complete contrast to both the AM3 and AM1 was the AM2, which appeared at the very end of 1932; Bristol's operating fleet decided they could

employ some more 20-seat one-man-operated buses, so, four years after the model had formally been discontinued, Bristol built a further batch of eleven 2-Tonners! In appearance, they were particularly attractive small-scale versions of their AM1 and AM3 brethren!

Meanwhile, in June 1932, the first G-Type double-decker emerged. This forerunner of many BBW double-deckers carried an individual style of body. It followed contemporary fashion for double-deckers by incorporating the so-called 'piano front' effect. In this, the front panelling of the body, between the upstairs windows and the cab, was shaped rather like an upright piano. The bus was to become a Bristol demonstrator, before being placed in service in Bristol with Greyhound.

By this point in Bristol's history, changes had occurred to the company's establishment and its relationship to other concerns. In 1929, the railway companies were empowered to acquire a shareholding in the bus companies operating within their territories, in return for which the railways' bus services would be transferred to those operators. Bristol Tramways & Carriage Company was not eligible for involvement in this transaction, not for any lack of Great Western Railway bus services in their area (far from it!), but because the activities of BT&CC were too diverse. The business involved the operation additionally of trams, taxis and a contract fleet, as well as the manufacture of vehicles. BT&CC, however, decided on a voluntary sale of a shareholding to the GWR. Following the death of Sir George White in 1916, his shares, which represented just over 50% of the share capital of the company, had remained with his family, many of whom were in positions of authority. It was these shares that were now offered to the GWR.

The offer was taken up, but in 1931, the GWR decided to transfer them to the Western National Omnibus Company. The latter had only been created in 1929 to take account of the acquisition of a shareholding by the GWR in the relevant area of the widespread National Omnibus & Transport Company. As it happened, 1931 had already seen Western National's remaining shareholding pass to the control of Thomas Tilling Ltd and, through Western National's controlling interest in Bristol Tramways, a Tilling director joined the Bristol board in 1932. Thomas Tilling had once been one of the largest operators of buses in London after the London General Omnibus Company, but following agreement made with the LGOC over Tilling's activities in London, Tilling had developed its expansionist policy as one of investment in provincial bus companies and was now becoming known as the Tilling Group.

The interest that both Western National and Tilling had in Bristol was to have a major effect on the future of the company's business, particularly the MCW's activities.

To start with, Western National ordered 39 Bristol H-Type chassis, of which nine were to receive Bristol AM3 bodies.

BBW was not to be favoured with many orders from Tilling Group companies as it transpired, as there was another coachbuilder within the Group. That was the Eastern Counties Omnibus Company, whose factory was at Lowestoft. This plant had been set up and owned – until 1931 – by United Automobile Services, who had themselves bodied no fewer than 130 Bristol B-Type chassis there in 1929 for their own operations, some of which were now under Eastern Counties administration. United Automobile continued their operations in north-east England and was now a Tilling-associated company; furthermore, they now had 20 H-Types being bodied at the same Lowestoft factory, by Eastern Counties. For a while, BBW's output became almost exclusively to the order of BT&CC themselves.

(The full history of the Lowestoft coach factory, under administration by United Automobile, Eastern Counties and, from 1936, Eastern Coach Works, is told in *Eastern Coach Works, Volume 1* by Maurice Doggett (Transport Publishing Co, 1987); *ECW 1946-65* and *ECW 1965-87* by Maurice Doggett and Alan Townsin (Venture Publications, 1993 & 1994, respectively). In many ways, particularly since 1946, BBW's history is tied in with that of Eastern Coach Works.)

The first production J-Types passed through BBW in 1933. Several received dual-doorway versions of the AM3 body, while others, for the Greyhound fleet, received a new coach body, the AM5. This was similar in general outline to the AM3, but had a hinged entrance door at the front and was appointed luxuriously with 26 seats.

In time for exhibition at the 1933 Commercial Motor Show, BBW had built a new and eye-catching design of double-deck body on chassis G.104. This owed virtually

**144.** The spring of 1932 saw BBW introduce a new range of bodies. These were principally to be mounted on the new family of G-, H- and J-Type chassis, but as the MCW were still happy to receive orders for the established B- and D-Type chassis as well, bodies of the new type were also designed to suit these two models. The new bodywork featured all-metal construction for the framework, in association with Accles & Pollock subsidiary Metal Sections Ltd, of Birmingham. The frames were supplied to Bristol's specification and assembly took place as usual at BBW. New codes were devised for these all-metal bodies – starting at **AM1** for the 30-seat, two-doorway bodywork for B- and D-Type chassis. Seen here on 23rd May 1932, posed against Arno's Castle (or the Black Castle), a folly almost next-door to Brislington depot, is B.785, due to become BT&CC's HY 6030. The body took the lead of the prototype all-metal L7 body, shown in Plate 129, in the use of larger windows, but was considerably tidied up in appearance in respect of the rear profile, the door valances, the canopy fairing and, in particular, the finish to the front dome. The latter now incorporated the destination box very tidily, although the outcome did produce a slight scowling effect. The AM1, unusually for a dual-doorway body, featured a central rear emergency door.

nothing to the piano-fronted body on G.101 and possessed a smooth, gently sloping frontal profile, combined with a gradually curved rear outline. The outcome was very much up to the times in terms of styling and construction and was a world away from BBW's first double-deckers, the Manchester A-Types, built only six years before! The body on G.104 had seating for 48 (influenced by current taxation classes) and was coded AM6.

Also on display at Olympia was the first Bristol to be powered by an oil engine. The chassis was designated JO5G and it was, in fact, a re-engineing of H.101, which had received an AM3 36-seat body earlier in 1933.

In the spring of 1934, chassis JO5G.2 emerged with a breath-taking coach body. The features were rounded to the point of exaggeration, yet most tastefully executed. Designated Q3, this 32-seat coach was supplied to the ever-faithful A & R Graham of Kirkintilloch. The idea for its styling was only to be repeated on two more bodies, sadly.

In contrast, the much more functional looking AM5 coach was supplied in 1934 to the Tramways fleet, which also received several AM3 34-seat two-doorway saloons, all on J chassis. One further saloon appeared in 1934, under the designation AM8, a one-off front-entrance variant, built on an experimental J.MW chassis with a new four-cylinder petrol engine. It was supplied to Doncaster Corporation.

The year 1934 saw production of the acclaimed B-Type chassis draw to a close. The large majority latterly had been built for BT&CC themselves, with AM1 bodies, but two similar buses were supplied to Coast Line of Musselburgh, near Edinburgh, in 1932. Aberdare UDC continued to specify the earlier pattern of body for its final B-Types of 1932 and 1933 and a final AM1 body was built in 1935 on what had been an instructional chassis, now registered for the first time as BHU 635.

**145.** In June 1932, Coast Line of Musselburgh received two more Bristol B-Types (see Plate 131), this time featuring **AM1** dual-doorway bodies, with 31-seats. After the first 14 AM1 bodies had been built on B-Type chassis (including the new body for B.705 – see Plate 134), the new, slender, EV radiator was introduced as standard, from B.789. The Coast Line buses were on chassis B.816/7, the latter, registered SY 4731, being shown here.

**146.** It was very uncommon for BT&CC to arrange for their official photographer to capture the *off*-side rear aspect of a vehicle; indeed, the vast majority of photographs, as reproduced in this book, were taken from a nearside-front angle. Therefore, this view of the other Coast Line **AM1-Type** Bristol B, SY 4730, especially deserves to be included. It will be seen that the top line of the rear windows actually prescribed a gentle curve. A spare wheel was able to be located within the aperture beneath the emergency door. *(M J Tozer Collection)*

**147**. This is a picture of the interior of an **AM1-Type** 30-seat dual-doorway body on a Bristol B-Type chassis for BT&CC's own fleet. It shows the light and spacious nature of the body, partly created by the large windows and slender pillars. The smooth lining panels of the ceiling also help the appearance. Clearly seen is the angled front door, still glazed to the ceiling, and the rearward-facing seat backing on to the driver's cab. Although the use of an internal screen to separate passengers who smoked from those who preferred not to smoke had been discontinued, a line was painted across the ceiling behind the second pair of forward-facing seats, with a notice at the side which read, 'Smoking Prohibited Forward of this Line'. A notice in the window of the front door stated, 'Hire Bristol Coaches for Outings of All Kinds'. The manufacturer's plate, of the same type as described for the L7 body in Plate 130, was fixed to the front bulkhead.

**148**. It is interesting that Aberdare Urban District Council continued to specify the previous design of bodywork for its three 1932/33 B-Types, despite the introduction of the AM1 model. The actual body code has not been verified, but their 1931 example was given as **L10-Type**, rather than the L5 for one-man-operation, as previously chosen by AUDC (see Plate 123). Certainly, these later three did not have the facility for the driver to take the fares, nor did they have the external signwriting, yet the front doors closed across the foot of the steps in the manner of the L5. In common with the AM1, an emergency door was now located in the rear wall. Note the addition of the AUDC sign above the destination screen. For the 1933 pair, a new type of seat was installed, featuring a separate grab-rail across the top. It will be seen that, even with the EV-Type radiator, the base-line of the windscreen was horizontal, unlike that on the modified L6-1 body for Doncaster shown in Plate 134. The bus shown here is No.28 (TG 5568) on chassis B.867 – only 11 more B-Type chassis were to be built after this one. The scene for this 1933 photograph is a new location, in the Hengrove area of Bristol – this bus was the only B-Type known to have been photographed at this spot.

**149**. Bristol Tramways' Motor Constructional Works introduced their H- and J-Type chassis in 1931, to meet a newly permitted maximum length for single-deck four-wheel buses of 27ft 6ins (instead of the 26ft length applied to the B- and D-Types). The BBW body in the new all-metal range that was designed for the new chassis was termed **AM3-Type**. The first vehicle completed, in February 1932, was on chassis H.102. The body was of rear-entrance layout and the effect of the extra length meant seating could be provided for no fewer than 36. Basically, lengthening was achieved, in relation to an AM1, by the insertion of an extra side window.

Having the entrance at the rear resulted in the emergency door being sited on the offside at the front. That, in turn, enabled the oval rear window to be restored to the design! Note that on the AM3, only two steps were required to reach the saloon, deep though these steps were. H.102 was registered as HY 7537 late in 1932 and ran on demonstration for a while.

**150**. Chassis H.101, which had appeared on Bristol's stand at the November 1931 Commercial Motor Show, eventually emerged from the Body Building Works carrying a very similar body to that on H.102 seen above; its official code was **AM3/36**, to reflect the seating

capacity. This photograph of the completed H.101 was taken in October 1933, in the grounds of Arno's Castle; the railway beyond was the Bristol and North Somerset line, which also passed behind the MCW. The bus was painted for demonstration work and carried a roof luggage rack, with a rear access ladder. It will be seen that the front destination indicator was not blended into the front dome in the way of the AM1 bodies. This particular AM3 benefited from more opening windows than the example on H.102. Despite the use of a 4-cylinder engine, the H-Type shared the use of the taller JV radiator with the J-Type. In time for the Commercial Motor Show

of November 1933 though, H.101 had become the first Bristol to be fitted with an *oil* engine – a Gardner 5LW unit. As such, the chassis was renumbered in January 1934 to JO5G.1 (J-Type, Oil, 5-cylinder, Gardner), not being registered until June, as AHW 393.

**151**. In December 1932, the MCW built a special batch of 11 more 2-Tonner chassis – the first since 1929 – for BT&CC's own needs. They were registered HY 7641-7651. BBW responded with a 20-seat version of the all-metal body, designated **AM2-Type**. This was fitted for one-man-operation, so had a front entrance, with folding doors, and a rear emergency door. Each of the three main windows on either side opened for ventilation. The styling was clearly akin to the AM1 and AM3, although the destination box resembled the fitting in the latter rather than the former. Even the radiator shroud was brought up-to-date – all in all, a very appealing little bus, yet, despite their special place in the fleet, they were declared surplus from 1939 and had all been sold by 1942. Most then became showman's vans.

**152**. The first double-deck body to be built by BBW since Manchester Corporation had received its Bristol A-Types in 1927 (Plates 81-83) was mounted on chassis G.101, as shown by this photograph dated June 1932. Ideas about styling, of double-deckers in particular, were moving forward in great strides ... while also bowing to the dictates of fashion! So, while it was now customary to project the upper saloon forward over the cab, the frontal panelling was shaped in such a way as to earn the nick-name 'Piano-front'. This was as much a requirement for the fashion-conscious operator as was the oval back window on single-deckers! The cab and bulkhead treatment was very similar to BBW bodies on D-, H- and J-Type single-deckers of the time, although the use of three windows across the front of the upper saloon was not common. The bus was incomplete at this stage, even lacking seats. The registration HY 3630 had been allocated.

**153**. This broadside view of the first G-Type double-decker shows that, since Manchester's A-Types had been built, the staircase had become enclosed by the bodywork. The staircase can be seen to turn through 90 degrees after the fourth step, while an opaque window on the offside gave extra lighting to the stairs. The rear profile was very upright, although a slight tuck-under was applied to the foot

of the rear panel. The side windows were longer than on the single-deck bodies and an unusual feature was that the lower saloon contained conventional half-drop windows, while those upstairs were of a full-depth sliding arrangement. The reader's attention is drawn to the finish to the body-side trim below the trailing upper-deck side window, whereby the upper beading is brought down to merge with the lower beading through a negative curve. Such a feature was to occur on later BBW double-deckers, as we shall see. Similarly, a development of the treatment of the fairing to the rear platform was to appear on later bodies.

**154**. Following changes to the ownership of the Bristol Tramways & Carriage Company, through which it was now effectively under the control of the Western National Omnibus Company and a member of the Tilling Group of operators, Western National placed an order for a quantity of Bristol H-Types, nine of which were to receive Bristol **AM3/36** rear-entrance bodies. Seen here at Hengrove in June 1933 before delivery was the third bus of the batch, on chassis H.105. The body is very similar to that on H.101 seen in Plate 150, except for a slightly more straight-forward treatment to the cab nearside window. This picture clearly shows the slight cut-away to the

panelling over the windscreen, in contrast to the AM1 (144 & 145). The livery was light-green and white, with a dark-green waistband. The bus was registered FJ 8932 in Exeter, where Western National and its sister company Southern National had their headquarters; oddly, though, none of their services radiated from there, as Exeter was comprehensively served by Exeter Corporation (city services) and Devon General (rural services). Instead, Western/Southern National covered most of the rest of south-west England!

**155**. The first AM3-Type bodies to be built in two-doorway format were produced for BT&CC's own fleet in 1933, with more following in 1934. The extra doorway reduced the seating capacity to 34 and the body was accordingly coded **AM3/34**. The location of the half-drop windows reverted to the third and fifth 'bays' (as each window-sized section was termed), as on H.102 in Plate 149. It will be seen that the two leaves of the rear door opened outwards on AM3 bodies, with handrails attached to the inside of the leaves for use when open. At last BT&CC had decided to dispense with the roof luggage carrier on their service buses! The 1934 bus shown here was mounted on 6-cylinder chassis J.153 and it was later registered AHU 503.

**156**. An all-metal coach body was introduced in 1933, coded **AM5-Type**. Its general characteristics were similar to the AM3, except that it was of front-entrance layout and the side window-pillar spacing was increased. By adopting this arrangement, the back of each double-seat lined up with a pillar, to give passengers in the window seats an unobstructed view. The use of full-drop windows also aided clear vision. Despite being mounted on the longer J-Type chassis, the seating capacity was still 26, as in many an earlier coach. There was a sliding head to the roof and a small roof luggage-carrier. This photograph dates from July 1933 and shows J.123, one of six coaches for Greyhound Motors (becoming HY 9379). Note the list of sea-side resorts served by Greyhound, applied to the glass louvres over the side windows.

**157**. Early in 1934, BT&CC took delivery for its own coach operations of a fleet of 18 Bristol J-Types with **AM5/26** coach bodies. This photograph of J.129 (which was registered AHW 540) shows that, although they were very similar to those built for the company's Greyhound subsidiary, BT&CC's examples were plainer, with none of the lining-out (which had even included the luggage-carrier on the Greyhound coaches) and without facilities for route boards to be attached to the sides of the roof. Whereas BT&CC's buses proudly carried the city's coat-of-arms on the side panels, coaches wore an emblem of the intertwined letters BT&CC. The lower corner of the leading window in the cab has been rounded, in the style of the AM3 body on H.101 in Plate 150.

**158**. This snap-shot, taken on Grand Parade, Bath, during an outing in the late 1930s, luckily captures the rear aspect of a Bristol **AM5-Type** coach body on J-Type chassis. It is the leading vehicle in this pair and is registered AHU 804. It will be seen that while these coaches carried the BT&CC emblem on the sides, the rear emergency door was adorned with the Bristol scroll. To the left of the door can be seen the four tip-up steps (one in the white waistband) arranged in staggered fashion, to reach the ladder to the roof luggage pen. The livery has been slightly revised since the coaches were built, to incorporate white surrounds to the side windows. The coach standing astern is HY 6229, a 1932 D-Type with **Q2-Type** coachwork, as illustrated in Plate 142. *(B.V.B.G. Collection)*

**159**. Double-deck styling had advanced so much by October 1933 that the second BBW body to be built on a G-Type chassis (G.104) was very much more modern than that built on G.101 a little more than one year earlier and shown in Plates 152 & 153 and was thus a world away from the Manchester A-Types of six years earlier. The latest body was classified **AM6/48**, with the 48 seats split equally between the two decks – a very spacious layout, but governed by the bands of taxation in force at the time. The body had a smooth, sloping front end, with a gentle curve through the panelling in plan view. The two front upperdeck windows were set in a shallow V formation. The front of the roof projected slightly, to overhang these windows, a similar effect being given by the panelling over the windscreen. Note the top pane is open slightly, highlighting the style of glass, with the bottom edge dipping to a point, that had been in use on BBW bodies since 1928. Three half-drop windows were installed on each side of each deck, those upstairs having metal louvres at the top, while downstairs the metal louvre continued above all five bays. Permanent ventilation slots were installed above the lower-deck windows. By looking through the cab it can be seen that the tops of the windows on the offside are in line with the tops of the saloon windows, a feature evidently not well received by the drivers.

**160**. At the rear, the **AM6/48** body featured a continuous curve through its entire height. The upper corners to both rear windows (that on the upper deck opened for emergency use) were rounded with generous curves, while their lower corners were square. The trailing upper-deck side window was of an outline usually referred to as D-shaped and this outline would be featured increasingly on buses in the 1930s. Note in particular the treatment of the paint-work on the contrast band below this D-shaped window; it had the same characteristic as the beading in the same location on the body built on G.101 and described in Plate 153. The staircase again turned though a right-angle after the fourth step, but there was no offside window to add light. This vehicle, on chassis G.104, initially started work as a demonstrator and was registered AHW 74 in 1934.

**161**. Bristol's MCW was very involved with the design and testing of new types of engines around 1933/34. Besides installing the Gardner 5LW oil engine, which altered chassis H.101 into chassis JO5G.1 (Plate 150), the MCW was still experimenting with new petrol engines of its own make. This was met with more detailed chassis codes and it was decided to drop the type-letter H and standardise on the J-Type, however many cylinders – 4, 5 or 6 – the engine contained. A new 4-cylinder petrol engine, designated MW-type, was installed in 1934 in

a chassis which thereby received the number J.MW.1. It then received an all-metal body, becoming the sole example of the **AM8-Type**. As can be seen, it was a front-entrance version of the AM3. The emergency door was sited in the rear wall. There were half-drop windows in the 3rd and 5th bays, although an extra half-drop was installed towards the rear on the offside. The bus was completed around May 1934 to the specification of Doncaster Corporation as No.44 (DT 4793) with only 31 seats. Note the route-number indicator fitted on top of the front destination box.

**162**. In May 1934 there appeared a most remarkable new coach from the Body Building Works. It was very impressively styled, with flowing lines, windows that had a strong rounded theme, a luggage-carrier that was blended into the roof and a sliding entrance door. The body was coded **Q3-Type** and it was built for A & R Graham of Kirkintilloch (SN 6309) on a very early oil-engined chassis, JO5G.2. The faring from the underside of the canopy was continued down to meet the front wing and was used as the starting point for body-side flow-lines. The front door slid between internal and external glazed panels. Round-cornered windows had been introduced by the Q1 and Q2 bodies, shown in Plates 140-143, but the corners of the Q3 windows were rounded to the point of exaggeration. The frontal profile was kept very smooth, with a tall windscreen. The destination screen received a route-number sight alongside. The sliding head to the roof was neatly housed beneath the luggage-carrier when opened. Curtains were fitted to the windows and yet, despite its opulence, it carried 32 passengers.

**163**. This shows the interior of A & R Graham's **Q3/32** coach. The seats were deep and were fashionably trimmed with vanity mirrors, coat-holder rails and arm rests. Lamps within stylish shades were attached to each window pillar, there were curtains to the windows, a clock and mirrors were placed on the front bulkhead, and the underside of the generous parcel racks and the ceiling were trimmed and decorated in the best of taste. The circular device in the centre of the bulkhead is a Clayton heater. The bulkhead itself was covered in deep moquette, which would have helped to soften the noise of the Gardner 5LW engine.

**164**. The rear view of the **Q3/32** unveiled a mastery of craftsmanship in the sheer perfection attained in shaping the metalwork around the beautiful tail end of the coach, with its soft and gentle curves. The whole of the rear of the roof was in one piece – perhaps even down to the foot of the rear panels – and it was all shaped by hand, as no other coach quite like this one was to follow. As if the metalworkers' abilities were not remarkable enough, there were the painting and polishing skills that followed. Even the large Graham name across the rear panel was a work of art. Tip-up steps and hand-rails were necessary to reach the roof luggage-carrier, yet even these were installed with compassion. The rear window, it will be seen, utilised curved glass. It was perhaps unfortunate, though, that the coach was mounted on a JO5G chassis, as noise and vibration produced by the Gardner 5LW were not inconsiderable. Interestingly, the emergency door, located on the offside at the front, was sited in the rearward of the two shorter bays.

# Chapter 7

BBW started to build double-deck bodies on G-Type chassis in the late summer of 1934. At first, quantities were small, but customers and styles were varied. The first three double-deckers were mounted on the first three GO6G chassis, which were powered by six-cylinder Gardner 6LW engines. This engine was rather longer than the five-cylinder 5LW unit that was beginning to become popular with several customers and which fitted into the engine compartment of the G- and J-Types quite comfortably. The installation of the 6LW meant revisions had to be made; as the radiator could not be moved forward, because that would result in the vehicle exceeding the permitted maximum length, the bulkhead between engine and saloon had to be moved rearward. In consequence, the first body pillar was relocated by the same amount to the rear, with compensation being made to the size of the window bays. At the front of the body, a distinct rearward curve was given to the front window pillars and dome.

The first body on a GO6G was given a new code, which was over-simplistic, but remained the style used for all future BBW production; it was coded DD1, DD obviously standing for Double Decker. The customer was Pontypridd Urban District Council, while interestingly, near-neighbour Aberdare UDC received the second DD1-bodied GO6G immediately afterwards. The third example followed straight on, as a demonstrator, before entering BT&CC's own fleet.

The AM6 double-decker, for five-cylinder GO5G or petrol-engined G-Type chassis, started its own production run with another demonstrator (a GO5G) which was soon bought by Doncaster Corporation. In 1935, more AM6 bodies were built, mainly on petrol-engined Gs for Bristol's own fleet, but including two GO5Gs for that division as well.

An order for four GO5Gs from Exeter Corporation followed the demonstration of a Weymann-bodied example there, but happily the body order for these four was placed with BBW. They were built to Exeter's specification and were termed AM9. The principal difference was that the buses had a straight staircase.

Several developments were taking place on single-deck chassis in 1935. Firstly, an entirely new coach design emerged. The most noticeable characteristic of this was that the front bulkhead windows sloped back to match the rake of the windscreen. The entrance was located at the rear on this occasion and a novel feature for the time was that the door was a sliding unit. Seating was provided for 32 and the body was coded Q4.

Western National placed its second order with BBW in 1935. In common with many companies, Western National was updating the appearance of its buses and coaches – as designs had moved ahead so rapidly of late – by having new coachwork mounted on five- to ten-year-old chassis. In the case of this 1935 contract, 1928/29 chassis were required to be rebodied. The chassis were Tilling-Stevens B10A2 models that had been acquired from the North Western Road Car Company, another Tilling-controlled operator. As the chassis-maker's name indicates, Thomas Tilling initially had a major involvement in this manufacturer and several Tilling Group fleets bought Tilling-Stevens chassis in the late 1920s. The make then fell from favour and its place was subsequently taken by Bristol, on a much more widespread basis.

The new BBW bodies built on the Tilling-Stevens chassis for Western National were equipped with 32 coach-type seats, but the styling of the body was totally unlike any other. They had rather shallow roofs and outswept skirt panels, while the window pillars gradually broadened towards the top. Interestingly, this latter feature was also incorporated – though somewhat more subtly – into the first batch of Eastern Counties-bodied Bristol J coaches for Western and Southern National's newly acquired, prestigious, Royal Blue express coach fleet. Over a two-year spell, no fewer than 40 Tilling-Stevens were rebodied by Bristol in this way.

During 1935/36, BBW produced some saloon bodies for J-Type chassis that were very similar to – and every bit as attractive as – the L4/L10 range of bodies on B- and D-Type chassis introduced in 1930. The new bodies were even more rounded in outline and benefited from a neater finish to the front dome. Most noticeably, they reverted to the use of permanent vents over the side windows. There were three variations of this design. Two went under the code AM7 and differed only in being to single- or dual-doorway layouts; these were supplied to BT&CC's own fleet. The third version was ordered by West Hartlepool Corporation, who required two buses with front entrances. Despite the similarity in appearance to the AM7, the West Hartlepool examples are presumed not to have been all-metal products, as their classification was L12.

The reign of the AM7 body, although supplied across 1935 and 1936, was to be curtailed by the introduction of yet another new design, the S1, before 1935 was out. Inasmuch as the AM7 was good-looking, the S1 was regarded by many as ungainly! Had the S1 followed the AM3, the contrast would not have been so great. The S1 (S meaning Single-decker) had the taller side windows, but the most notable feature was that it was finished with outswept side and rear panels. The windscreen was rather too upright and the roof too shallow and somehow the outcome failed to achieve the right balance. The initial S1 body was mounted on chassis JO5G.15, which became a demonstrator before joining the company's own fleet. Production started in 1936 and, curiously, for a while, S1s and AM7s were supplied alongside each other in that year! Both appeared on some of the last petrol-engined Js as well as on a few oil-engined examples, but all were built just for the Bristol fleet. A demonstrator, built later in 1936, although essentially similar to the S1, was coded S2. This differed in being of rear-entrance layout, as it was destined to be shown to Western National, who preferred this configuration.

By all accounts the framework of the new style of bodies, starting with the S1, reverted to the use of timber. Early metal frames from some manufacturers were found to give rise to problems of corrosion and durability later and maybe BBW was aware of such drawbacks. Nevertheless, their all-metal bodies appeared to achieve full service lives, given the reduced amount of attention paid to them between 1940 and 1945.

Meanwhile, BBW produced two more individual luxury coach bodies, containing the exaggerated round theme that was the basis for A & R Graham's Q3 body on JO5G.2 in 1934. Chassis JO5G.41 appeared in September 1935 with one of the new bodies, under the

banner of the 'Golden Demonstration Coach', which may give a clue to its colour! This was a 28-seater and the body was coded as L13. Then, completed in time for the 1935 Commercial Show – the last to be held at London's Olympia – was an even more flamboyant version, coded Q5. This 26-seater was built on the very last petrol engined J-Type chassis to be built.

Revisions were made to the double-deck body for GO5G chassis in 1936 which caused the coding to be changed from AM6 to DD2. The most noticeable visual change was seen at the back, where the upper-deck rear emergency window gained a pronounced curve to its top edge, a development of the shape that had appeared on the three DD1 bodies. The fourth and final DD1 body, on the fifth and final GO6G chassis, was built later in 1936, once again for Pontypridd UDC.

A much more obvious change to the double-decker occurred in the summer of 1937, when the DD3 appeared, featuring a severe slope to the body's front panels. This was not a particularly attractive aspect, yet remained in vogue for all further double-deck bodywork until the Second World War affected production.

The 1937 version of the single-deck body on J-Type chassis was coded S3, but was generally similar to the S1.

**165**. Double-deckers started to figure more regularly in BBW's output from 1934, on Bristol G-Type chassis powered by a variety of engines. The first completed were on GO6G chassis (G-Type, Oil, 6-cylinder, Gardner), one each for Pontypridd and Aberdare Urban District Councils. Whereas the 5-cylinder Gardner motor fitted into the same sized engine bay as the Bristol JW 6-cylinder petrol engine, the same could not be said for the 6-cylinder Gardner 6LW engine. Such was its length that, in order not to exceed the vehicle's permitted maximum length, the front bulkhead had to be set back a little. This reduced the length of the lower saloon marginally and each side window would have been fractionally shorter, though this was imperceivable. What was more obvious, as shown in this August 1934 view of GO6G.1 for Pontypridd (21: TG 8256), is the broader painted cover between the unpainted, machine-turned bonnet and the bulkhead and a greater gap between the front wing and the bulkhead. The body designed for the GO6G started a new system of designations – **DD1-Type**, DD meaning Double Decker, of course. This bus seated 48 passengers, with 24 on each deck.

**166**. Hard on the heels of Pontypridd's GO6G.1 came an identical **DD1/48** body in September 1934 on GO6G.2, for Aberdare, as No.2 (TG 8389; both councils registered with Glamorgan County Council). Other than the fact that Pontypridd's livery was deep-blue and white and Aberdare's was crimson and white, with a silver roof, even the elaborate painting styles were extremely similar. The DD1 possessed a smoother frontal profile than the AM6 body, with glazing flush with the metalwork. Indeed a sense of streamlining was given by the fact that the front upper-deck pillars were gently curved rearwards. Permanent ventilation to the upper saloon was provided by the two slots in the face of the front dome; these were hidden underneath the overhanging dome in the AM6. The rear upper-deck window was graced by a gentle curve through its top line, while downstairs, the platform window was frosted in line with the handrail, to afford decency for ladies climbing the stairs. Notice that the treatment of the paintwork below the D-shaped upper-deck side window was a variation of the earlier theme. The faring to the canopy and over the platform was a development of that first seen on G.101 (Plate 153), with a horizontal extension from both front and rear bulkheads before starting the upward incline. Aberdare specified a side destination indicator, but did not take advantage of the spacious front panels to incorporate the AUDC display as carried on their 1933 B-Types (Plate 148).

**167**. The **AM6-Type** double-decker was still produced for G-Type chassis with engines other than the long Gardner 6LW. This photograph was taken at Hengrove in August 1935 of an AM6/52 body on GO5G.30, destined for BT&CC and registered BHW 639. Compared with the first AM6 body, on G.104 in Plate 159, the front had a slightly increased slope. Also, the canopy faring was curved down to the front wing and an extra opening window installed in the lower-deck. These items were not present on the immediately preceding AM6/48 bodies of Bristol's BHT-registered batch.

**168**. This photograph from the rear captured the same bus in service in 1938, standing at the Clyde Road terminus of the 20, in Redland. It shows that the **AM6** retained the straight top to the upstairs back window – itself rather an unusual choice for the location of the rear route-number stencil! – and that the guttering from above the nearside upper-deck windows was taken across the back panels in a most untidy way. Since the bus was built, the frosting to the platform window has been removed. The picture also shows the way that the tops of the windows in the driver's cab were as low as those in the lower saloon. Notice that the livery has been altered, with respect to the application of the areas of white, and that it carries fleet-number C3024, allocated in the 1937 renumbering scheme, the C-prefix indicating that the bus was assigned to Bristol 'City' work. *(S. Miles Davey)*

**169**. Following the operation of a Weymann-bodied Bristol G-Type demonstrator, Exeter Corporation placed an order with BT&CC for four GO5G chassis, with BBW bodies. Several special features were incorporated to Exeter's requirement and accordingly the body was coded **AM9-Type**. The most notable feature was that the staircase was straight, permitting a spacious platform. There were five half-drop windows on the nearside of the upper saloon, although on the offside they were only installed in the first three bays, due to the intrusion of the stairs. For the same reason the lower deck totals were three and two, respectively. Exeter Corporation used route *letters* rather than numbers and specified the fitment of a separate box for their display. A repeater box was placed in the window alongside the platform, but in a further photograph taken after blinds had been fitted, the box had been removed to the *first* side window. The batch was numbered 45-48 (BFJ 155-8) and shown here, in the grounds of Lawrence Hill bus depot, unusually, is number 48, in October 1935. The livery was green and cream; the name Exeter Corporation was carried across the upper panels, as the buses carried no external advertising.

**170 & 171**.  Shown here are the interiors of the upper and lower saloon of an Exeter Corporation **AM9/48** body. The staircase intruded so far into the upper deck that there was only room for four pairs of seats on the offside. For all that, 26 passengers were accommodated on that deck, as the rearmost seat provided four places. The route-letter box and winding handle can be seen at the front of the upper saloon, just above floor level. The staircase also intruded into the lower saloon, reducing the capacity there to 22; it will be noticed that a single, inward-facing seat was installed below the stairs. Note the polished grilles on the inside of the permanent ventilators above the lower saloon windows. The opening windows used a snap-type catch at the top, but there was a regular tendency in later years for the opening panes to skew and become stuck.

**172**. BBW did not always build bodies of a well-balanced design, or with the opulence of the Q3 coach shown in Plate 162. The **Q4/32** coach was a case in point. This appeared about March 1935 for BT&CC's own needs, on a batch of J-Types with 6-cylinder petrol engines (although one chassis was re-engined with a 4-cylinder Dennis oil engine before being licensed, to become chassis JO4D.1). They were registered BHU 294/5, 388 and 636-652. The most notable feature of the design is that the rake of the windscreen was matched by the rake to the windows in the front bulkhead. This was reflected by the faring down to the front wing and by the pillar in the cab near-side windows. The destination box was blended smoothly into the front dome, but such aerodynamic features were somewhat spoilt by the clumsy roof luggage carrier and the upright pillars and straight lines of the side windows. The waistline was rather high, being level with the top of the bonnet. Note the sliding rear entrance door and the fact that, unusually for a coach, the Bristol coat-of-arms was carried on the side panels. It is interesting that all of these bodies were selected for replacement as early as 1941-1945, by new bus bodies built to wartime utility standards; it is wondered if the structure of the Q4, particularly around the disjointed front bulkhead, may have become weak.

**173**. There was no shortfall in the standard of trim applied to the interior of the **Q4/32** coach. There was a sunshine roof, embossed material on the ceiling, with polished wood trim, single-panel opening windows and the usual mirrors, curtains and moquette-lined body walls and bulkhead. The subject for these photographs was BHU 639; as the MCW was introducing more variety in the engines offered, the G- and J-Type chassis with the original specification 6-cylinder JW petrol unit were recoded to match the fuller descriptions now in force; accordingly, the chassis number of this coach was J.JW.185.

**174.** It has already been stated that bus and coach bodywork styling was moving ahead in great strides in the early 1930s. This had a negative effect, though, in that many coaches of six to ten years of age looked 'dated' to prospective passengers, even though probably perfectly sound. Among the operators who decided to overcome this problem by fitting new coachwork to these young chassis were Western and Southern National. An order was placed with BBW in 1935 for the first of no fewer than 40 new 32-seat coach bodies, for mounting on six- and seven-year-old Tilling-Stevens chassis. The chassis had actually been acquired second-hand from fellow Tilling Group operator, North Western, and Western/Southern National prepared them for rebodying with an overhaul and the fitment of a more modern radiator. Unfortunately, the Tilling Stevens B10A2 was an old-fashioned chassis in any case and the front end, even in revised form, still looked dated. Furthermore, the design of the new body, which was completely unlike any other produced by BBW, was not particularly glamorous, with a high waistline, a shallow roof and oddly shaped windows. These had larger-radius corners at the top than at the bottom and pillars that broadened towards the top. The latter was a feature that had a certain amount of popularity, but was usually carried out with rather more finesse, especially by the Tilling Group's principal bodybuilder, Eastern Counties – see pages 75 and 91 of *Eastern Coach Works, Volume 1* by Maurice Doggett, published by TPC. These BBW coach bodies had canvas roofs, which could be rolled back – an idea that was itself somewhat dated!

**175.** BBW built another coach body with well-rounded corners to its windows, in the fashion of A & R Graham's Q3 coach, shown in Plate 162. The newcomer was slightly less elaborate, as this photograph, dated 13th September 1935, shows. The front profile was not so smooth, there was no roof luggage carrier, there were no curtains and ventilation slots were placed above the side windows.

Also, there was a destination indicator placed in the rear dome. It is interesting that the body was not coded among the Q-class reserved for coaches, but instead was the **L13-Type**. For all that, it was named as 'The Golden Demonstration Coach' and received an eye-catching metallic gold paint scheme. As in the case of the Graham coach, it was mounted on a chassis powered by a Gardner 5LW oil engine that no doubt made its presence felt! The chassis was number JO5G.41. Seating was provided for 28 and the coach was registered CAE 154.

**176**. The interior of the **L13/28** 'Golden Demonstration Coach' shows that plenty of luxury was applied within. The decoration of the ceiling and under-side of the parcel shelves was of the quality that was only to be expected at the time, as was the lighting. The bulkhead, similarly, carried the usual array of mirrors and a clock. The seat uprights were covered in leather, leaving cloth to be used only for the cushions. The emergency door, as in the Graham coach, was located in the second offside panel. This coach featured a divided rear window using flat glass, unlike the Graham coach. Following demonstration work, it passed into the BT&CC fleet.

**177**. Closely following the 'Golden Demonstration Coach' came another luxury coach, this time designated **Q5/26** and painted black and ivory. It was the third and – sadly – final coach on this particular theme and was probably the most luxurious! As the destination indicator suggests, it was finished for display at the 1935 Commercial Motor Show, which was the last to be held at London's Olympia exhibition hall before Earl's Court became the regular venue. The Q5/26 was mounted on a quiet-running petrol-engined chassis; in fact, the last petrol-engined Bristol to be built, J.JW.226. It was later licensed as CHW 567. This coach was rather tall, as the waistline was level with the top of the bonnet (giving the windscreen a horizontal base-line), there were route display screens placed above the side windows, which in turn allowed a two-tier destination indicator to appear at the front, and there was a luggage-carrier blended into the roof. A large faring was applied between the canopy and the front wing, with an unglazed window to permit some side-ward vision. The steps to the roof luggage-carrier were installed in the body side this time and the pillar between the fourth and fifth windows was broadened to take account. Rather than being slightly curved under, the rear of the body was swept outwards. Internally, the coach was not dissimilar to the L13/28 shown above, except for the use of pale leather for the seats and the fitting of curtains. The lack of permanent vents above the side windows meant very deep parcel shelves could be fitted.

**178.** Having written the caption to Plate 174 about the advances in bodywork styling, BBW – doubtless unintentionally! – helped to stall the advance with the introduction of the **AM7-Type** bus body in June 1935. This body restored the splendidly rounded character of the 1930 L4/L10 range, as best depicted in Plate 126. Indeed, if anything, these new bodies were even more rounded! They were certainly every bit as attractive. Permanent vents were reintroduced above the side windows, but a more modern feature, even in comparison with an AM3 body, was the much neater treatment at the front of the roof, although the well-inclined face the destination indicator now received would have made the display more difficult to read due to reflections. The oval back window also returned to dual-doorway bodies, as seen here, although this was the last BBW model to remain in production featuring this attractive item. In the dual-doorway form, 34 'Pell' tubular seats were installed, that opposite the rear doorway taking three. This AM7/34 is BT&CC's BHU 980, mounted on 4-cylinder chassis J.NW.71.

**179.** The **AM7-Type** was also built as a front entrance bus. In this form, the space occupied in the dual-door version by the rear door and small trailing window was combined, with one long window. The emergency exit was placed in the rear wall. Oddly, there were only 32

seats in the single-doorway form. This AM7/32 body was mounted on one of chassis numbers J.NW.67, 69, 70 and 72, later registered BHW 431/0/2/3, respectively. All AM7 bodies were supplied to BT&CC, comprising six AM7/32 models and 31 AM7/34 types. Most were supplied on J.NW and J.JW chassis during 1935/36; the 1936 buses differed by having the side-lights repositioned to the cab dash and the front bulkhead. One each of types AM7/32 and AM7/34 was mounted on the first chassis to receive 6-cylinder 7.7-litre oil engines

by AEC (JO6A.1 and 2). Also, one body was mounted on an experimental chassis, powered by the Bristol Axial or rotary engine, and was registered BHW 429. Unfortunately, after its clutch disintegrated during testing, the experiment was concluded and its AM7/32 body dismantled!

**180.** West Hartlepool Corporation returned to BT&CC in 1935 after a break of seven years. They placed an order for two J-Type single-deckers, complete with BBW bodywork. The chassis were 4-cylinder models, numbered J.NW.52/3. Despite the similarity in appearance to the AM7/32 shown above, it is interesting that the bodywork evidently was not from the all-metal family. The designation was **L12-Type**. Only two principal features distinguished the L12 from the AM7/32. Firstly, the pillar-spacing was slightly increased, leaving

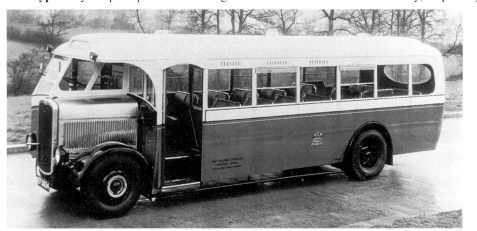

a shorter trailing side window; and secondly, the emergency door was located at the front of the offside, resulting in the installation of the oval back window. An extra roof ventilator was fitted and the windows in the side of the cab restyled. Seating was provided for 36, by including a rearward-facing triple seat backing on to the front bulkhead; this still left 12ins of access at foot level to the emergency door. The passenger door was a folding unit, closing across the foot of the steps. Seen here is the first of the pair, EF 5634.

**181**. A JO5G demonstrator was built in 1935 and registered BHY 691. A new style body was built for it and brought to single-deckers the new type of coding that had been started with the DD1 (Plates 165 & 166), namely **S1-Type**. The styling of the S1 never gained the affection given to the AM7-Type seen in Plates 178 & 179. The windscreen seemed a little too upright, the roof too shallow and the waistline too high, although, as the saying goes, all things are relative! A new idea for BBW, although already specified by Western National for the coaches started earlier in the year (Plate 174), was the use of outswept or flared side panels. This was another of those fads of fashion that were to have a great impact on body styling. The earliest

known photograph of the first S1 is this view, taken during the Second World War. It shows the bus, now numbered 2002 in the BT&CC fleet, standing in Queen Square, Bristol, with a route-board on the side for city service 146. It will be seen that, although the front door is still placed at the top of the steps, there is a sliding door at the rear entrance. A simple valance adorns the front porch. A route-number box has been added to the roof since the bus entered service. There is evidence of minor collision damage, probably incurred during wartime black-out conditions, and the white paint in the livery has been covered with a coat of grey, to minimise detection by enemy aircraft. *(Peter Hulin)*

**182**. The **S1-Type** entered production in the spring of 1936. Curiously, the eight bodies built in 1936 were thoroughly intermingled on a

batch of J.NW chassis with some of the last AM7-Type bodies! Seating was again provided for 34 in a dual-doorway body. The sliding rear door was open for this picture and, as can be seen, it slid inboard of the trailing side panel. Careful study will show that the centre bay of both the S1 and AM7, in which the route board was located, was actually slightly longer than the rest. This photograph, taken in July 1936, also shows that, at the time, BT&CC's fleetnumbers were derived from the Bristol chassis numbers, although sometimes, as here, in abbreviated form; this bus is N86 (CHW 51), on chassis J.NW.86.

Sister vehicle N100 (CHW 49) was actually completed as the sole J.PW model, with Bristol's last new design of petrol engine.

**183**. The offside aspect and rather upright front profile of the **S1-Type** are captured in this view. The photograph was taken on 16th

July 1939, by which time the bus, CHW 52, was already on its third fleet-number. Originally numbered N87 to reflect its chassis number of J.NW.87, it became C629 when the entire fleet was renumbered in early 1937; the C-prefix indicated City fleet, for Bristol Joint Services work. After that, a Gardner 5LW oil engine was installed in May 1939, resulting in a further renumbering, into the appropriate series, as C2702. The location is Durdham Downs, at the top of Blackboy Hill, and the terminus of new Tram-Replacement Route 7 to Zetland Road and The Centre. *(S. Miles Davey)*

**184**. In 1936, the double-deck AM6 body was succeeded by one of slightly revised appearance, to which new classification **DD2-Type** was applied. The changes are shown in this view of GO5G.132 (DAE 374) at the Clyde Road terminus of the 20 in Bristol. The rear upstairs window took on an attractive new shape, as a curve was applied to the top edge, this being even more pronounced than on the DD1 body. Metal louvres were now fitted above all the main side windows, not just above those that opened. On the lower deck, the window in the first bay reverted to a non-opening type. The most beneficial change, though, was felt by the driver, as the cab's offside window, forward of the door, had its top raised, to line up with the top of the windscreen. It is interesting to note that when some AM6 bodies were rebuilt during or after the war, the tops of their cab offside windows were raised to match the DD2 style. Twenty DD2-Type bodies were built, all for BT&CC. The first ten, with DAE registrations, had an unusual seating layout, as there were fewer seats upstairs than down – 26 against 28. Note the larger destination screen, with a route-number box located above it. The bus in the distance is AM6-bodied GO5G.125 (CHY 120). *(S. Miles Davey)*

**185** (right). In the summer of 1937, new GO5G chassis for BT&CC appeared with a body further revised in appearance. The most noticeable feature of this, the **DD3-Type**, was the severe slope applied to the front profile. This reduced considerably the length of the leading upper-deck side window. The front dome appeared to overhang the front windows more than previously, giving rise to a scowling effect. The windscreen was set back from the front dash in the manner last seen on L1-family bodies up to 1930, although the dash on the DD3 carried a rounded shoulder. The windows in the front bulkhead became rectangular, but in the interests of fashion, the leading and trailing side windows downstairs became D-shaped; note, however, how the louvres above the glass in these windows did not over-run the curved edges. The leading cab offside window, short though it now was, received similar shaping. It will be seen that larger destination boxes had at last started to appear and a route-number box was positioned above. The latter, though, was given a more upright face, probably in the interests of clarity. Interior lights were positioned at the tops of the window pillars. This bus, EAE 286, entered service as No. 3077 in BT&CC's new numbering system. It is seen at Weston-super-Mare. *(A.G.Vowles)*

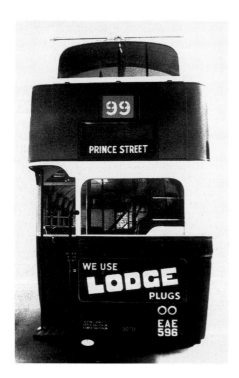

**186** (left). This photograph depicts the rear aspect of the **DD3-Type** body on the 12 GO5G chassis delivered to Bristol Tramways in the summer of 1937. The attractively shaped rear windows upstairs and on the platform were the same as introduced on the DD2-Type (Plate 184), but rain-water channelling and other items had been tidied up. Service 99 had once been worked by Greyhound Motors, but that concern was absorbed by BT&CC in 1936. The subject for this study is 3070 (EAE 596), a country services bus rather than one allocated to Bristol Joint Services for city work, so the destination display was probably only applied for the photograph. Incidentally, an oil or diesel-engined bus would have no need for Lodge sparking-plugs! *(M.J.Tozer Collection)*

**187**. This is a well-known photograph, but serves well to illustrate the features of the **DD3-Type**. The prominent frontal slope is shown clearly, as is the D-shaped window in the cab and the bulbous front dash. The windscreen was shallower as a result of this and, also, the opening upper part of the screen dispensed with the dip at the foot of the glass that had been featured since 1928. BT&CC's 3079 (EAE 288) is shown in Swindon in war-time grey paint, but with unmasked headlamps and only a hint of white on the tips of the wings and life-rail. *(R.H.G.Simpson)*

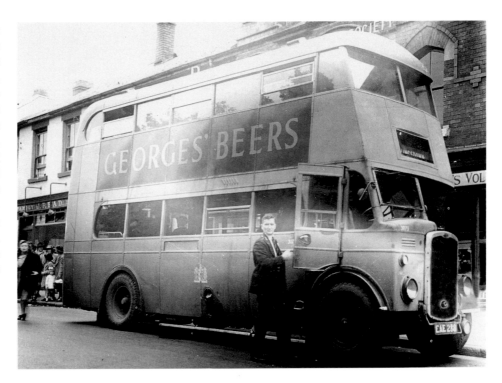

**188**. The single-deck bodies built on JO5G chassis for BT&CC in 1937 incorporated several slight differences from the 1936 S1 batch, shown in Plate 182, and were afforded the classification of **S3-Type** (there had been only one S2 body, a rear-entrance 34-seat version for demonstration purposes, registered CHY 821). There were four principal revisions taken into the S3. The face of the front destination box was made more upright, to improve clarity. The faring below the canopy was made smoother and was continued down to the front wing. The faring over the front porch was made slightly more prominent. Finally, and most significantly, the rear doorway reverted to the hinged type placed at the top of the steps. All of these features are shown here on 2059 (EHT 97), standing without destination blinds on Bristol's Tramway Centre shortly after entering service. Note that a recess is provided in the waistband to carry the side route-board. Also, it will be noticed that the bonnet is painted. *(A.G.Vowles)*

**189**. This photograph taken inside the Body Building Works shows an **S3-Type** body under construction, in 1937. The craftsman's use of a mallet and chisel by the front porch is fairly strong indication that the framework was once again made from timber! The outline of the vertical destination box can be seen and the edging for the canopy and bulkhead faring is in place, though with a temporary stiffening brace. It can be seen that a thin rail of wood was applied below the waistrail, for the attachment on the finished bus of the beading that marked the foot of the waistband. The upright pillars have all been carefully fabricated to capture the outward flare at the base. *(M.J.Tozer Collection)*

**190**. To depict the rear aspect of the S1-S3 family of single-deckers, we need to turn to a post-war photograph, of a bus in BT&CC's then-new Tilling-green livery, with a cream waistband. The subject is an **S3-Type** on 2075 (EHT 537). The main feature was that the oval

back window had gone for ever. In its place were two panes, which prescribed a fairly even arc through the top of the pair. The destination box was inclined in line with the dividing pillar of the windows. Originally, a route number box was also carried at the rear, placed in the waistband. A recess was still provided for the under-body mounting of a spare wheel. At the time, Robertson's Golden Shred Marmalade was made in Bristol. Thirty S3 bodies were constructed, six of which were the first Bristols for the Gloucester City fleet, which BT&CC now managed on behalf of Gloucester Corporation; these six, with Gloucester BFH registrations, were based on chassis JO4D.2-7, with 4-cylinder Dennis engines. *(Mike Mogridge)*

# Chapter 8

BBW was involved in 1937 in further programmes to update seven- to nine-year-old chassis for related operators. Western and Southern National were included again, but before their work was commenced, another Tilling company was catered for. This was the West Yorkshire Road Car Company. The acquisition of this customer was particularly interesting. BT&CC's current General Manager was the influential Major Frank J Chapple who had moved to Bristol from the same post with West Yorkshire. Significantly, West Yorkshire had been one of the first Tilling Group companies to standardise on Bristol chassis. Major Chapple had shown strong ideas on single-deck body styling at West Yorkshire (involving Eastern Counties-bodied Bristol Js in particular), this having a hint of the front-entrance design evolved by the rival BET Group and brought by Major Chapple from his previous post with Yorkshire Woollen District, a BET company.

In view of this distinctive West Yorkshire single-deck pattern, it was therefore surprising that the new BBW bodies did not conform to Major Chapple's standard of appearance. Most notably, these bodies, which were mounted on 1928/29 Tilling-Stevens B10A2 chassis, featured a *rear* entrance. They were of a well-balanced design, but were akin to products of the Eastern Counties factory for *other* customers in 1932/33.

Western and Southern National were also now beginning to evolve their own individual design. They had two consignments from BBW in 1937, one batch again reclothing chassis built around 1929, but the other comprising new small buses.

The rebodying was carried out on AEC Reliance and Leyland Lion chassis, with a couple of Leyland Tigers included as well. The body style was generally conventional, but incorporated a moulded panel above the side windows for advertising purposes, together with outswept skirt panels, similar to the contemporary S3 body being built for BT&CC. They seated 32 with a rear entrance.

The small, 26-seat bodies built for this customer were on Dennis Mace chassis. This model and its normal-control equivalent, the Ace, were well suited to Western and Southern National for their many services traversing narrow lanes in sparsely populated countryside. The BBW bodies were clearly related to those built on the AEC and Leyland chassis, although the doorway was located towards the front of the saloon.

The Commercial Motor Show of 1937 moved to a new venue in London, at Earl's Court. Bristol's stand at this show was taken up entirely with examples of the new range of oil-engined chassis, the K-Type double-decker and L-Type single-decker.

For the K-Type double-deckers ordered for BT&CC's own fleet for 1938, BBW merely adapted the sloping-fronted DD3 body as built for their final Gs. The only significant alteration was made to the front of the cab, due to the fact that the radiator of the K-Type chassis was more stocky than that of the G. The dash was moved rearward, with a sharper edge to the 'lip' beneath the windscreen. Slight changes were later incorporated before production was geared up to start building a large fleet of K5Gs for Bristol's tramway replacement.

For the L-Type single-decker, BBW introduced the S4, another dual-doorway product. Essentially, this was the outcome of moderate restyling of the S1/S3 built on J-Type chassis, yet the improvement in appearance was most satisfying. In fact, however, the restyling had been done earlier, although the initial outcome had been disguised by operator-requested details. To be precise, the S4 shared its profile and the shape of its side panel curves and sweeps with the bodies built the previous year on the Western National AECs and Leylands!

Bristol Tramways was one of several Tilling operators who agreed to obtain a batch of Dennis Lancet single-deckers, probably for evaluation against the Bristol L. Three were delivered and entered service in 1938 with BBW bodies. These were adapted from the S4 and coded S5.

For its Bristol L-Type buses in 1939, BT&CC decided to return to the front-entrance layout. These bodies, designated S6, actually incorporated several subtle styling improvements. A somewhat less subtle styling revision – perhaps more correctly described as a revision in construction methods – affected the double-deck body from August 1938. The five-bay layout employed ever since G.101 appeared in 1932 was replaced by a six-bay configuration, which resulted in a rather more fussy appearance. Small revisions were later made to detailed points and body designations progressed through to DD6.

Output was now at a high level as the replacement of Bristol's trams got under way. Neighbouring Bath Electric Tramways and Bath Tramways Motor Company had been acquired by Bristol Tramways & Carriage Company in 1936 and in 1939 the removal of Bath's trams was achieved with a fleet of 30 new double-deckers. Only 14 of these were on K-Type chassis, as the other 16, although visually similar, had 1936 G-Type chassis. These chassis had been traded in, after two years' service, against new K-Types by Maidstone & District and Chatham & District, the G-Types henceforth being put to good use by Bath Electric Tramways with new Bristol bodies.

In the period 1938 to 1942, the number of BBW double-deck bodies built on K-Type chassis, or used for rebodying G-Types, amounted to no fewer than 242 units! Only five examples did not enter the BT&CC group's fleets; these five – two in 1938 and three in 1940 – were supplied to Pontypridd UDC.

Similarly, L-Type chassis receiving BBW saloon bodywork, although in significantly smaller numbers, were also almost entirely directed towards BT&CC. The exceptions included three buses which went to Doncaster Corporation – in fact, these were diverted from a BT&CC order – and a sole rear-entrance version that, once more, was delivered to Pontypridd UDC. In 1940, however, work started on more orders for Western/Southern National. These amounted to 18 bodies on L5G chassis, together with 39 similar products with which to rebody their entire batch of H-Type chassis new in 1933; this of course resulted in the replacement of their nine Bristol AM3 bodies. The new bodies, like the Pontypridd L-Type, were of six-bay layout with a rear entrance, but there the similarity ended, as they were finished very much to Western/Southern National's distinctive appearance, including the application of advertising panels as on their 1937 Bristol bodies.

**191**. The West Yorkshire Road Car Company followed the example set by Western and Southern National by ordering new bodies for mounting on earlier Tilling Stevens B10A2 chassis (Plate 174). In this case the 1928/29 chassis had not been modernised and the buses retained the antiquated radiator. The order called for 25 bodies, which were in build in January 1937. They were 31-seaters, but bore no resemblance to any other BBW product. Indeed, their appearance was most closely akin to Eastern Counties bodies built for North Western around 1932 – compare this picture with that on page 51 of Maurice Doggett's *Eastern Coach Works to 1946*, published by TPC. Relevant features are the curved-under side panels, the raised, half-round section waistband, the small-radius curves to the lower corners of the side windows, the D-shaped trailing side window, the well-raked windscreen and the overhanging destination box. The type of destination indicator used by West Yorkshire consisted of painted boards, with separate leaves hinged across the middle and turned like a book – hence their name 'Bible Boards'. Shown here is K255 (WW 7122), which entered service in the Keighley-West Yorkshire section of the fleet on its return. The photograph was taken at Hengrove in January 1937, but it is sad to record that this set of photographs was the last that BT&CC commissioned on a regular basis.

**192**. The interior of the 1937 body on Keighley-West Yorkshire K255 (WW 7122) shows the neat but functional lines of the body. The roof-sticks were still exposed, but they were finished with polished wood facing strips. A bell cord ran the length of the ceiling, close to the hand-rail, and was attached directly to a gong inside the cab. Although the vehicle was intended merely for local bus work, the seats were of a particularly comfortable design and they were trimmed – as was the bulkhead – in an attractive floral-pattern material. West Yorkshire was one of several operators who believed in high standards of trim for even the most mundane of duties.

**193 & 194**. Western and Southern National returned to BBW for more rebodying in 1937. The bodies this time were 32-seat bus bodies, which were mounted on seven- to eight-year-old chassis, comprising Leyland Lions, Leyland Tigers and AEC Reliances. They were completed between April and August and totalled 26. These nearside and offside views show Southern National 2977, which had a 1930 Leyland Lion LT2 chassis and was registered in Somerset as YC 9412. The radiator is a replacement unit, available for modernising the looks. The body styling contains several features recently introduced by W/SNOC, for incorporation by each of the bodybuilders supplying to the firm. The features governed the body-side trim, the advertisement display panels, the destination-box and surround and the D-shaped window ahead of the driver's door. The trim on the sides contained an area of white relief to the green paintwork and swept down at the back. It also curved down to the front wing on the nearside, but on the offside it was continued straight forward and round to meet the radiator. An area along the sides of the roof received a more upright face, for the display of advertisements; as the offside view shows, this was indented, while beading was extended fore and aft to enclose white relief. At the front, the company's distinctive two-aperture destination box was contained within a flat panel, which was again painted white. The roof contour was gently curved and the way the side panels curved inwards before the outward flare at skirt level was well balanced and attractive. In the photograph from the offside, the vehicle on the extreme right of the picture is an earlier Leyland Lion, with a body also built in 1937, but by Mumford of Plymouth and yet, as it was again to W/SNOC's requirements, it clearly resembles the BBW product. These photographs were taken in August 1952. *(Both photographs – Alan B. Cross)*

**195.** The offside rear aspect of one of the 1937 bodies built as part of Western and Southern National's rebodying programme is captured in this photograph of 3546 (DR 5476), which had a 1929 Leyland Tiger TS1 chassis. The bus in its original form had been acquired with the business of Southern General of Plymouth. One can see that the BBW body contained a large, single-piece rear window, with a continuous curve through the upper edge, although other builders used twin rear windows. The elliptical, white-painted panel below the window was stipulated by the company. Note a roof luggage carrier was still being called for, complete with a fairly sturdy-looking ladder. The side windows were rather numerous; the first bay was short as it contained the emergency door on the offside. Then there were four principal bays with opening windows. The next bay, ahead of the rear entrance, was interesting as it was of variable length, according to the dimensions of the chassis; the Lion in Plates 193 & 194 was slightly shorter than the Tiger seen here, so this window in the Lion was considerably reduced in length. Note that the louvres, above the windows, are made of glass and dip to their centres. This is another 1952 photograph, but pre-war, the window surrounds would have been included in the area of white paintwork. *(Alan B. Cross)*

**196 & 197.** In June and July 1937, BBW built the bodywork on 17 little Dennis Mace chassis for Western National. They were 26-seaters for the bye-ways and remote villages so numerous in the West Country – the bus seen here at Penzance, 636 (CTA 529), is *en route* for the most famous of Cornish villages, Mousehole. The Dennis Mace was unusual in having the front axle set back, which resulted in excellent manoeuvrability, although the front doorway had also to be set back a little. The styling had strong similarities to the full-sized bodies shown in Plates 193-195, although the front entrance resulted in the emergency door being placed in the centre of the rear wall. The front door was again a sliding unit that ran inside the panel to its rear. In these buses the door seems to have been mechanically operated – the label on the glass requested passengers to wait until the *driver* or conductor opened the door. W/SNOC's two previous batches of Dennis Maces had been bodied by Eastern Counties and Brush, and were quite similar to each other, but BBW's batch conformed to W/SNOC's own new styling ideas. Interestingly, BT&CC took a batch of Dennis Maces for their own fleet in 1937, yet chose to have them bodied by Duple! *(Both photographs – Alan B. Cross)*

**198 & 199**. It is very gratifying that amateur bus enthusiasts sometime took the trouble to photograph the interior of buses, especially where no official photographs seem to exist. These views capture the same 1937 Western National Dennis Mace 26-seater, No.36 (CTA 529). The forward view shows that, in common with the preceding Eastern Counties and Brush-bodied Maces, there was a rearward-facing seat across the front bulkhead. This was chosen to overcome the intrusion of the wheel arches from the set-back front axle. The seat took four people, as the area between the bulkhead and the front door was of use only as a luggage pen, for which bars were added to protect the windows from damage. The rearward view shows the attractive cloth and leather seat trim, as well as showing that the lining panels around the rear corners and on the emergency door were also trimmed in moquette. The first nearside seat was out of alignment with the others, due to the intrusion of the enclosure for the sliding door. *(Both photographs – Alan B. Cross)*

**200**. The 1937 Commercial Motor Show was used by BT&CC to launch their new K-Type double-deck and L-Type single-deck oil-engined chassis. The K-Type chassis that was displayed, number K5G.42.23, later received a BBW body to become Bristol Tramways' C3094 (EHU 229) as the last bus in a batch of 12. It is seen here not long after entering service in January 1938, at Avonmouth Church on route 28. The body was identical to the DD3-Type for GO5G chassis – as illustrated in Plate 187 in particular – with one exception. The radiator on the K-Type (and L-Type, too) was of a new pattern, designated KV-Type. It was thicker-set than the JV radiator of the G-Type (and J-Type). Accordingly, the front dash of the cab was set back, causing the forward end of the front wing to protrude underneath the dash, while there was a smaller, and squarer, lip to the top of the dash. This batch had the same destination equipment as the DD3 body, with a separate and slightly more upright route-number-stencil holder. Note that the recess in the lower waist rail for a route board is not being used. *(A.G.Vowles)*

**201**. In May 1938, BT&CC placed in service another 22 BBW-bodied K5Gs, at the commencement of the massive programme to replace the trams in the city of Bristol. Over the next few years, BBW built as many bodies as they could on new K5G chassis, but such were the numbers required that Eastern Coach Works was needed to help out; indeed, on this occasion, 18 ECW-bodied examples were also activated. The BBW buses were numbered C3095-C3116 (EHY 557-578) and this photograph shows C3115 on Tram Replacement Route 1, crossing Durdham Downs (route 2 was introduced in the same scheme). It is at The White Tree, which is seen behind the bus; the trunk was painted white as an aid to visibility at a busy and unlit cross-roads with North View/Parrys Lane. These buses contained two main differences from the bus shown in the plate above and, although no accurate record now exists, it is firmly believed these bodies were coded **DD4-Type**. The destination indicator was modified, with the removal of the separate route-number box, while the blind box received rounded corners. Secondly, the louvres above the upper-deck windows were extended over the end windows. A less obvious but significant change was that the lower corners of the side windows received a small-radius curve. *(Peter Clare, courtesy Peter Davey)*

**202**. Despite the pressure on BBW to build for Bristol's tram-replacement programme, an order was still accepted from Pontypridd Urban District Council for two double-deckers on K-type chassis. The council may have preferred Gardner 6LW engines, as in its previous two Bristols (Plate 165 & Plate 310 on p.166), but they received standard K5G chassis. They may well have been asked to accept standard BT&CC-specification BBW bodies, because the outcome, including the destination screen, was identical to Bristol's EHY-registered batch, believed to have been coded **DD4-Type**. They were nevertheless painted in Pontypridd's version of

deep-blue and white, together with all the lining out, and were numbered to follow the GO6Gs as 23 and 24 (DNY 684/5). Shown here is 23 in the town centre during the war, passing below trolleybus wires. *(Chris Taylor Collection)*

**203**. The new Bristol L-Type single-deck chassis received a body subtly restyled from that on its J-Type predecessor and designated **S4-Type**. This improved the controversial items such as windscreen rake, roof depth and side-panel curvature. If compared to Plates 181-183 & 188, the S4 can be seen to have a much more agreeable balance, especially in the deeper roof and the more gently outswept side panels. The side windows appear to have been placed fractionally lower and certainly there was a step in the line above these windows where they met the cab windows. The revised outline of the body may have been fresh to a new Bristol chassis, but, if this offside view, showing Bristol's 2086 (FAE 60) in post-war livery, is compared to the Western National rebodied Leyland in Plate 194, it will be seen that the outline is extremely similar! Both designs even shared the D-shaped window in the offside of the driver's cab, although in the S4, this was actually to match the double-deck bodies on K-Type chassis. The route number stencil sight was incorporated above the destination screen in an attractively shaped pressing. The box seems not to have been used after the war, though. *(R.F.Mack)*

**204**. The very first L-Type chassis, L5G.43.1, received an **S4-Type** body to become BT&CC's 2082 (FAE 56). The S4 was a dual-doorway body, but with only 32 seats. A curved base-line was reintroduced to the bulkhead windows. Still only two half-drop windows were applied to each side. This photograph was taken during the war years, as the bus was on lay-over from the service from Severn Beach, in Grange Court Road, alongside a depot in Westbury-on-Trym, Bristol. The distinctive depot buildings were sold in the early 1950s and refitted as a car show-room, remaining as such to this day. *(A.G.Vowles)*

**205**. Another post-war view is used to depict the rear styling of BBW's **S4-Type** body. Compared with the S3-Type in Plate 190, the back windows had a similar shape, but were not so tall, and the destination screen had received an upright face. Note that this indicator has been painted out – a sharp contrast to the 18in-deep display at the back of the 1950 ECW-bodied L-Type standing ahead! On the S4, three shallower steps were introduced to each doorway, instead of two. Twenty-seven S4-bodied L-Types were built, the first seven becoming 2082-8 (FAE 56-62). The next ten formed the first Bristols for the company's newest subsidiaries, Bath Electric Tramways Ltd and Bath Tramways Motor Company Ltd, since the latter had taken delivery of three BBW-bodied A-Types in 1927, as shown in Plate 84. The new L-Types were accordingly registered in Bath, as GL 6027-6036. The next seven were allocated to the Gloucester City division (on four-cylinder L4G chassis), and were registered in that city as CFH 19-25. The final three were delivered at the end of the year for Bristol Tramways Country Services, as 2122-4 (FHT 257-259). *(Peter Davey)*

**206**. When Bristol Tramways purchased three Dennis Lancet 2 chassis, undoubtedly as part of the Tilling Group's evaluation of this model in comparison with the Bristol L5G, BBW built the bodywork. The outcome was merely an adaptation of the 32-seat, dual-doorway S4, with the classification of **S5-Type**. The radiator of the Dennis Lancet 2 was mounted almost as high as the Bristol KV radiator, so BBW do not seem to have made more than slight changes to the cab. Even the bulkhead fairing was not altered, so just failing to match the shape of Dennis' front wing. The biggest alteration would seem to have involved the move of the access to the fuel tank to the nearside. 2089 (FHT 77) was new in July 1938, but is seen in post-war green livery at Axbridge. *(A. G. Vowles)*

**207**. The second batch of Bristol tram-replacement K5Gs, taking over in September 1938 on an extended (now cross-city) route 1, together with new routes 3 and 4, included 17 BBW-bodied buses, registered FHT 88-104. Shown here is C3172 (FHT 103) at the Victoria Rooms. These buses presented a marked change in appearance and are almost certain to have received the coding **DD5-Type**. Instead of employing five-bay construction, as had been in use ever since G.101 had appeared in 1932 (Plate 152), the bodies were of six-bay layout. The result of accommodating six windows along the sides instead of five was a more fussy appearance. The length of these windows was reduced from 3ft 3¼ins to 2ft 8½ins. The lower-deck windows, additionally, were

reduced in height, slightly, although the top of the window in the cab door was raised. Half-drop opening windows continued to be fitted to the first, third and fifth upper-deck bays and second and fourth bays on the lower-deck, but an additional roof air-extractor was introduced, in the third bay. The bulkhead windows now received very small-radius curves to the corners. The use of a route board on the offside of the bus was now discontinued, while that on the nearside was relocated next to the platform. *(A.G.Vowles)*

**208**. Another 28 similar double-deckers of the presumed **DD5-Type** entered service during the winter of 1938/39, with registrations FHT 119-130 and FHT 241-256. This picture was taken for a local press report covering the building of the new buses and shows the

rear aspect of the body, modelled by C3177 (FHT 122). It was generally similar to the DD3-Type shown in Plate 186, except that the platform window was reduced in height slightly, in accordance with the shallower side windows. The rear destination screen was projected within attractive moulding; this pattern had appeared on the buses presumed to be the DD4-Type (as shown in Plate 201), but on those bodies the box was set at the foot of the blue panel, whereas on this type, the box was positioned centrally. Another innovation was that the upper-deck rear emergency exit, incorporating the back window, was from here on hinged at the top instead of the bottom; its external handle can be seen directly above the destination box. Note the distinct shape of the faring above the platform in this picture and the plate above.
*(Peter Davey Collection)*

**209**. The appearance of the double-deck body was revised in three ways in April 1939. The most important change concerned the front destination box. As had already been found prior to introducing the S3 body in 1936, a box with a sloping face could be difficult to read, due to reflections. The front profile of the DD3 to DD5 range was severely sloped and the destination box glass had been in line with the profile; now, though, the face of the destination indicator was made upright. The panelling was attractively moulded round it. The second change was that the corners of the bulkhead windows received large-radius curves. Thirdly, the top corners of the windscreen became rounded; the effect was achieved by the addition of corner pieces to the polished surround, fitting square into the top outer corners of the frame, but giving a rounded finish where the glazing was held. This characteristic was to be a feature of the windscreens used in BBW bodies for many years to come. A change made inside the body was to revise the seating layout; the split of 28 in each saloon was altered to 30 upstairs and 26 down. The first buses to incorporate these revisions replaced Bath's entire tram network, in April and May 1939. The first of the K5Gs, numbered 3800 (GL 6601), is seen here in wartime conditions, with the substitution of grey for the white paint in the livery, yet with the addition of white to the wing-tips and with masks over the headlamps to leave just a narrow beam. *(The Omnibus Society Collection)*

**210**. Thirty new BBW-bodied double-deckers of the type described above were built to replace Bath's trams in April and May 1939. Only 14, however, were on K5G chassis. The other 16 were rather interesting, as their chassis were 1936 GO5Gs. These had originally been supplied, with bodywork by Weymann, to Maidstone & District and its subsidiary Chatham and District. In 1938 M&D traded in the GO5G chassis for new K5Gs, on to which the 1936 Weymann bodies were transferred (the work possibly taking place in Bristol). BT&CC was happy to use the GO5Gs in its large tram replacement programme, so the chassis were now put through BBW. Here they received the latest type of body, prior to becoming Bath Electric Tramways' 3814-29; they retained their Kent registrations

DKN 31-46. The body was identical to that on 3800-13 as in the plate above, except that the cab dash needed to be modified to suit the G-Type's more slender JV radiator. The dash was made more bulbous and was similar to that on the DD3-bodied GO5Gs as shown in Plate 187, although the upper strip of beading followed the line of the windscreen, rather than being parallel to the lower strip. The first of the batch of GO5Gs is shown here, on the Twerton route, outside Bath Abbey and with the Guildhall in the background. In addition to Bath buses 3800-29, Bristol's City fleet received 12 K5Gs with this particular body pattern, C3216-27 (FHT 260-271). *(Peter Hulin Collection)*

**211**. A new single-deck body, the **S6-Type**, appeared in the spring of 1939. With this, BT&CC decided – once again! – to go in for a single-doorway, front-entrance body. 32 seats were still installed. The S6 was further improved in looks over the S4/S5. The waistline was lowered and the pillar-spacing increased, resulting in larger windows, amounting to seven along the side instead of eight – an interesting contrast to the way double-deck styling had recently changed! The shallower waistband was now of curved section and the side route board was placed next to the front doorway. A slightly disappointing feature was that the base-line to the bulkhead windows was now made horizontal,

instead of curved. The windscreen was improved in appearance, by having rounded corners at both top and bottom. The rounding at the top was achieved in the same way as described in Plate 209. The window in the driver's door now had a polished frame, another feature that was to become a standard BBW fitting. Shown here is 2137 (FHT 284), awaiting custom for the Radstock 88 service at The Centre in Bristol (nowadays the amount of traffic passing this point would make it impossible to obtain such a photograph). *(A.G.Vowles)*

**212**. This interesting photograph provides a comparison between the 1939 **S6-Type** and one of the last S4 bodies, built at the end of 1938. It shows what a well-balanced design the S6 was. The larger and less numerous windows can be seen, as also the lowered waistline – compare the front corners of the two, by the front dash. The top of the side windows probably remained in the same position, but the beading above these on the S6 was sloped up before continuing over the cab, rather than stepping up as on the S4. The subject for the S4 body here is 2122 (FHT 257), while the S6 is 2136 (FHT 283). *(A.G.Vowles)*

**213**. Because the **S6-Type** body was a front-entrance model, the emergency door had to be positioned in the rear wall. The rear-end styling was nonetheless very attractive, with the tops of the windows on either side of the door having well-rounded outer corners. All three back windows had small-radius corners at the base. This post-war photograph shows Bath Tramways' 2250 (GL 6615), the first bus in a batch of ten. *(Peter Davey)*

**214.** The Gloucester City division required the dual-doorway layout for a further six buses in 1939 and these were again on L4G chassis (numbers 1253-8: CFH 603-8). The body design was a blend of S4 and S6 ideas, but sadly, few records of BBW's body designations of this period have survived. The pillar spacing was as found in the S4, but the body had the slightly lower waistline, with curved-section waistband, of the S6. The type of waistband made it necessary to place the handle of the emergency door lower down. Details of the windscreen and bulkhead patterns also matched the S6. Nos.1256-8 were transferred away from Gloucester in 1951 and were renumbered 2468-70 for country services (and they soon received 5LW engines!). They were fitted with the large, post-war-style destination box at the front and it is in this condition that CFH 606 is shown here, working a Bristol city service. *(S.N.J.White, courtesy Roy Marshall)*

**215.** In June 1939 two further revisions were introduced to the double-deck body and it is known that this version was designated **DD6-Type.** The changes were introduced with a batch of 30 buses, registered FHT 794-816/824-30. These were ready to implement Tram Replacement Routes 5 and 6 on enhanced services to Filton, where the works of the Bristol Aeroplane Company were becoming ever more busy as war once again threatened. The last-mentioned bus is seen here, though on Route 1 at Sea Mills Square early in the war. The more noticeable revision was that the roof-level air-extractors were repositioned into the second, fourth and sixth bays. The other alteration saw the introduction of rounded lower corners to the windscreen, as already in place on S6 single-deckers; compare with Plate 207. From this point on and until war-time conditions saw the introduction in 1942 of bodies built to a utilitarian standard, the double-

decker received no more changes. The DD6, therefore, saw a record production run, BT&CC taking, on new K5G chassis, no fewer than 110 bodies! In addition to the buses mentioned above, the bodies spanned the registration series GAE, GHT and GHU, with the last two examples being on HHT 141/2, new in January 1942. It is very fortunate that an example of the DD6 body has been magnificently restored by the Bristol Vintage Bus Group. The subject is C3336 (GHT 154), which originally entered service in November 1940. In fact, the restoration was achieved by meticulously combining parts of the last two surviving DD6-Types, during the 1970s and 1980s. *(A.G.Vowles)*

**216**. This is the interior of the upper saloon of the **DD6/56** body of the Bristol Vintage Bus Group's restored C3336 (GHT 154). The roof is still single-skinned, whereas the cove panels at the sides are double skinned and provide the basis for the light-bulbs and numerous black bell-push buttons. The opening windows are of the winding variety. There is polished wood applied to the face of the upright pillars, while all other trimming is in blue. *(Allan Macfarlane)*

**217**. An order was accepted from Pontypridd Urban District Council for three more BBW-bodied K5Gs, for delivery in 1940. As in the case of their 1938 pair (Plate 202), the buses were built to the BT&CC pattern and this is clearly shown by the inclusion of a recess for a route board next to the rear platform. The bodies were of the **DD6-Type**. The middle bus of the trio, No.29 (ETG 139), is posed here after being prepared for wartime black-out conditions, with masked headlights and (one) white wing-tip. The livery was still elaborately lined-out. *(Chris Taylor Collection)*

**218**. Plate 217 illustrates how Pontypridd UDC received K5Gs with DD6-Type bodies to BT&CC specification. In October 1941, Doncaster Corporation received three L5Gs with **S6-Type** 32-seat bodies, also to BT&CC specification. This is again borne out by provision for a route board next to the doorway, although this time the area was finished with flat panelling at the last stage of construction. The front destination indicator is also of BT&CC's characteristic shape. Careful study of the waistband shows this to have been flat, rather than curved-section, doubtless a concession to wartime restrictions in supply and finish that were in force by late 1941. The vehicle shown, No.19 (BDT 980), was the middle bus of the three. They had a remarkably long life, remaining in service for 20 years. Even then, two were transferred to the Corporation's Education Department, lasting there until 1967! *(M.J.Tozer Collection)*

**219 & 220**. These interior views of a Doncaster Corporation L5G not only typify the appearance of the **S6-Type** 32-seat front-entrance body, but also shows that, despite the fact that the second world war had been raging for two years now, the quality of trim was still high. The seats were quite tall and they were once again finished in leather and cut cloth. In the backs of the seats were circular ash-trays that could be swivelled up-side-down when being emptied. A Clayton circular heater was placed on the front bulkhead, a luxury not afforded to Bristol-area passengers! The high bulkhead window-line of the S6 will be apparent. By the late 1930s, parcel shelves had become standard and the interior lights were now placed on the underside of these shelves; as built, these lights were heavily masked, for black-out reasons, but after the war, ornate covers were installed. At strategic places under each shelf, small, raised and circular bell-push buttons were located, while at the top of the door pillar was a larger button, within a polished surround, for use by the conductor. All seats faced forward and single seats were used alongside the rear wheel arches. *(M.J.Tozer Collection)*

**221**. As BT&CC's need for double-deckers during this period was far greater than that for single-deckers, there was a break in the supply of Bristol L-Types for the fleet between the 1939 buses shown in Plates 211-213 and a small consignment delivered in late 1941. Twelve of the latter (five for the Country fleet, four for Bath and three for Gloucester) were S6-Type front-entrance buses. The City fleet, however, received six dual-doorway 32-seaters, as shown by this post-war view of C2706 (HAE 17). The bodies were generally similar to the dual-door buses built for Gloucester in 1939 (Plate 214), except the curved-section waistband was forsaken in the interests of economy. *(B.V.B.G. Collection)*

**222**. The final Bristol L-Type chassis built to peace-time standards after the start of the Second World War was L5G.54.100. This was

completed for Pontypridd UDC, with a unique body – the only *rear*-entrance version of the S4 to S6 family of bodies. It had seating for 36, reflecting the capacity popular around 1933/34. The framework was derived from that used for the dual-doorway body, as seen in the plate above, but the bulkhead window over the engine was able to be a single-piece fitting, with no door pillar to support. Interestingly, the rear entrance was protected by a sliding door. The bus was numbered 16 and registered ETX 322. It is seen here posed in Brislington depot yard. Despite wartime troubles, the bus was elaborately painted and lined out. Note that even the tyres carried a light-coloured ring on their sides! The route-number-holder over the destination box was not required in Pontypridd, so the chance was taken to display proudly the initials PUDC. *(A.G.Vowles)*

**223**. Western and Southern National had taken delivery of a number of Bristol L5Gs in 1938/39, for which the bodywork, finished to the operator's own particular styling, was built in Plymouth by Mumford. For the eighteen 1940 buses, the body contract was placed

with BBW. They later received DOD registration marks. The 1939 Mumford buses had been particularly elegant, with five bays between the bulkhead and rear door, but the Bristol bodies utilised six bays. As such, they resembled the 1938 Mumford examples. The operators' styling features that had appeared on the 1937 BBW products for rebodying older chassis, as in Plates 193-195, were still to be found, although the waist-level relief-band no longer dropped into the rear corner. A destination indicator was placed above the final side window ahead of the door. The seating capacity was 35. The buses were completed between May and July 1940 and Southern National 340 (DOD 529) is shown here in June 1943. *(The Omnibus Society Collection)*

113

**224.** As soon as BBW had finished bodying the 18 buses for Western and Southern National, as shown in Plate 223, they carried straight on into a further batch. These, however, were subtly different. The operator was still pursuing its policy of obtaining new bodywork for existing chassis and, in 1940, this programme turned to the 1933 Bristol H-Types. All 39 were to be dealt with by BBW and, although 30 had originally been bodied by Brush, the first nine had carried Bristol AM3/36 all-metal bodies! (See Plate 154) Most chassis had already had their Bristol LW 4-cylinder petrol motors replaced by Gardner 5LW oil engines. The new bodywork was little different from that on the L5Gs. To meet the slender JV radiator though, the dash was brought forward, producing a slightly longer window ahead of the driver's door, while the windscreen was able to be fractionally deeper, which improved the looks of the bus. The front wing did not protrude below the dash and as this wing was closer-fitting to the wheel, there was slightly deeper panelling between the wing and the white waist-band. Fifteen bodies were completed in 1940 – interestingly eliminating all AM3 bodies! – then the pace slowed and work was not completed until May 1943. Shown here is 126 (FJ 8956), with one of five bodies delivered incomplete by BBW in 1942 and finished by Tiverton Coach Builders in Devon. *(R.H.G.Simpson)*

**225.** One of Western National's 1940 L5Gs, 331 (DOD 516), suffered at the hands of an enemy air-raid on Plymouth in December 1941 and the body was burnt out. A replacement body was ordered from BBW and 331 was complete again in March 1942. The new body was finished to the original styling, except for a few concessions to wartime events. The glass louvres above the side windows were replaced by a continuous metal louvre, the side destination indicator was excluded, there was no roof luggage-carrier and there were only two opening windows each side, instead of four. The bus is shown here in the simplified post-war livery in July 1952. *(Alan B. Cross)*

# Chapter 9

From the 3rd September 1939, the United Kingdom was once more at war. Production at BBW and the MCW continued – falteringly – under peacetime processes for a few years, during what was known as the Phoney War, before enemy attacks on shipping or bombing raids radically altered the supply and usage of raw materials. The last Bristol bodies of peacetime appearance were outshopped on new K- and L-Type chassis in 1941/42, after which manufacturers were obliged to observe severe restrictions imposed by the Ministry of Supply. The new regulations governed such items as the materials used, seating type and capacity, the number of opening windows and the overall shape of the completed bus. Rounded panelling requiring skilled craftsmanship was to be superseded by flat panelling that could be achieved by unskilled workers. Bodies built for rebodying existing chassis were not, surprisingly, obliged to meet the full MoS utility standards and this included the new bodies on Western National's H-Type chassis, which continued in production until 1943.

From late 1941, though, once existing previously-obtained or manufactured parts had been used up and to comply with MoS requirements, BBW introduced utility versions of their bodies for K- and L-Type chassis. Only four such single-deckers were built, as double-deckers were much more in demand for wartime transport. These four were of front-entrance layout, carried squarer roof domes and lacked the outsweep to their lower panels. The Ministry of War Transport was involved in their allocation to operators and, although one bus entered BT&CC's own fleet and two went to Western National, the other bus had the unlikely customer of Edinburgh Corporation! The chassis of this and the two Western National buses, numbered L5G.56.006 to 008 respectively, were built during what was popularly known as the 'Unfrozen' period. The MoS had put a halt on all chassis manufacture a little earlier, but when it was realised that a number of manufacturers, such as Bristol, had sufficient stocks of parts to enable several more chassis to be completed, the stocks were 'unfrozen' and final assembly took place.

Bristol's double-deck bodies finished to MoS utility standards were also built on unfrozen chassis, in this case to the K5G's 57th Sanction (a fuller description of Bristol's Sanction system was given in *The Bristol Story – Part 1*, by Alan Townsin (Venture Publications, 1996)). These bodies had less of a resemblance to the pre-war pattern than even the L-types, by having a more upright and quite flat frontal aspect. A major difference from all other bodybuilders' MoS pattern double-deckers was the fact that Bristol bodies were based on the pre-war structure using six bays; the MoS instructions specified five bays. Twenty-one Bristol utility double-deckers were built, nine for BT&CC (including two as replacements for bodies destroyed in early air-raids), eight for Maidstone & District and Chatham & District (who had been standardising on Weymann-bodied Bristols) and two each for Pontypridd UDC and another previously-unserved customer, Colchester Corporation.

Once the MoS pattern bodies on unfrozen chassis were out of the way, floor space at BBW could come into line with the MCW by being devoted once again to aircraft production for sister company, the Bristol Aeroplane Company. BBW's job was the manufacture of nose and tail sections for the Bristol Beaufighter. These were then joined to the main fuselage sections, which the MCW were building at their Chatsworth Road works nearby. Completed fuselages were taken to Filton by road, on the back of a specially modified Bristol bus chassis.

Despite total involvement in aircraft production, the services of BBW as a bus body producer were still called upon during the war. There was no possibility of building bodies in Brislington, but there was a way round the problem. In 1930 one of the few major private operators of bus services in the Bristol area, W J Bence & Sons of Hanham, was acquired by BT&CC. It was run as a subsidiary until absorbed in 1936. Besides operating buses (and lorries, etc.) the Bence family had a coachbuilding plant situated at Longwell Green. This remained in the family's hands after the bus operating side of the business passed to Bristol Tramways. In 1942, a further link with BT&CC was formed when it was agreed that Bence Motor Bodies Ltd – as the factory was now titled – should build MoS-style single-decker bodies on behalf of BBW, to rebody several earlier chassis. The designs were quite clearly of BBW origin and contained several BBW characteristics within the utilitarian aspect.

Two types of body were built by Bence for the BT&CC fleet. The first type, unusually, incorporated a rear entrance, together with no fewer than 37 seats. This received the BBW designation of S13. Twenty-four bodies of this type were built, the majority being used for the surprising purpose of replacing the 1935 Bristol Q4 32-seat coach bodies on J-Type chassis.

The second type of Bence body, which carried BBW code S14, was a front-entrance version for mounting on B-Type chassis. These replaced fourteen 1929 coach bodies built by London Lorries, three of the five 1930 Bristol L9 bodies, two L10s, seven of the Northern Counties version of the Bristol L10 and six L6-1 bodies.

The name of Bence Motor Bodies Ltd was changed in 1944 to Longwell Green Coachworks Ltd. After the war, the company built itself up into quite a strong position, particularly in relation to Welsh municipal operators and only ceased bus body building in 1966. On three occasions after the war, Longwell Green became involved with BBW again, as we shall see. The company finally closed its doors in 1983.

The act of war involving this country did not stop engineers from focusing their minds on such items as bus body construction inventions. Although BBW had abandoned the construction of all-metal bodywork in 1936, the principle was still very much in the minds of the designers. So much so that in 1941 BT&CC and Arnold J Romer, the General Manager of the Motor Constructional Works, jointly lodged an application for a patent for metal framework of bus bodywork of an unorthodox design. In this, the sides of the body were to be formed of rows of T-shaped or cruciform *sheet* metal pieces, cantilevered and secured to each other to produce the body and window pillars. Cross-bracing frames would be worked into the uprights of the side pieces to form part of the body's roof and floor structures. Interestingly, it was proposed that a bus with this form of structure would need no conventional chassis, the running units being supported by the lowest cross-pieces; in other words, Bristol was proposing an integral all-metal double-decker in 1941!

The great advantage seen with this design of body was the significant increase in internal space created by the elimination of bulky wooden upright pillars and horizontal rails; even headroom in the two decks could be increased. No doubt the ideas generated during the design of this integral bus were incorporated into the development, post-war, of the Bristol-ECW Lodekka, in which Arnold Romer was a key player.

226. War had been declared in September 1939, but for the next two years, bus chassis and body manufacturers were left to continue building their products as best they could, given that it was becoming increasingly difficult to obtain the raw materials. Eventually, a halt was put on these activities, but then, as described in the heading to this chapter, the manufacture of chassis was 'unfrozen', while bodywork had to be built to a basic utility specification, including flat panelling and squarer roof domes. The first utility bodies from BBW were completed at the end of 1941 and mounted on three Unfrozen L5G chassis, numbers 56.006-008. The allocation of buses to operators was undertaken by the Ministry of War Transport, which resulted in many Bristols going to operators who had never received one before. The first Utility L5G was in this category – it was sent to Edinburgh Corporation! It was numbered X15 and registered DSF 987. The BBW body was adapted from preceding models and yet, although of front-entrance layout, it had the closer-pitched pillars of the dual-doorway examples (see Plates 218 & 221). The cab pattern was little altered, except that the dividing pillar on the nearside was made upright. The destination indicator was simple, but Edinburgh was allowed the separate route-number box. Amazingly, in 1948, Edinburgh Corporation rebuilt this body to rear entrance, with their preferred open platform layout, very similar to Manchester's M-Type body shown in Plate 101. The bus was adapted as a driver-trainer in 1953, but remained in the fleet until 1961 before being scrapped. *(The late D.L.G.Hunter)*

**227**. This offside view illustrates that these first Utility bodies retained much of their BBW character, although study of the rear profile shows the effect of the use of flat panelling. The second and third of the Unfrozen L5Gs were supplied to a familiar customer, Western National, although, with their front doorways and plain lines, they were a long way from the ideals which this operator had previously set! Seating for 34 was achieved by using inward-facing pairs over the rear wheel arches. Seen here in 1952 is 366 (GTA 391). A further identical body was built, on a slightly earlier chassis, for BT&CC's own fleet, becoming 2167 (HHT 150) in 1942. *(Alan B. Cross)*

**228**. Demand for double-deckers during the war was, naturally, much greater and more parts were in stock to be unfrozen. BBW bodied 19 of the 85 Unfrozen K5Gs with a very distinctive utility body (another two received DD6 bodies). The Ministry of Supply laid down

guidelines over the design of utility bodies and one requirement was that the framework should be of five-bay layout. BBW, however, based their utility double-decker firmly on the DD6, with six bays and retaining rather small windows. The outcome is shown here on the second Unfrozen K chassis (57.002), Pontypridd UDC 18 (ETX 764). It will be seen the front profile sloped somewhat less than on the pre-war bodies – indeed, the windscreen is more upright still. The front panelling in plan view was flat and the front dome did not overhang the windows. These windows received inward-tilting opening ventilators at the top, a design that was to be featured in utility double-deckers from many bodybuilders. Curiously, the first upper-deck side window received a vertical leading edge, which left a triangular solid panel ahead of the window. The trailing window was similarly upright. Only one window on each side of each deck was allowed to open. At this stage, the upper-deck emergency exit was not glazed. Details around the cab were all that offered respite to the squareness. Despite the austere times, PUDC still insisted on the application of its finely lined-out livery. *(Chris Taylor Collection)*

**229**. Maidstone & District and its subsidiary Chatham & District had taken a number of K5Gs into stock since 1938 (bodied by Weymann) and they were allowed an allocation of Unfrozen Ks. The bus shown here was delivered to Maidstone & District as DH17 (GKR 747), but is seen after being transferred to Chatham & District in 1945 and repainted into their green, light brown and cream. This picture shows well the angular rear to the roof. Note that there is no provision for applying the relief colour above the windscreen.
*(London Trolleybus Preservation Society)*

**230.** Curiously, the seven utility bodies built on Unfrozen K5G chassis for BT&CC themselves, as 3622-8 (HHT 143-8 and HHU 351), were finished with a full complement of half-drop windows and with D-shaped frames to the end windows on the lower-deck and at the back of the upper-deck. They also lacked the front tip-in ventilators. Shown here is 3628, in the wartime khaki camouflage livery in which it was delivered, standing at The Centre. Note the treatment of the platform faring is like that on pre-war bodies, while the canopy faring has taken on a shape similar to that first seen on the DD1-Type in 1934 (Plate 165). The MoS relaxed its rulings when new bodies were built for mounting on existing chassis, which is why BBW could produce the bodies for Western National's H-Type chassis to their pre-war style. Similarly, after five BT&CC G- and K-Type double-deckers were severely damaged by early air-raids, BBW built new DD6 bodies for them as late as 1942. However, when they built more bodies for this purpose later in 1942, for two fairly recent K5Gs, these bodies were of the utility style shown here. *(Peter Hulin)*

**231.** In 1943 a new Bristol design of single-deck utility body emerged – not from Brislington, where both BBW and the MCW were fully engaged on the production of aircraft parts for the Bristol Aeroplane Company, but from Bence Motor Bodies Ltd of Longwell Green, to the east of Bristol; the bus operation side of Bence's business had passed to BT&CC in the 1930s. These bodies were given the BBW designation of **S13-Type.** Although built exclusively for BT&CC's fleet, they featured a *rear* entrance, but that enabled seating to be provided for no fewer than 37, the largest capacity single-deck BBW bodies yet. They were built to the MoS utility specification, with angular domes and so on, but the cab side windows and the end windows to the saloon were D-shaped. The two-tier destination display was still used, but within a more angular surround. The shape of this was affected by the roof being deeper. Note the smooth front to the cab, which blended attractively with the JV radiator of the 1935 J-Type chassis, and the tiny side-lights and small, masked headlamps. *(Peter Hulin)*

**232.** This nearside view of an **S13/37** single-decker shows that the base-line of the simple bulkhead window was curiously high. The rear entrance was provided with a hinged door at the top of three steps, as usual. The twin back windows were similar in shape to those on the S1 to S4 (see Plates 190 & 205), but curved in less sharply, resulting in wider glazing. Twenty-four S13 bodies were built during 1943-45 (although one is on record as having been built in 1941) and 19 were chosen to replace the 1935 Q4 32-seat coach bodies, as described in Plate 172. (The other Q4 had already been replaced in 1942, by a second-hand body.) The S13 posed for this photograph in January 1943 was 2035 (BHU 638). The petrol engines in the J-Type chassis carrying the Q4 bodies had been replaced by Gardner 5LW oil engines between 1937 and 1940. Of the other S13s, one was mounted on 2000 (AHW 393), with chassis JO5G.1 (see Plate 150), one on C2700 (CHW 50, this one, after the war, being rebuilt to dual-doorway layout) and the other three on 1939 L5Gs 2126/55/6, whose original bodies had been destroyed by enemy action. *(Peter Hulin)*

118

**233**. Two styles of body were built by Bence Motor Bodies Ltd on behalf of BBW, the other version receiving the BBW code of **S14-Type**. The S14, which accounted for 32 bodies, contained the basic features of the S13 seen in Plate 232, but differed in being of BT&CC's conventional front-entrance layout and mounted on 1929-31 B-Type chassis. This resulted in the seating capacity being limited to 34 – nevertheless two more than had been previously attained in B-Types. In fact, several S14s were built with only 29 seats, but these were arranged around the perimeter of the saloon, to enable as many standing passengers as possible to be carried on these buses during the war. The

lower bonnet and radiator of the B-Type enabled the windscreen to have a level base. A very interesting feature was that the opening windows were of the top-sliding variety, an innovation that had appeared in a small way just before the war. There were three sliders on the off-side and two on the near-side. Shown here after the war is Bath Tramways 385 (HW 9497), which originally carried a Northern Counties version of the Bristol L10 body (see Plate 127). *(A.G.Vowles)*

**234**. Bristol Tramways and Arnold J Romer, the General Manager of the MCW, jointly applied to the Patent Office in May 1941 for a specification for Improvements in or relating to Frameworks for Vehicles. The invention concerned a structure of considerable strength for its weight, while providing the maximum width and height available for the accommodation of passengers. It was proposed that the framework would comprise a number of sheet metal sections, each with cantilever arms, that, when combined, would result in the vertical arms being arranged so as to provide window pillars. A drawing made to accompany the application is

reproduced here. The bus was clearly based on a DD6 in outline – interestingly, it was still of six-bay configuration. It will be seen that the sections were either T-shaped or cruciform. The upright arms provided the foundation for the cross-members of the frame, on to which the upper-saloon floor and roof would be placed. The cross-members below the lower saloon would be of double depth, to support the running units normally carried by a chassis, which could then be dispensed with. The outcome would be a lightweight and more spacious bus, with the capability of an increased seating capacity. The continuation of the war did not offer much chance to put the theory into practise and, even after peace returned in 1945, the idea was not developed. *(Allen Janes Collection)*

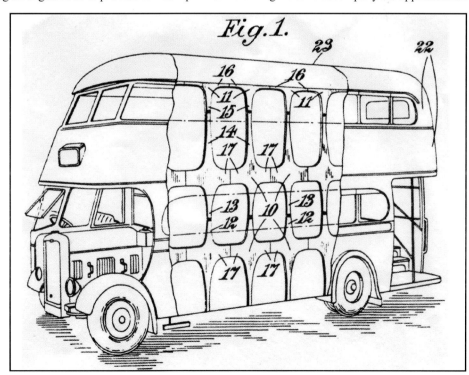

# Chapter 10

Although the war in Europe came to an end in 1945, there was a lot of work to do in Bristol before bus body building could restart. The body shops in Brislington bus depot were still geared up to the production of aircraft parts, so these premises had to be cleared out and re-equipped. While this was taking place the body department was called upon to build a batch of five double-deck bodies for fitting to 1936 G-Type chassis, whose original Bristol AM6 bodies would be moved to the company's earliest Gs, now numbered C3000-4. As Brislington was as yet unusable, agreement was reached with Longwell Green Coachworks to manufacture the bodies there. This was an extension of the wartime agreement whereby Bristol-designed utility single-deck bodies had been built at the same factory by Bence, as these five double-deckers were also of BBW design.

They appeared in September 1946. The styling was largely derived from the pre-war body for the K-Type chassis, apart from displaying a welcome return to five-bay layout. Most notably, though, they were of *lowbridge* construction – the first ever lowbridge bodies of BBW origin!

Inasmuch as BBW had shown individuality in the styling of its wartime double-deck bodies, its 'cousin' within the Tilling Group, Eastern Coach Works, had also shown individuality. The bodies from that plant were very much less severe than the average utility body and were generally known to be acting as prototypes for a completely fresh set of designs, planned for introduction once the war was over. Indeed, the new ECW bodies introduced in 1946 bore absolutely no resemblance to pre-war ECW products and henceforth a much higher degree of standardisation was made. The double-decker was of five-bay layout, seating 56 in highbridge form or 55 when of lowbridge layout (when mounted on standard Bristol K-Type chassis), while the saloon was also of five-bay configuration and was a 35-seater, with a rear entrance (for mounting on the Bristol L-Type). All three were exceptionally attractive and had a fresh, modern appearance, while most other manufacturers simply seemed to dust off their pre-war designs. The single-deck body featured perpendicular cant panels for the application of advertisements, although this had the result of producing a slightly 'square-shouldered' look. The cant panels and window surrounds were painted cream in the Tilling Group's standard livery schemes, while the double-deckers' cream relief (after some experimentation) was applied in two bands, one above the lower-deck windows and the other below the upper-deck windows. The new ECW bodies were officially described as being of 'Tilling Standard' configuration. Any other bodybuilders supplying bus bodywork to members of the Group, in the ensuing four or five years, were normally called upon to comply with the Tilling Standard appearance. Examples of Tilling Standard designs emanated, in small numbers, from Beadle, Willowbrook and Strachan ... and in large numbers from BBW! Each manufacturer was permitted some individuality of detail design as long as the overall appearance was to the Tilling Standard. Each make of body was thereby quite easily recognisable. Further details of ECW's post-war bodies and comparisons of the Tilling Standard bodies from the other builders can be found in *ECW, 1946-1965* and *ECW, 1965-1987* by Maurice Doggett and Alan Townsin (Venture Publications, 1993 & 1994, respectively).

Bristol drew up plans for new Tilling Standard bodies in 1946. BBW's function in bodybuilding differed completely from pre-war years; because many buses had been neglected and had suffered badly under wartime operating conditions, new bodies were to be built on chassis dating from the 1930s. Such was the number of old chassis chosen for rebodying that BBW's output was almost entirely turned over to this programme. Indeed, in the 1946-1951 period, BBW bodied more than 160 old chassis and yet they built on only 27 new chassis ... more remarkably, not one of those 27 was a Bristol! Initial production was directed exclusively at BT&CC's own fleet, while new chassis for the company were to be bodied by Eastern Coach Works – the first time that the Lowestoft concern was contracted to body the entire intake of new Bristols for BT&CC!

An interesting feature of post-war production was that the appearance of Bristol bodies happened to be revised almost annually. That is rather convenient, because records are now missing of BBW's DD- and S-series designations for the period, so it is therefore easiest to identify and refer to the bodies by the general year of production, e.g. '1949-Style bodies', even though building may have started and/or ended in the adjacent years. Consequently, the first Tilling Standard designs are referred to *here* as 1947-Style bodies, although it is known that, in this case, the designation S15 was applied to the single-deckers.

The design of the 1947-Style saloon complied with Tilling Standards exactly in respect of the side and end profiles, pillar spacings, seating layout and canopy and bulkhead fairings. However, all other features were exclusive to BBW – the detailed design of the cab, bulkhead, side windows, entrance and rear-end, for example. One of the points affecting cab design was that the J-Type chassis chosen for fitting with these bodies retained their high radiators. The principal identification feature of the 1947-Style body was the appearance of the side windows. All had square top corners, and the deep sliding ventilators, which were applied in the Tilling Standard positions, were also square-cornered items.

When the design work for the 1947-Style body was completed the Brislington plant was still not ready to resume manufacture. Therefore Longwell Green was again sub-contracted. Production got off to a flying start with no fewer than eight bodies appearing in service in December 1946, all on 1933/34 J-Type chassis converted to 5LW power. Production then slowed considerably, although it did move into Brislington at last. The other eight bodies took the whole of 1947 to emerge, and again 1933/34 J-Types received these bodies. The majority replaced Bristol AM5 coach bodies (which had worked as buses during the war), together with four AM3 saloons.

The double-deck 1947-Style body contained several of the features of its single-deck counterpart, naturally, including the deep, square-cornered sliding ventilators. It was of Tilling Standard five-bay layout and the relief colour was provided by two cream bands. There the similarity to ECW bodywork ended, though, as it had a rather more upright front than the ECW product and at the rear the profile took a detectable 'kink' at each cream band, rather than being gently curved. In plan view the front was absolutely flat, the three-piece dome somehow emphasising this. No ventilators were fitted to the front upper-deck or lower-saloon bulkhead windows. The shape of the bulkhead windows was, interestingly, exactly the same as on the final pre-war double-deckers.

The entire run of 12 of these bodies was built for BT&CC on new chassis ... not Bristols, but Leylands! They were of the Titan PD1 model. The Tilling Association had ordered 150 Leyland Titans for their member companies for 1947/48 delivery; Bristol Tramways took 50, which were bodied in equal numbers by ECW and BBW. The initial 12 received 1947-Style bodies between August and December that year. The first to be completed was proudly shown off to the Press at Brislington depot on August 8th 1947. The construction or finishing work of some of the dozen bodies was undertaken by Longwell Green Coachworks and it is known that Longwell Green transfers were applied to the bodywork!

Following completion of these 12 bodies, production of a further batch of double-deckers commenced. These, however, were of a subtly revised styling and heralded the arrival of the 1948-Style body. In this pattern, the main side windows took on a completely new appearance. The entire window pans were of propriety manufacture and came with a shallower setting to the glazing and with well-rounded corners, both top and bottom. The integrated sliding ventilators, with rounded top corners, were of the same distinctive pattern as used by several other coachbuilders about this time, particularly those supplying single-deckers built to the BET Federation design, such as Brush. The shallower setting of the glazing in the side windows – including the trailing upper-deck window – obviously increased the width of the window 'sill' internally. In all other respects, the double-deck body was unchanged, including recessed windows with small-radius corners around the front of the upper-deck!

A further 13 new Leyland PD1 chassis received these 1948 bodies, together with five Bristol G-Type chassis dating from the 1930s. The first 12 of the PD1s entered service between 1st January and 1st July 1948, then came the G-Types. One was a 1932 oil-converted bus, most recently carrying a 1936 Bristol AM6 body that had been displaced from its original chassis by a Longwell Green-built lowbridge BBW body in 1946. The other four were 1936/37 GO5Gs which had carried Bristol DD2 bodywork. The final Leyland appeared on 1st October.

The single-deck 1948-Style body was produced over a twelve-month period from March 1948. It had the same rounded side windows as fitted to the double-deckers, with the same shallow setting. Thirty bodies to this design were built for mounting on J-Type chassis dating from 1933-35, plus one 1936 model, and also on one of BT&CC's two surviving H-Types, 2157 (AHT 659), which also was now fitted with a 5LW engine.

Amid all the bodybuilding that was being carried out during this period, further political changes were affecting the overall management of Bristol Tramways & Carriage Company. The Tilling Group, which had controlled BT&CC since 1932, took the controversial decision in 1947 to accept an approach from the current Labour Government for acquisition by the State. This new Government very much favoured public ownership of utilities and transport. Indeed, Britain's railways were nationalised in 1947, so from then on railway shareholding in bus companies was held by the new British Transport Commission. On 1st January 1948, Tilling's shareholding in bus companies was also placed with the BTC. No changes to everyday running were to be seen and controlling decisions were still handled by the Tilling Group Management Board, though now within the BTC.

A 1949-Style body made its debut in December 1948, when an ambitious new double-deck rebodying programme was commenced. It was decided to give new bodies to 38 pre-war K5Gs. Two distinct batches of chassis were chosen – the earliest examples of 1938, which included the very first chassis, belonging to C3082 (EAE 280), while the rest had EHU and EHY registrations; and seven buses from a 1939 batch with FHT marks. All chassis were given post-war type PV2 low level radiators and bonnets on being prepared for rebodying and all displaced bodies were of BBW origin. The appearance of the body was again revised. Perhaps surprisingly, the side windows reverted to the 1947 shape and setting. However, a different type of square-cornered sliding ventilator was fitted. This was shallower, had polished metal framework, and was actuated by the forward section sliding back over the rearward part.

It was to be March 1950 before the last of these rebodied Ks took to the road. In the meantime, a smaller programme was started involving a few of their single-deck counterparts, L5Gs, among yet more J-Types. Again PV2 radiators were fitted to the chassis before the new bodies were built.

The first two 1949-Style saloon bodies, despite appearing four months after the first double-deckers, were very distinctive in retaining 1948-Style side windows, with rounded sliding ventilators. But from the third body, the shallow, polished, square sliders were installed. Another feature of the 1949 single-deck bodies (which were coded S18) was that several were built to a *two-doorway* layout, for the first time since 1941. ECW had built some two-door bodies on new Bristol Ls in 1947 exclusively for BT&CC, with others following in 1949/50, and the twelve 1949 Bristol bodies to this layout were the only other examples on vertical-engined chassis supplied to a Tilling operator after the war.

The buses that received the first two 1949 bodies, i.e. those with the 1948 side windows, were numbered respectively 2084 and 2082 (FAE 58/6), 2082 possessing, in fact, the very first L-Type chassis (coincidentally, the very first K was numbered, as stated above, C3082!). The first five bodies were two-doorway 33-seaters, after which nine rear-entrance 35-seat bodies appeared, before production reverted in January 1950 to two-door bodies. This brought BT&CC's total of 1949-Style single-deckers to 21 by April. Although several 1938/39 Ls were rebodied in the programme (losing S4 and S6 coachwork), there were also plenty of J chassis involved – no fewer than 13, in fact. Most were of 1936/37 vintage (losing AM7, S1 and S3 bodies), but two early chassis went through the process. One of these was the very first J chassis, J.101, new in 1931 (2057: HY 6504), so it will be seen that the first J, the first K *and* the first L were all rebodied by Bristol to the 1949-Style!

A milestone was reached in 1950 as it was in that year that the first post-war Bristol bodies appeared for a customer other than Bristol Tramways. Two 1949-Style single-deck, 35-seat bodies were ordered by Red & White Services of Chepstow, for mounting on 1937/38 Albion Valkyrie chassis, 331 (BAX 331) and 736 (EXF 263). This order had come very soon indeed after the Red & White Group had sold its British bus operations to the British Transport Commission in February 1950. Until that time, the Red & White Group had been the largest independent bus group in the United Kingdom. Now, under BTC control, Red & White and its associates were to place a considerable amount of work in the hands of BBW.

235. The first BBW bodies to be designed following the end of the Second World War were built by Longwell Green Coach Works, as an extension to the arrangement that had seen the same factory, then named Bence Motor Bodies Ltd, produce the Bristol S13- and S14-Types during the war (Plates 231-233). In 1946 Longwell Green built five double-deckers for mounting on 1936 GO5G chassis. The new bodies were of low-bridge layout – the first such bodies designed by BBW! To enable buses to pass under low bridges, a sunken gangway ran along the *side* of the upper saloon. The seats therefore carried four abreast, below the lowered roof. BBW's styling was derived from the DD3 to DD6 family, shown between Plates 185 & 217, reverting to five-bay construction; the destination screen, though, was placed flat on the sloping front. There were no D-shaped side windows, but the cab and windscreen details were similar to the pre-war patterns. The cab dash was attractively shaped to suit the JV radiator. The rear upper-saloon window was now rectangular, with small-radius curves at each corner. At the end of the war, BT&CC had forsaken the deep-blue and white livery for 'Tilling green', with cream relief, and the five lowbridge buses were delivered in this livery. *(Peter Davey)*

**236**. A new Tilling Standard body pattern was introduced after the war and each bodybuilder supplying to the Tilling Group was expected to comply. BBW's first post-war single-decker, the **S15-Type**, matched the Tilling Standard well, in respect of profile, the five-bay layout, sliding ventilators in specific windows, a rear entrance, the area of cream relief and even the shape of the bulkhead faring. In detail, however, the S15 differed in several ways from the ECW version, which should be taken as the yardstick (photographs of ECW Tilling Standard bodies, to compare with BBW versions, can be found in *ECW 1946-1965* by Maurice Doggett & Alan Townsin

(Venture Publications, 1993)). For example, BBW continued to use a hinged door at the top of the entrance steps. Also, BBW initially built only on older, J-Type, chassis with high radiators. Shown here is what can also be termed a **1947-Style** body, in which the distinguishing feature was the shape of the side windows. The top corners of these were square and they used deep, square-cornered sliding ventilators. Note the side destination box, with a paper display. The bus shown is 2018 (AHT 968), with a body built by Longwell Green in December 1946; the 1933 chassis had previously carried a Bristol AM5 coach body (see Plate 157). *(M.J.Tozer Collection)*

**237**. At the back of the BBW version of the Tilling Standard body, the rear window was deeper than on ECW bodies, continuing down to the waist-line. The upper corners of this window were of a larger radius than the lower corners. Unlike ECW, BBW did not include a rear boot on its service buses, so the back panel was a single sheet. The number-plate was situated in the lower corner, as found only on the first of ECW's post-war bodies. 2369 (HY 9378) was originally a Greyhound coach, again with an AM5 body, as in Plate 156. *(Peter Davey)*

**238**. Not very long after receiving their new **1947-Style** bodies, the J-Type chassis were updated by being fitted with post-war-style PV2 radiators and low-level bonnets, with longer front wings. The cab had to be rebuilt. Due to the more stocky nature of the radiator, the dash needed to be moved rearward, resulting in a much more upright windscreen. A new bottom half was made for this, with a horizontal lower edge, but it retained its original top half; note the *square* top corners, which matched the side windows (this enabled the writer, when only five or six years old, to make positive identification from dead-ahead!). Another former Greyhound coach, 2373 (HY 9382), demonstrates the 1947-Style body in its most familiar form. *(Peter Davey)*

**239**. The double-deck **1947-Style** body was clearly related to the single-decker. It also complied to Tilling Standard five-bay construction, a 56-seat capacity (30 up, 26 down), and painting with the cream relief applied in two bands. On the double-decker, the sliding ventilators had polished frames, while the top corners of the fixed windows had small radii to match the lower corners. The front of the body was rather upright and the panels were quite flat – the wide centre panel of the three-piece dome somehow emphasised this. The bulkhead design was exactly the same as in the DD6 and the cab leading window was also still D-shaped. The polished frame to the window in the cab door is another item continued from before the war. The twelve 1947 double-deckers were among the small number of post-war BBW bodies to be mounted on *new* chassis, none of which were Bristols! In this case, Leyland Titan PD1 chassis received the Bristol bodywork. A feature almost universal on PD1s bodied by any coachbuilder – other than Leyland themselves! – was that the lower edge of the windscreen was horizontal, due to the shape of the dash plate supplied with the chassis. The second 1947 BBW Leyland, BT&CC's C4001 (KHW 242) is seen on The Centre (Broad Quay) soon after entering service, on a branch of tram-replacement route 2. *(M.J. Tozer)*

**240**. The rear styling of the **1947-Style** double-decker matched the Tilling Standard in having rectangular windows to both decks. The upper-deck back window on the BBW body, though, had slightly larger corners at the top than at the bottom and somehow looked more aggressive than the window on the ECW body, in which all four corners were of uniform radius. The prominent rain-deflecting louvre above the window soon gained an uneven nature. The two Leyland PD1s seen here are the former C4001/3 (KHW 242/4), photographed in 1966 after joining a fleet of buses providing internal staff transport at the Filton plant of the British Aircraft Corporation, formerly the Bristol Aeroplane Company. Inside the hanger beyond the buses, a prototype Concorde was taking shape! *(Allan Macfarlane)*

**241**. The upper-deck interior finish of the early post-war BBW body appeared rather more basic than the ECW body. This was due to the application of flat panels above the side windows, into which light-bulbs were placed, without reflectors – in this instance no bulbs are fitted. One of the small, black, bell-push buttons can be seen on the offside, just above a window pillar. Curiously, passengers were not provided with any poles to assist them along the gangway and the seats were only fitted with grab plates on their outer corners. The roof was now double-skinned, although the front and rear domes, more prone to being damaged, were still single-skinned. On the lower deck, the corners of the ceiling above

the windows were curved, though quite sharply, there was a raised strip above the corner panels to carry the light-bulbs and bell-push buttons, and two wooden grab-rails ran the length of the ceiling, either side of the gangway, as again there were no upright poles. *(Allan Macfarlane)*

**242**. What can be regarded as a **1948-Style** BBW body appeared in the January of that year, on the first of 13 more new Leyland Titan PD1 chassis. A significant softening of the appearance was achieved by the use of side windows that featured well-rounded corners, both bottom and top. Windows of this design were also supplied to other coach-builders, notably to Brush and Roe for the single-deckers built for operators within the BET Group. The new side windows featured a shallower setting from the exterior (with a consequent increase in the breadth of the window surround inside the bus). The windows around the front of the upper deck, however, were exactly the same as used in the 1947-Style body, with smaller-radius corners and a deeper setting! The bus shown here, outside St Philip's Library in Trinity Street, Bristol, is C4031 (KHY 400). The delivery to BBW and ECW of the chassis for BT&CC's fleet of 50 Leylands was fairly random, but registrations and fleet-numbers were generally allocated in chassis-number order. *(S.N.J.White, courtesy Roy Marshall)*

**243**. Before the last of the 25 Bristol-bodied Leylands entered service, five similar **1948-Style** double-deck bodies were built on Bristol G-Type chassis. These retained their high and slender JV radiators, so the front of the cab was adapted to take account. The lower edge of the wind-screen was horizontal, unlike that of the single-decker bodies on the equivalent J-Type chassis. Shown here is C3052 (DAE 375), which had a 1936 chassis and originally had a BBW DD2 body, such as shown in Plate 184. *(M.J.Tozer)*

**244**. As with the J-Types exemplified by Plate 238, the chassis of the five G-Types with **1948-Style** bodies were soon updated with low-mounted PV2 radiators and so on. This, however, caused a problem when rebuilding the cab, as the windscreen and dash needed to be moved back slightly; the front of the body was already very upright, so when the new items were fitted, the upper panelling was left overhanging the windscreen a little! Seen here is C3055 (DAE 372), speeding down Cranbrook Road, Redland, in May 1954. Note the pattern of the fairing to the canopy and platform, both having a characteristic shape evolved by BBW since the early 1930s. *(Peter Davey)*

**245**. The **1948-Style** single-decker, using the same pattern of side window as the 1948 double-decker, with boldly rounded corners, appeared in March 1948, as the programme to rebody J-Type chassis continued. This view of 2017 (HY 8260), whose chassis was already 15 years old at rebodying, shows that the lower edge of the windscreen sloped down towards the outside pillar in Tilling Standard fashion. The top corners reverted to being rounded by the addition of the corner plates, as described in Plate 209, so matching the rounded top corners of the side windows. Note that although all the side windows have the large-radius corners, the top of the trailing window has one square corner! *(M.J.Tozer)*

**246**. Typifying the **1948-Style** single-decker after the updating of the chassis with a PV2 radiator is 2351 (AHW 534). As in Plate 238, this picture shows that the original top half of the windscreen was retained after the front of the cab was rebuilt. The bulkhead window can be seen just clearly enough to show that this was not modified when the lower bonnet was affixed, retaining a high, sloping base-line. Unlike on ECW bodies, this window was non-opening and the top corners were square. Note the runners of the rounded sliding ventilators no longer lined up with the base of the side destination box. A new type of seat was installed in these bodies, with a separate hand-rail above a gently curved top. *(M.J.Tozer)*

**247.** The emergence of a **1949-Style** body coincided with a new wave of rebodying, in which the chassis were equipped with PV2 radiators and low bonnets *before* entering the Body Building Works. Additionally, the chassis chosen were generally of the more-recent K- and L-Type models. This picture shows 1939 K5G C3240 (FHT 806) about to leave Broad Quay on The Centre on a summer's evening and it shows well the features of the 1949-Style body. The side windows, it will be seen, reverted to the square-topped variety, at the deeper setting, as found in the 1947 bodies – see Plate 239. The sliding ventilators, however, were shallower and in these the front half slid back over the rear half. The front upper-deck windows were of a new pattern, with their own frames or pans, and these had a shallow setting. The cab leading side window and the bulkhead window now came within polished frames, to match the windscreen and the cab door; note the slight change made to the shape of this door. Altogether, 38 of the 1949-Style double-decker bodies were built on pre-war K5G chassis. Before very long, a structural weakness was detected at the front of the post-war BBW bodies and, on rebuilding, the front and leading side windows were mounted flush with the exterior panels. *(M.J.Tozer)*

**248.** At least six of the first twelve **1949-Style** double-deckers were even more like the 1947 bodies than the rest, by having side windows and ventilators that were identical to the 1947-Style. This is demonstrated by C3093 (EHU 228), which is shown after repainting in the brighter livery adopted for a while around 1951. If compared to Plate 239, not only does this picture show the deep ventilators, in which the rearward half opened, but even that the top corners of the fixed windows on the lower-deck and at the rear of the upper-deck were rounded, unlike the 1949 bodies with the shallow vents. Six buses known to have these features were BT&CC's C3088/90-3/7. *(S.N.J.White, courtesy Roy Marshall)*

**249**. Side windows of the 1948-Style, with the well-rounded corners, were a feature of the first and second single-deck **1949-Style** bodies. They were mounted on 1938 L5Gs 2084/2 (FAE 58/6), respectively, and seen here is the first-built. This picture also shows that a dual-doorway (33-seat) layout was chosen. The front door, like that at the back, was again at the top of the steps and the bulkhead window was once more split, to support a door pillar. By having PV2 radiators mounted before the bodies were built, the cab front was able to retain the Tilling Standard degree of rake. The windscreen was not as deep as that used by ECW, yet it gave a distinctive look to the bus. 2084 stands at the exit of Weston-super-Mare's Beach Bus Station, with displays for a town service that featured 1949-Style two-doorway rebodied Js and Ls until its conversion to Lodekka operation in 1957. As a single-deck route, the terminus faced the woodwork room of the Grammar School and, during the route's last few months as such, the buses for one 11-year-old pupil were a much greater attraction than planing and dove-tail joints! *(S.E.Letts)*

**250**. For the remaining 21 of the **1949-Style** single-deckers built for BT&CC, the square-cornered sliding vent was used, as in the equivalent double-deckers. Among them were ten more 33-seat dual-doorway bodies, five of which were mounted on Js of the City fleet. Illustrating the variant is C2701 (CHW 51), now looking very different to the form in which it was shown in Plate 182! The bus is seen here leaving The Centre in the evening peak, when the only other traffic on the move consisted of a bicycle, a Ford 10 and a Hillman Minx! Note that the side destination box, which had been used rarely, was now omitted. Due to a surplus of single-deckers in the City fleet, these five Js (C2701-4/31) were transferred to Bath Services in 1952 and renumbered 2215-9, although they ended their lives in the Bristol Country fleet, including work on Weston-super-Mare's route 90. *(M.J.Tozer)*

**251**. Nine rear-entrance, 35-seat, versions of the **1949-Style** single-decker were built, between two batches of dual-doorway models. Six were mounted on Js and Ls in the Gloucester City division, but seen here is one of the three Country buses, 2063 (EHT 547), a 1937 JO5G. Note the large, fixed, bulkhead window, with its polished frame. Of the Gloucester buses, 1245 (BFH 521) had a different set of windows which, although still square-topped, had a shallow setting and carried slightly deeper sliding ventilators, which opened from the rear. *(Mike Mogridge)*

**252**. In 1950, BBW outshopped their first bodies since the war for an operator other than BT&CC themselves. Two 35-seat, rear-entrance bodies of the **1949-Style** were constructed for Red & White Services Ltd, of Chepstow. They were mounted on the 1937/8 Albion Valkyrie CX11 chassis – with Gardner 5LW engines – of 331 (BAX 331) and 736 (EXF 263); the latter bus is shown here. The front axle and the dash plate were further forward than on the Bristol J or L chassis and the cab was elongated slightly. The bonnet was a little higher and came close to the base of the windows; the windscreen needed to be raised marginally. The bulkhead window carried an inward-tilting ventilator of the type that had been widely used in wartime utility bodywork, such as shown in Plate 228. The fuel tank on the Albion was located on the nearside. Red & White's destination screen was just slightly smaller than that used by BT&CC, so the box itself was the same as on bodies for Bristol. These two buses were renumbered in 1951 into Red & White's distinctive new system, in which the last two figures indicated the year the vehicle was new, so they became S1437 and S3838. *(S.N.J.White, courtesy Roy Marshall)*

**253**. Shown here is the interior of the **1949-Style** single-deck body seen in the plate above, as built for Red & White on an Albion Valkyrie chassis. Note the way the under-side of the parcel-shelf was curved down to the top of the windows, as also practised by ECW. Polished steel grab-rails ran the length of the shelves. The seats were of the type introduced in 1948, but the light-covers, the tip-in front ventilator and the circular Clayton heater on the bulkhead were to Red & White's specification. Directly above the window at the back of the cab is a hatch with a lift-up cover, to enable the conductor to speak to the driver. *(Chris Taylor Collection)*

# Chapter 11

The biggest change yet to the pattern of post-war Bristol bodies occurred in May 1950. Since 1946, their bodies had been timber framed (and unfortunately, by necessity, using less than the most durable quality of wood), but with effect from this date BBW re-introduced a body using metal framework. The parts for this were, in fact, supplied by Eastern Coach Works, who had turned over to metal framing in 1949. In the 1950-Style BBW body, ECW characteristics were also adopted, although by no means exclusively. This style therefore saw the introduction of the ECW pattern of cab, bulkhead, entrance and rear-end. On the other hand, the side windows were identical to the 1949 Bristol body, with the square-cornered sliding vents, so the origin was unmistakable. As this latter feature was retained and as the Tilling Standard outline was already in existence, the changes for 1950 were not quite so dramatic as might be imagined.

The first ten 1950-Style bodies to be built – in May and June 1950 – were most interesting in being fitted with 31 coach seats and painted in a brighter livery. The seats were all forward-facing and were of the same pattern as used in ECW's equivalent express vehicles built since 1947. Like those ECW coaches the external side panels were painted cream, but with a green 'flash' thereon. This flash was derived from that used by ECW, but was simpler in outline. The ten J-Type chassis that received these bodies were all new in 1937. Nine of them were from a batch of 14 Duple coach bodied Js (six were JO6As, the rest JO5Gs), namely 2201-9 (DHY 653-661), plus one Bristol S3 bodied JO5G saloon, 2060 (EHT 98). The bodies' life as coaches was not to be very long, for by the autumn of 1954 they had been downgraded to 35-seat buses and repainted in bus livery, the external brightwork being overpainted.

In July 1950 a stage-carriage version of the 1950-Style body appeared. Thirty-five bus seats by Deans were installed, being of the curved top pattern that first appeared in 1948. Thirteen such bodies were constructed between July and November, the majority of chassis receiving them being 1937 JO5Gs of the EHT batch.

Production then continued unabated into a 1951-Style body ... and with it the metamorphosis was complete! Because, in the 1951-Style body, the side windows and sliding vents were pure ECW, resulting in a body looking as much like an ECW product as it ever would. Production ran to 27 bodies. The last appeared in June 1951 and with it the post-war rebodying programme for the Bristol Tramways fleet was completed. A total of 108 J-Types, 38 K-Types, eight Ls and six Gs had

been rebodied by BBW since the 1947-Style body first appeared. (Additionally Eastern Coach Works built new bodies on 28 J-Types and 93 G-Types for BT&CC.) The last 27 chassis rebodied were again principally 1937 JO5Gs, but there were still some older Js worthy of receiving new bodies; for example three 1933 chassis – a mere 18 years of age! – were included in the programme.

By no means was BBW left idle following the completion of the 1951-Style single-deckers. Already they were well into the production of coachwork for Red & White and its old associate United Welsh. Again the programme involved rebodying older chassis and more variety was achieved by these being the products of Albion and Guy.

For double-deck bodywork, Red & White only sent Guys to BBW. Although the chassis were wartime Mark I and Mark II versions of Guy's Arab model, they had been updated by receiving the latest Mark III low-level radiators and bonnets – the Guy equivalent of Bristol's PV2 upgrade. The Red & White contract was novel in one major respect – the bodies were to be of *lowbridge* layout. They became, in fact, the first ever lowbridge bodies to emerge from Brislington (the 1946 bodies to this configuration had been built at Longwell Green, of course). Seating for 55 was provided, with 27 in the upper saloon and 28 in the lower. The initial batch of four lowbridge bodies for Red & White was built by early 1951. The styling was derived from BBW's 1949-Style (suitably amended), so the buses had a family resemblance to Red & White's two Albion single-deckers with 1949-Style bodies.

United Welsh's first consignment also comprised 1949-Style double-deckers completed during 1950/51, but this time to conventional highbridge layout (seating 30 over 26). Three were on 1940 Albion Venturer CX19 chassis and two on wartime Guy Arab IIs. More significantly, though, two *new* Guy Arab III chassis were also given Bristol bodies of this pattern. These Guys were the only new double-deck chassis other than the 25 Leylands for BT&CC to be bodied by Bristol in post-war years – a curious state of affairs! The Arab IIIs became United Welsh 1200/1 (HCY 295/6). They were delivered on 8th May 1951 and were this operator's last new double-deckers before Bristol *chassis* with bodywork by *ECW* became the norm. Fortunately, records survive of BBW's classifications for the bodies from this date. The highbridge bodies built on the United Welsh Albions were coded DD14, those on their Guy Arab IIs were DD17 and on the new Arab IIIs, DD19.

The reason for much of the rebodying was to replace pre-war coachwork that had become time-expired. During the difficult wartime and early post-war years, routine maintenance of bodywork had taken a back seat (pardon the pun!). There was now a considerable need to apply a thorough overhaul to bus bodywork and a number of businesses around the country specialised in the work of 'rebuilding' pre-war bodies. BBW also offered its services and in 1950/51, several vehicles visited BBW to have their timber framework renewed, interior fabrics re-trimmed and scuffed panelling replaced, before the vehicles were repainted. Among the visitors, sent by BTC fleets from around the country, were Plaxton-bodied AEC Regal coaches which Lincolnshire Road Car Company had acquired with the business of Enterprise & Silver Dawn, and some Thames Valley Leyland Tigers which carried ECW bodies, but of the BET Federation pattern. A Bristol/ECW K5G from United Counties was sent for rebuilding after being involved in a serious collision with another double-decker.

**254**. In May 1950, BBW produced its first metal-framed bodywork since 1936, with the introduction of its **1950-Style** single-deckers. The first products to the new design were eye-catching Express-service 31-seat coaches. Parts for the metal framework were supplied by Eastern Coach Works and the design of the cab, the front bulkhead, the rear entrance and the back end were also to ECW's pattern. Nevertheless, the side windows, with their square upper corners, were exactly as had been used in BBW's 1949-Style bodies, as shown in Plates 247, onwards. The first ten 1950-Style bodies were coaches and they were completed in May and June 1950.

All were mounted on 1937 chassis, six of which were uncommon JO6As. The coach here was a JO5G, 2060 (EHT 98), which formerly had an S3-Type dual-entrance bus body, as in Plate 188. The other nine coaches were 2201-9 (DHY 653-661), which originally carried Duple coach bodies. 2060 is seen on the public weighbridge in The Horsefair, Bristol; the tree-lined park beyond it shortly disappeared as work started on building the huge Lewis' Department Store (later taken over by John Lewis and, in 1998, by Bentall's). *(Mike Mogridge)*

**255**. This nearside view of a **1950-Style** coach body illustrates, together with the plate above, the incorporation of the ECW pattern of cab, front bulkhead and sliding rear entrance door. The window in the bulkhead featured a push-out ventilator, a major characteristic of ECW bodies since 1946. Another ECW feature was that the external handle for the off-side emergency exit was located at the foot of the door, instead of being at waist-level. Since 1948, ECW themselves had built several Express-service coaches, mainly on new Bristol L-Type chassis, and their practice of painting the side panels cream was echoed by BBW. The shape of the green 'flash' on these panels differed between the two builders. As can be seen, its polished surround dipped below waist-level only once, until curving down at the front of the body; on ECW bodies, the beading dipped a second time, in the middle of the centre bay. BBW coaches lacked the extra panelling attached to the life-rail between the wheels and no extra sliding ventilators were installed. The near-side aspect of the coach is given by 2201 (DHY 653), a JO6A; the spindle for the crank-handle on AEC engines protruded through the radiator. *(Peter Davey)*

**256**. At the rear, the BBW coaches looked exactly the same as the ECW versions. This was not only due to the use of the shallower ECW type of rear window and the placing of the number-plate below this window – compare with Plate 237 – but by the use of the same shape of polished beading across the back, the provision of a rear boot, with twin doors, and the fitting of a rear bumper-bar, flimsy though that item was! 2205 (DHY 657) was another of the JO6As. *(Peter Davey)*

**257 & 258**. Following completion of the ten Express coaches, BBW turned in July 1950 to a service-bus version of the **1950-Style** body, termed the **S20-Type**. One item to note is that the runners for the driver's signalling window in the cab door had a hammered metal finish, instead of being painted. This matched ECW's new 'Thin-wall' bodies, which featured flush interior panels and rounded pillar-cappings, although internally the BBW bodies followed ECW's previous practice, as shown in Plate 259. For comparison, the insert shows a **1949-Style** Bristol body (on Gloucester city 1255, CFH 605, a 1939 L4G), while the main picture shows a **1950-Style** body; by continuing to use the same type of side windows, in an outline that already complied with the Tilling Standard, the inclusion of the ECW features did not make a great difference. The 1950 body is on 2264 (EHT 551), a 1937 JO5G which, as it turned out, was to be the only 1950-Style body ever to carry Bath Services fleetnames. *(Insert – S.N.J.White, courtesy Roy Marshall; main picture – Mike Mogridge)*

**259**. The interior of the **1950-Style** single-decker had clear similarities to the contemporary ECW product, particularly about the bulkhead windows and the use of the push-out ventilator. The light-fittings and bell-pushes, too, were now of ECW's pattern and position. The window pillars and bulkhead mouldings were square-cornered, as in ECW's first metal-framed bodies of 1949, rather than the rounded patterns that ECW adopted soon afterwards. There was, however, no mistaking BBW's square-cornered sliding ventilators. The curved-top seats were to BBW's favoured pattern and there were two other points that distinguished the BBW bodies. Firstly, whereas ECW applied fabric to the under-side of the parcel shelves, BBW painted the shelves white; moreover, the finish to this paintwork had an amazingly deep and long-lasting lustre

– this photograph was taken after the body had seen 19 years of every-day service, yet the shelves still showed clear reflections. The second point concerned bells for passenger use; on ECW bodies there were just the two under the nearside parcel shelf – BBW provided an extra bell, under the *offside* parcel shelf, opposite the doorway and of great benefit for passengers at the rear of a crowded bus. *(Allan Macfarlane)*

**260**. In November 1950, a straightforward set of revisions to the single-decker heralded the arrival of the **1951-Style** body. The alterations were simple – the incorporation of ECW's pattern of side windows and round-cornered sliding ventilators – but the outcome was to produce a body that closely resembled the ECW product! Two ways to identify the BBW version were that the nearside side-light was mounted on the bulkhead, rather than on the faring as in ECW's case – see also Plate 255 – and that there were no boot doors. As on

ECW's latest bodies, where the side destination box had been discontinued, an extra sliding ventilator was installed. This bus was 2370 (HY 9379), whose J-Type chassis had been found worthy of rebodying even after 18 years' service! Some details of the cab should be noted in relation to the standard L-Type; the Gardner 5LW was mounted slightly higher in the J-Type, needing the steel fire-wall separating the engine from the cab to be taller. The result was that the cab nearside window had a higher base-line than the L-Type. Also, the base-line of the windscreen was slightly higher and clear of the beading beneath it. These details were found on both ECW and BBW bodies on J-Type chassis; BBW did not rebody any Ls to the 1950- or 1951-Styles. *(Mike Mogridge)*

**261**. The offside aspect of the **1951-Style** body looked very similar indeed to ECW's Thin-wall bodies of 1949/50, with the hammered-finish metal runners to the driver's signalling window. The fractionally shallower windscreen, with straight beading beneath it, was a consequence of being mounted on a J-Type chassis and, as ECW rebodied no J-Types for BT&CC with Thin-wall bodies, this product must be from BBW! Another tell-tale feature was that BBW applied a strip of unpainted aluminium around the edge of the off-side front wing and this is clearly seen here. Internally, the curved-top seats, the deep-lustre paint on the under-side of the parcel shelves and the extra bell-push identified the BBW product. This bus had a 1937 JO5G chassis and was number 2066 (EHT 100). *(Mike Mogridge)*

**262**. As shown in Plate 252, BBW had built its first bodies for Red & White – the two 1949-Style single-deckers – during 1950. At the beginning of 1951, BBW completed four more bodies for Red & White. This time they were double-deckers, though again to the **1949-Style**. Of particular interest, they were the first *lowbridge* buses to be built at Brislington (BBW's 1946 lowbridge buses had been constructed at Longwell Green). They were clearly lowbridge versions of the bodies for BT&CC as shown in Plate 247. Note the safety rail on the inside of the windows alongside the sunken upper-deck gangway. Red & White supplied four wartime Guy Arab I and II chassis, which had been updated with Arab III-style low radiators and bonnets. On Guys, these were even lower than the PV2 patterns on Bristol chassis. The bus that had originally been numbered 491 (EWO 491), but which became L1043 in 1951, shows Red & White's livery featured pale-cream around the windows rather than on two bands, though the beading was nevertheless applied for the latter. The bus is set to work a Gloucester to Quedgeley service, on the English side of the River Severn. *(Surfleet/Chris Taylor Collection)*

**263**. Before selling its British bus operating interests to the State, for placing under the wing of the British Transport Commission, Red & White had controlled several small operators in south Wales and southern England. The biggest was Swansea-based United Welsh, which had been closely allied to Red & White, to the extent that fleet-numbers were co-ordinated between the two fleets. United Welsh shared in the 1950/51 programme of fitting new **1949-Style** Bristol bodies to earlier chassis, although in this case they were highbridge buses. The oldest chassis treated were 1940 Albion Venturer CX19s, of numbers 653-5 (DWN 157-9). Again adapted from the BT&CC pattern of body, the windscreen needed to be reduced in depth, due to the higher radiator and bonnet of the Albion. Like Red & White's buses, as seen in the plate above and in Plate 252, the front windows on both decks had inward-tilting ventilators and the cream relief was applied to the window surrounds. It is interesting that the fleet-number on the front of 653 here is applied in BT&CC-type transfers! Happily, records have survived of the BBW classifications for bodywork from this stage and these United Welsh Albions were of the **DD14-Type**. *(Roy Marshall)*

**264**. Two further 1949-Style double-deck designs were built for United Welsh, designated the DD17- and DD19-Types. Two bodies were built on wartime Guy Arab II chassis and comprised the **DD17-Types**. As it happens, the chassis of 687, shown here, had originally been Red & White's 497 (EWO 497), from the same batch of 1943 Guys as shown in Plate 262 and, like those buses, now updated with a low Mark III radiator. Note the extra cream relief in this instance. Following 687 is an Arab I also transferred from within the Red & White Group, this time from Cheltenham District (EDG 969) and here carrying new bodywork by Lydney Coachworks, of which more anon. *(Roy Marshall)*

**265**. This photograph of the only other **DD17-Type** body, on United Welsh Guy Arab II 678 (DWN 380), was taken in the 1960s and enables a comparison to be made between the post-war standard styling from BBW and from ECW (on a Bristol K-Type, one of several that United Welsh had recently acquired, this one, LAE 314, originating with Bristol Tramways as it happened). Both bodies comply to the Tilling Standard, though BBW's body is somewhat harsher in appearance. The subtle difference in the shape of the upper-deck rear window can be detected (see also Plate 240). Note the distinctive shape to the platform faring. Neither United Welsh nor Red & White used rear destination indicators. *(Chris Taylor Collection)*

**266**. It was very interesting that United Welsh decided to award BBW with the job of bodying two *new* Guy Arab III chassis in 1951! They became the last double-deck chassis of this make delivered to United Welsh before the BTC-standard Bristol/ECW combination made its impact. The two bodies were coded **DD19-Type** and were the last new models to be based on the **1949-Style** body. The DD19s differed from the DD17s, as shown in Plate 264, in that the cab dash was brought forward to meet the protruding radiator. Consequently, the DD19 had a gentle slope to the front profile. The two buses had an unladen weight of 7 tons 18 hundredweight (8 tonnes) and were delivered in May 1951. The second of the pair, 1201 (HCY 296) is seen here, in central Swansea, where there is evidence of the wartime bombing suffered by the city. *(A.R.Packer/Chris Taylor Collection)*

# Chapter 12

In July 1951 a substantially revised lowbridge body appeared for Red & White, with the code DD18. Most noticeably the front and rear profiles contained a pronounced curve, particularly at upper-deck window level. This resulted in a somewhat less severe looking bus than the lowbridge 1949-Style body. Another remarkable point is that the body featured an enclosed platform with folding doors. This was an option that was only just beginning to gain popularity on buses operated on country services; Red & White was among the first companies to standardise on enclosed platforms.

In the DD18 bodies, all glazing – except the traditional polished-framed cab windows – was rubber mounted and set flush with the exterior panelling. Corners were rounded both bottom and top, with a fairly small radius. The five DD18 bodies carried a distinctive pattern of sliding ventilator. This was not only rounded at its top corners but at its lower corners as well. The fixed parts of the windows beneath the ventilators also had rounded top corners. It is interesting to note that these ventilators were identical in design to those in Red & White's famous Duple-bodied Guy Arab IIIs built in 1949/50 and in their new Leyland Royal Tigers emerging from the local Lydney Coachworks.

Also for Red & White, a single-deck body was evolved, with the designation of S23. This combined features from several recent BBW designs: it had the sliding entrance door and shallower back window of the ECW-influenced BT&CC single-deckers of 1950 and 1951, while utilising the flush window settings of Red & White's 1951 DD18 double-deckers. The sliding ventilators, however, were of a new pattern, incorporated into the main glazing and of generous depth. The chassis chosen to receive S23 saloon bodies were Albion Valkyries. These had been built as recently as 1946/47; unfortunately for Red & White it had already been found desirable to replace their original Pickering bodywork. This order called for no fewer than 45 bodies, which took up production from the Autumn of 1951 to late 1953. Thirty of them, however, had been completed by August 1952.

During the Spring of 1952 BBW started work on two more types of double-decker for Red & White and United Welsh. Again based on modernised wartime Guy Arabs, the DD20 was a highbridge, open-platform body for United Welsh, while the DD21 was a lowbridge, enclosed-platform version for Red & White. The highbridge DD20 body bore the same basic profile as the previous post-war BBW double-deckers, but was to appear much more up-to-date for two reasons. The first was the use of the new flush glazing method, with the deep sliding ventilators as introduced on the S23. The second was that the slope of the frontal profile was improved, due to bringing the dash forward to meet the projecting Guy radiator, in the same manner as used on the two DD19 bodies on the Arab III chassis. The DD21 lowbridge body had the same pronounced curve to its end profiles as the DD18 and differed only in that the latest type of side windows were incorporated. Ten DD20s were built by the Spring of 1953, while 14 DD21s took until June 1954 to complete.

267. In July and August 1951, BBW built five double-deck lowbridge bodies of a revised styling for Red & White. They were coded **DD18-Type** and, as they were still based on the 1949-Style, they contained wooden framework. The main characteristic of their appearance was that both ends of the body featured a pronounced curve, particularly at upper-deck window level. This is clearly shown by this photograph of L1243 (EWO 494), on a sister Guy Arab II chassis to those in Plates 262 & 264. The cab dash was brought forward towards the radiator,

as in the United Welsh Arab IIIs with DD19 bodies (Plate 266), so the front panels of the body gained more of a slope. Another major change was that the windows were now mounted flush with the exterior panels. An innovation was that the rear platform was enclosed and protected by a two-leaf folding door. This kept the bus somewhat warmer in winter, but the day on which L1243 was photographed was particularly hot, as shown by the fact that the deep upper half of the windscreen was wide open! The DD18 featured an unusual type of ventilator in the side windows. In this, not only did both halves slide, as shown, but it was rounded both top and bottom, with a matching radius to the corners of the fixed glazing immediately below. Exactly the same design of ventilator appeared in other Red & White buses of the period, notably their many Duple-bodied Guy Arab IIIs. *(Mike Mogridge)*

**268**. The five DD18 bodies were followed, through to the end of 1951, by the first 12 of a consignment of 45 further bodies for Red & White, this time single-deckers, which were coded **S23-Type**. Red & White found it necessary to have new bodies built for a large batch of Albion Valkyrie CX13s, delivered only in 1946/47 and numbered, in the 1951 scheme, S1-3046 and S1-1547. Bristol's S23 body was to the existing Tilling Standard outline, but had a number of influences. It had flush glazing as in Red & White's DD18s, shown in Plate 267, it featured the ECW-influenced sliding entrance door, shallower back window and waist-level registration plate, as introduced on BT&CC's 1950- and 1951-Style bodies, and yet the frame of the unusual single-panel windscreen, as well as the polished surround to the window in the cab door, continued the patterns that had been in use since before the war. Beyond that, there was a new feature – a new style of deep, round-cornered sliding ventilator, with polished runners. Note the pale-cream relief was limited to the window surrounds and, note in particular, the tiny side-lights! S747 (FWO 656) seen here was delivered on 29th November 1951. *(B.V.B.G.)*

**269**. In 1952, United Welsh started to take delivery of more rebodied Guy Arab IIs, with a body that was coded **DD20-Type**.

By incorporating all the recently-introduced features – the flush-mounted glazing, the deep, polished ventilators, and the sloping front – the DD20 emerged as the most attractive and up-to-date of all the post-war designs of BBW origin. Ten of these bodies were built (by reflecting the seating capacity still, the full designation was DD20/56) and were delivered over a twelve-month period. Shown here is 681 (DWN 431), one of four on chassis that originated with United Welsh, the other six having been transferred, three each, from Cheltenham District and Red & White. *(Roy Marshall)*

**270**. Fourteen more lowbridge bodies were built for Red & White from the spring of 1952, although deliveries stretched through to mid-1954. These bodies were classified **DD21-Type**. Although essentially similar to the DD18 bodies as shown in Plate 267, the DD21 incorporated the latest type of sliding ventilator. As this photograph clearly shows, both halves of the slider could be opened. Note that the canopy faring still retained the characteristic BBW shape. The DD21/55 body is modelled here by L342 (EAX 646), which had an Arab I chassis. *(Aviation & Transport Photographs)*

**271**. This photograph of Red & White's L1943 (EDG 975 – originally delivered to Cheltenham District), was taken after Red & White had adopted the Tilling Standard livery pattern, with cream relief carried by two bands. The rear upper-deck window now had four matching

corners, though of a smaller radius than used by ECW (see Plate 265). Enclosing the platform resulted in the installation of an emergency door in the rear wall; open-platform buses were not required to have such a door as long as the opening continued into the rear wall by the designated amount. This picture shows the window in the emergency door is balanced by a window to light the stairs, although the outcome left a wide pillar between the two. Note the shape of the rain guttering over the platform area. L1943 was captured standing at Cardiff Central Bus Station. *(Chris Taylor Collection)*

138

# Chapter 13

The next chapter in BBW's history came about as a result of a rationalisation of the Red & White Group's interests following transfer to State ownership. The Group was the sole shareholder in a small bodybuilding plant at Lydney in Gloucestershire, known as Lydney Coachworks Ltd. This company's main activity was the rebodying of chassis for the Group. They were instrumental, however, in gaining an order from Leigh Corporation in 1949. (Several of the 1949/50 Lydney bodies, incidentally, employed exactly the same pattern of side windows and sliding ventilators as used in BBW's 1948-Style bodies!)

After passing to British Transport Commission control it was hoped that a large share of the BTC's bodybuilding requirements would be directed towards Lydney. However, due to many problems, including the supply of parts and materials and the passing of bodies by the Eastern Coach Works Inspector who was sent there to ensure the Tilling Standard was met, deliveries were very slow. Eventually it was decided to close the plant in March 1952. Many chassis were at the factory at the time, bodies being in various states of construction. It was decided that BBW should take over lock, stock and barrel and complete the vehicles at Brislington. This was a massive project, involving the transporting of part-completed vehicles, all raw materials, tools, plans and several bare chassis across to the other side of the Severn, presumably by road via Gloucester.

The chassis of these vehicles were of a new model, the underfloor-engined Leyland Royal Tiger. Production had started at Lydney in 1951 and 20 bodies had been completed and delivered before the March 1952 closure. The first five comprised buses, which were originally numbered 1001-5 (JWO 121-5); before long the Red & White fleet was renumbered, using a unique system which quoted the year in which the vehicle was new (or, at least, for which delivery was planned!). These buses became U1-551, i.e Underfloor-engined buses, sequence 1 to 5, for 1951. They were followed by fifteen coaches (1006/7, later UC2/351, plus UC4-1651: JWO 126-132/213-220). In 1952 some of these Lydney-bodied examples needed to go across to BBW for remedial work.

The vehicles which required completion by BBW were of both 45-seat bus type and 41-seat coach variety. In either case the design was very similar. The most unusual feature of both versions was that the entrance door, placed ahead of the front axle, as was generally adopted with the underfloor-engined layout, was a *sliding* unit. It is believed that this was a unique configuration. The five main side windows were fitted with sliding ventilators

of the rounded upper-and-lower-corner type, as already described for Red & White's Bristol DD18 bodies.

The first Lydney bodies to be completed by BBW for despatch by August 1952 were six coaches for Red & White, together with a further two examples for United Welsh. The Red & White coaches were numbered UC17-2251; they were registered JWO 543-8. The United Welsh coaches were numbers 999 and 1000 (GWN 863/4): until 1951 both companies had shared a common numbering system and indeed it was stated above that the Red & White vehicles were initially allocated 1001 onwards.

The remainder of the body parts recovered from Lydney Coachworks were not assembled and completed until late 1952 through to mid-1953. This consignment included the 45-seat buses for Red & White, U651 to U3751 (JWO 221-242 & 549-558).

The bodies of Lydney origin employed metal framework which, following earlier negotiations, was actually of Leyland design. It had been Lydney's intention to build their coach bodies to the Leyland *styling* as well, but in practice the only bodies built to this pattern were four which were mounted not on Leylands but on Guy Arab UF chassis! These were assembled by BBW for South Midland, a former Red & White Group company now under Thames Valley control; they were delivered in March to May 1953. They were central-entrance 41-seaters, which followed the Leyland design quite closely. The unusual Leyland front profile was used, incorporating well-raked windscreens with small additional glasses carried in the upright panelling immediately below them. One major difference from Leyland products was that the side windows were set flush with the exterior panelling and fitted with sliding ventilators.

BBW actually gave designation codes to the two types of Lydney body they were involved in constructing (as distinct from finishing off). The 45-seat bus body on Leyland Royal Tiger chassis for Red & White was coded UF1, while the 41-seat central-entrance coach on Guy Arab UF chassis for South Midland was UF2.

The last Lydney-originated bodies were outshopped by Bristol in the summer of 1953 and brought to an end BBW's only affair with underfloor-engined chassis. Meanwhile construction of S23, DD20 and DD21 bodies, also for Red & White and United Welsh, continued.

While analysing which of their earlier buses needed to receive new coachwork, Red & White earmarked three 1947 Leyland Tiger PS1/1 models from their associated fleet, Griffin Motor Company of Brynmawr (which, indeed, was to be absorbed in January 1953). It was planned that BBW should build new 35-seat saloon bodies to the same general styling as the S23-bodied Albions and an order was placed in October 1951. In the event, the bodies were not built at Brislington and the work was once again sub-contracted to Longwell Green Coachworks. A theory for the reason behind this is that BBW had plenty of work in hand and building just three bodies modified to suit the Leyland front end configuration would have been time-consuming and not cost-effective.

At the same time, it is known that Longwell Green Coachworks had considerable spare capacity following the end of the post-war boom in bus and coach building. Longwell Green therefore built the bodies to BBW design, the first late in 1952 and the others early in 1953. There is no doubt that these Longwell Green bodies were coded by BBW as the S24 model.

**272**. Lydney, to which this Red & White vehicle was bound, is a small town on the western banks of the River Severn in Gloucestershire. A major employer in the town used to be Lydney Coachworks, a member of the Red & White Group. After Red & White passed to the BTC, the situation at Lydney Coachworks was assessed, with the unfortunate result that the factory was closed down. All work in hand at the time – March 1952 – was transferred to Brislington, for BBW to attend to. Lydney Coachworks had largely been involved in rebodying chassis for the Red & White Group (see Plate 264), until being caught up in Red & White's desire to place in service a fleet of new Leyland Royal Tigers. These were of the then-novel underfloor-engined layout, built to the recently relaxed dimensions of 30 feet long and eight feet wide (9.14m x 2.43m). Production had started at Lydney in 1951 and five buses and fifteen coaches had been delivered by the March 1952 closure. BBW was then able to finish a further eight Lydney coaches quite quickly: these were delivered by August. These included six for Red & White, which carried numbers UC1751-2251 (JWO 543-8); UC1951 is seen here. *(Chris Taylor Collection)*

**273**. Two more Lydney coaches were completed by BBW for United Welsh. These had the numbers 999 and 1000 (GWN 863/4), both the fleet- and registration-numbers having been allocated ahead of those for the two Guy Arab IIIs with Bristol DD19 bodies, as described in Plate 266, that were delivered a year *earlier*. Leyland coach 999 is seen here, painted cream, with red wheel arches. The top half of the driver's windscreen was well-raked, to minimise reflections on the glass from interior lights at night; the driver no

longer sat in the confines of his own cab. A feature that was probably unique on underfloor-engined vehicles was that the front door was a sliding affair; the width of the opening hardly seems adequate, though. Furthermore, it was considered suitable to locate the offside emergency-exit door alongside the driver's seat. The sliding ventilators in all these Lydney-style bodies were of the same pattern as used in the Bristol DD18 bodies built for Red & White. These coaches, however, had the addition of glass louvres over the tops, which are more clearly seen in the plate above. Seating was provided for 41. *(Roy Marshall)*

**274**. BBW soon started to build complete bodies from the stock of parts recovered from Lydney Coachworks. Again they were mounted on Leyland Royal Tiger chassis, some of which had been standing in the open at Lydney for some time. Due to the amount of work involved, delivery of finished vehicles to Red & White did not commence until November or December 1952 and was not completed until July 1953 – remember, these had been ordered for 1951 delivery and that was reflected by their fleet-numbers! The batch comprised thirty-two

45-seat buses and BBW gave them the designation of **UF1/45**. They were numbered U6-3751 (JWO 221-242/549-558) and U651 is seen here. On the outside, the bus body looked very similar to the coach version, especially as the livery was the same, as shown by Plate 272. The bus, however, had less elaborate brightwork on the front panel and beneath the windscreen and cab windows and it lacked the bulbous wheel arch moulding, the extra panelling between the wheel arches to conceal the life-rail, and the glass louvres above the sliding ventilators. *(Chris Taylor Collection)*

**275**. If the idea of Bristol-bodied Leylands is not bizarre enough, then think about Bristol bodies to a *Leyland design* on Guy chassis! Lydney Coachworks had negotiated to use Leyland-designed framework and to follow Leyland styling for the completed coaches, but in practice developed the finished job to its own (or Red & White's) requirements. Eventually, though, BBW built a batch of bodies to the Leyland coach pattern. BBW coded the four coaches as **UF2/41**. The outline matched Leyland's coaches and the unusual windscreen arrangement, with well-raked main windows supplemented by small upright glasses below, was exactly as found on the Leyland body. In other respects, the Bristol body was very different. The deep window to the rear of the front corner window was only half the width, then there were two main side windows ahead of the door instead of only one, placing the door more centrally. The

windows were flush-mounted and fitted with sliding ventilators, instead of being recessed and winding down. Other items, like body-side trim and the position of the headlights, also differed. Thames Valley had ordered the coaches from Lydney in December 1951 and they were delivered by BBW about a year later to the South Midland subsidiary – the latter had formerly been a Red & White Group company and it was fitting that the link was extended. They were numbered 86-89 and registered in Oxford, in South Midland tradition, as SFC 501-4. *(W.J.Hayes)*

**276 & 277**. On 18th May 1952, a group of bus enthusiasts undertook a formal visit to BBW, where these two photographs were take vehicles captured in the photographs were for Red & White. The picture on the right is dominated by three of the Lydney coach-bodi seen that they were fitted with sliding heads to the roofs. The other two vehicles in the right-hand picture comprise an **S23/35** on an Albi To the extreme left of this picture, though, can be seen another DD21/55 Guy and a further S23/35 Albion. *(M.J.Tozer Collection)*

**278**. In October 1951 Red & White had decided that, in addition to rebodying the 45 Albion Valkyries, they would like BBW to rebody three 1947 Leyland Tiger PS1/1 models, which belonged to an associated fleet, Griffin Motor Company of Brynmawr. As events turned out, the three Tigers were not bodied by BBW, but by Longwell Green Coachworks and they were delivered, in Red & White livery, in the winter of 1952/53. The bodies were built to the same pattern as BBW's S23-Type, although adapted to suit the Leyland chassis. Without doubt, they received a BBW designation of **S24-Type**. At the front, the bodies carried a *divided* windscreen with *square* corners which, being coupled to a Leyland dash-plate of that period, had a horizontal base-line – see Plate 239. The box for the destination

indicator was smaller than on the S23. At the back, instead of the single, fairly shallow back window, there were two, slightly taller windows, as shown here. It is interesting to note that when ECW had bodied Leyland Tigers in 1946-48, such as those for Western Welsh, some of these also had two similar windows. Seen here is S2547, with Brecknockshire registration EU 8437. *(B.V.B.G. Collection)*

y were members and guests of The 'Bristol' Interest Circle, which keenly followed all aspects of Bristol Tramways' business. All the
~land Royal Tigers which BBW was finishing off. Note that the nearest coach still has no seats or glazing, yet is painted. Also, it will be
~kyrie chassis and a **DD21/55** on a Guy Arab II. The same five vehicles are also captured, from a different point, in the left-hand photograph.

**279**. The interior of the Longwell Green **S24-Type** seen in Plate 278 is shown here, showing that this, and the BBW S23, retained the

Tilling Standard appear-
ance – compare with Plate
259. The mounting of the
window glazing flush to
the exterior, though, re-
sulted in broader surrounds
on the inside, these being
finished off with square
corners. The lights are of
a different style, with
rectangular covers, and are
slightly further from the
windows than on 1950-
Style BBW bodies. The
brackets for the grab-rails
along the parcel shelves
are more upright. The high
base-line to the windows
in the front bulkhead is the
result of being built on
Leyland Tiger chassis.
*(B.V.B.G. Collection)*

# Chapter 14

There was a sense of expansion in BBW's work in 1954 because two customers from the past, together with two brand-new customers, came Bristol's way. The returning customers were Western and Southern National, who last had Bristol bodywork early in the war – including on one chassis now making a return visit! These twin operators required six new double-deck lowbridge bodies and four single-deck bodies, all on reconditioned Bristol chassis. All ten bodies, together with those for the new customers, were to be built to resemble ECW products very closely. For all that, each could be instantly identified as a Bristol body.

The six 55-seat double-deckers were coded DD22 and were almost identical to the bodies built by ECW on K-type chassis back in 1950. They were of five-bay layout, with ECW-style sliding vents, together with push-out vents in the windows at the front of the upper-deck and in the lower-deck front bulkhead. Internally, the body was finished to match ECW's 'Thin Wall' styling, whereby the window glass was set flush with the smooth lining panels. The DD22 bodies, however, incorporated the latest Tilling Standard destination indicator, comprising three separate sights – terminal point, places served and route-number. The seats, also, were of the latest type.

The DD22 bodies were mounted on six Bristol K5G chassis dating from 1938 to 1942, each modernised with a PV2 radiator. The chassis which received the four single-deck bodies, although dating from the same period generally, were more extensively updated. They were rebuilt to LL-Type configuration, in order to receive bodies 30 feet in length, instead of the original 27 feet 6 inches. Three chassis were unfrozen 1942 products (one of which originally bore a Bristol utility body), while the fourth was a post-war L6A, whose original Royal Blue coach body had been burnt out in an accident.

The four 30-foot long bodies were designated S25 and had a capacity of 39 seats. The extra length was obtained, in exact ECW manner, by inserting a 2' 6" section with window between the fifth bay and the rear entrance. The overall appearance of the body was almost precisely that for the ECW LL body, updated in respect of the seats and destination boxes, in the same way as the six DD22 double-deckers.

The United Counties Omnibus Company became a customer of BBW bodywork in 1954 for the one and only time. Five double-deck lowbridge 55-seaters were built on updated, Unfrozen Bristol K5G chassis (two bodies) or on wartime K6A chassis which were now also fitted with 5LW engines. All were delivered in July. BBW

classified these as DD23 because, although essentially similar to the DD22, a most significant difference was that they were constructed to the latest maximum width of eight feet, instead of the seven feet six inches of all Bristol bodies since the 1930s. The DD23 bodies were the only BBW bodies (other than those with Lydney connections) built to this width. They were virtually identical to some eight-foot wide bodies built by ECW in 1952/53 and were of five-bay layout, so in side view were indistinguishable from DD22 bodies built for Western and Southern National. Looking from either end, though, the extra width was easily discernible and the shape of the windscreen and bulkhead windows was quite different from the narrower bodies.

The second new customer for BBW in 1954 was Western SMT, a member of the State-controlled Scottish Bus Group. Western SMT had contracted ECW to rebody several older chassis in 1951-53 and now sent twelve 1946 AEC Regal single-deck chassis to Bristol, where new *double*-deck bodies were built for them, under the code DD24. These were 53-seat lowbridge bodies, again built largely to the ECW styling. They were generally similar to the Western/Southern National batch, but Western SMT specified considerably fewer opening windows. Construction of the bodywork was well advanced before the AEC chassis actually arrived in Bristol. The last of the completed buses were despatched from BBW in March 1955.

Work was now scheduled to build a further nine DD22-type bodies for Western and Southern National. Instead, that contract was switched to Eastern Coach Works! They built the bodies (with body numbers 8418-26, Series 2) to the same design as the Bristol DD22, despite the fact that ECW's own styling had been updated considerably since then, principally in the adoption of a four-bay layout, not only on new chassis of the KS/KSW variety, but on reconditioned examples of the K-Type. This batch of bodies for Western and Southern National thereby once more resembled the 1950 ECW product, while also lacking the tell-tale features that distinguished BBW's DD22.

Bristol did build a further three single-deckers for Southern National, however. These were coded S26 for, although again measuring 30 feet long and mounted on lengthened L5G chassis (in this case 1938 former Eastern Counties vehicles) these 1955 bodies were unique, not only to BBW but also within the Tilling Group. They were built with a specially high saloon floor, this largely eliminating the intrusion of the rear wheel arches. As a result, all seats could face forwards and, with a rearward repositioning of the entrance, an amazing total of 43 seats could be accommodated! Because of the higher floor level the whole body above this point was pro-portionately raised. It retained the general appearance of ECW bodies, but the cab styling was completely different and reverted to a 'traditional' Bristol fashion.

It seems strange that these very individual 43-seat bodies were built to total just three and that it was as late as 1955 that the 'experiment' should take place, when the likelihood of any more half-cab bodies being built was small. Indeed, the seven 1954/55 Bristol S25 and S26 bodies and six 39-seat saloons built by ECW in 1955 also for Western/Southern National, turned out to be the last half-cab single-deckers built for the BTC group. Furthermore, with the completion of the last S26 in July 1955, bus body building at Brislington came to an end.

**280**. Western and Southern National returned to taking BBW bodies in 1954, after a break of 11 years. The bodies were again for rebodying older chassis, in this case Bristol types of the late-1930s/early-1940s. BBW built the bodies very much to the ECW pattern, although there were tell-tale signs of the Bristol involvement. Four single-deckers were completed in February and March 1954, under the code **S25-Type**. They were built on L-Type chassis that had not only received PV2 radiators, but had been fitted with new, longer frames, to produce 30ft-long 39-seaters. The S25 bodies were very similar to ECW bodies built in 1950-52 on LL-Type chassis, including the insertion of an extra short window ahead of the rear entrance – compare to Plate 260. The three-part destination indicator (front and rear) was as introduced as standard for Tilling fleets in late 1951, so found on few examples of the LL-Type as distinct from the wider LWL model, by which the LL was generally succeeded. As in the 1950/51-Style BBW bodies, the nearside side-light was mounted on the bulkhead, rather than on the faring. Seen here, about to be driven away from the Brislington depot yard after completion, is Southern National 373 (GTA 395). *(Graham Brooks/B.V.B.G. Collection)*

**281**. An offside view of Southern National 373 (GTA 395) when in service. The chassis had been new in 1942, with a Strachan utility body. The most distinctive feature of the BBW **S25-Type** body and most noticeable in this view was that the windscreen's base-line was appreciably higher than that on any ECW bodied L-Types; indeed, higher even than on ECW or BBW bodies built on J-Type chassis – see Plate 260 again. A study has been made of the cab of this vehicle, but no explanation can be found. *(T.G.Partridge)*

**282**. Following the four S25/39 bodies came six **DD22/55** lowbridge double-deckers, in March to May 1954, also for Western and Southern National. These bodies resembled the ECW products on K-Type chassis last built in 1950, before the advent of the longer KS and KSW models, for which ECW introduced four-bay construction, with deeper windows. However, the DD22s had the latest style of seat and the three-piece destination boxes; at the front, the latter was mounted up against the upper cream band, which was to be an identifier. Careful study will show that over the rear platform, the guttering takes an unusual course, arching through the cream band to join the upper beading. This distinguished 1954 BBW bodies from ECW examples. Seen here about to leave on its delivery run is Southern National 359 (FTA 642), which had an updated 1941 K5G chassis. *(Graham Brooks)*

**283**. In 1954, BBW built its only batch of bodies to the width of eight feet (2.43m) that had been generally permissible since 1950. (This is other than bodies built with parts obtained from Lydney Coachworks.) Further, they were the only bodies built for United Counties of Northampton. The batch comprised five double-deckers, classified **DD23-Type**. They were very alike bodies built by ECW in 1951-53 for Eastern Counties and Eastern National, and for United Counties on some K5Gs transferred from Eastern National. Like those ECW bodies, the tops of the bulkhead windows were lower than on the narrower K-Types (compare with the plate above) and there was a curve through the base-line, both as found on the ECW body for the KSW. Similarly, the windscreen's frame had a curved base-line and was of half-round section, but in other respects, like its intrusion into the cream band and the profile of the cab front, the bodies complied to the standard K. The only clear way to distinguish a DD23 from an ECW version was by the guttering over the rear platform. Seen newly completed in July 1954 is United Counties 703 (BRP 232), on an Unfrozen 1942 K5G chassis, further modernised by replacing the Autovac tank on the bulkhead with a conventional fuel pump. *(Graham Brooks)*

**284**. From the offside, the **DD23-Type** seemed identical to the ECW examples built shortly beforehand – except that there was the tell-tale unpainted aluminium strip encircling the front wing! From this angle, the eight-foot width (2.43m) seems very noticeable. The white steering wheel was to remind drivers of the extra width of the bus. Curiously, the destination box was central on these bodies, unlike on the DD22. It is interesting that the sliding ventilators did not carry the glass draught-excluders on their trailing ends; this was a specific requirement of United Counties, who had dropped the item on buses from ECW in 1952. (The excluders were completely discontinued by ECW in 1954.) United Counties 704 (BRP 233) is seen at work in Bedford. *(R.F.Mack)*

**285**. Another once-only customer for BBW was Western SMT, whose territory covered the south-west of Scotland. In 1954/55, BBW built new lowbridge double-deckers for 12 of Western's 1946 AEC Regal *single*-deck chassis. The bodies were coded **DD24-Type** and reverted to the 7ft 6in width (2.286m). Although built generally to the ECW pattern, Western SMT specified only 53 seats (27 up, 26 down) and far fewer opening windows; fewer, even, than on the ECW bodies built for rebodying other Western SMT chassis types in 1952/53. Although built after the United Counties DD23 bodies, the sliding ventilators incorporated the draught-excluders. Other notable points concern the windows in the cab; it will be seen that the windscreen frame reverted to the traditional BBW pattern and is virtually identical to that on the Albions with DD14-Type bodies, as shown in Plate 263. Also, the cab side windows were set within polished frames again. Greenock-based GC284 (BAG 82) was one of the first completed in July 1954. *(Allan Macfarlane)*

**286**. A nearside view of **DD24/53**-bodied 1946 AEC Regal C308 (BAG 112), outside the Body Building Works in March 1955, about to be driven north to Western SMT on Ayrshire trade-plates. A sister bus can be seen behind, standing in the doorway of the body shops, and this was no doubt C309 (BAG 113), as these two had the last BBW double-decker bodies to be built. Note the application of *three* cream bands to the dark-red livery, the top one being deeper than normal, while the canopy faring was also deepened. Furthermore, the BTC's Scottish Bus Group operators, of which Western SMT was a member, tended to include cream-based advertisement panels as part of the livery and the corners of these panels were indented. The faring over the rear platform is the same as in the DD22 and DD23 bodies. *(Graham Brooks)*

**287**. In 1955, nine more DD22-Type bodies were planned by BBW for Western and Southern National. In the event, the bodies were built by **Eastern Coach Works** at Lowestoft, in June and July, receiving ECW body numbers 8418-26 Series 2. It is believed parts for their construction were retrieved from Brislington and they were again built to the 1950 ECW pattern. In appearance they matched the DD22, as shown in Plate 282, except that they lacked the characteristic BBW guttering over the rear platform and the unpainted beading over the offside front wing. Also, ECW was able to place the front destination indicator centrally. The ECW version of the DD22 shown here was on Western National 1945 K6A chassis 353 (FTT 704), seen after restoration by the Bristol Vintage Bus Group, together with their DD6-bodied 1940 K5G, outside the main gate of Bristol

Commercial Vehicles on 23rd October 1983, during a special visit to mark the end of bus manufacturing in Bristol. *(Phil Sposito/B.V.B.G.)*

**288**. It was a well-known fact that the Body Building Works were to close and yet, as if to show that the plant could always build something special, the *last* bus bodies built by BBW, in July 1955, were three single-deckers of a special high-capacity nature. The bodies were designated **S26-Type** and were mounted on more Southern National L-Type chassis that had been lengthened for 30ft bodywork. In the S26, the saloon floor was raised, to minimise the intrusion of the rear wheel arches, thereby enabling all seats to face forward. As a result, the capacity totalled 43 instead of 39, the highest ever achieved in a 30ft single-decker with a vertical front engine! The whole body was raised to relate to the higher floor, hence the large space between the bulkhead window and the bonnet. This is emphasised by the unique livery on completion, whereby cream was applied around the bulkhead window, as well as extending round the cab nearside window and the windscreen. The rear doorway needed to be moved back slightly and was reduced in width; compare with the S25 in Plate 280. The chassis of Southern National 375 (CVF 844), seen here, was new in 1938 to Eastern Counties. *(Graham Brooks/B.V.B.G.)*

**289**. Southern National 375 (CVF 844), with its 1955 **S26-Type** 43-seat body is seen again here, in service at Barnstaple. From the offside, the extra height was emphasised by the waistline at the front corner curving down. The seats can be seen to be getting slightly higher towards the back of the saloon, indicating the flooring beneath them still needed to be gently ramped to overcome the rear wheel arches. The seats themselves were non-standard and were probably of a lightweight type, to counter-balance the extra capacity. The windows of the cab deserve to be mentioned, as it was fitting that the last bodies to be built by BBW were able to feature windscreens and cab side windows of patterns that had become established BBW features, rather than of the ECW types! *(T.G.Partridge)*

# Chapter 15

The Nationalisation of transport and public utilities in the early post-war years has been mentioned in Chapter 10, as affecting the Bristol Tramways & Carriage Company. A considerable number of long-distance road-haulage businesses were also Nationalised and, similarly, placed under British Transport Commission control. These operations were henceforth carried out under the fleetname of British Road Services and a uniform livery of red was adopted for acquired and new lorries, throughout the country. There was a marked shortage of maximum-capacity heavy haulage lorries among the acquired stock, so BRS started to buy new 22-ton gross eight-wheel lorries with some urgency. Types such as the Leyland Octopus and AEC Mammoth Major fitted the bill, but the BTC, having a chassis manufacturing plant of its own in Bristol, directed BT&CC to design and build a similar chassis. The outcome was the Bristol HG6L (Heavy Goods, 6-cylinder Leyland engine) and the first chassis was built in 1952. Cabs were to be built by several constructors, including Eastern Coach Works, while among those to build the platform bodies was Bristol's own Body Building Works.

Full details of the Bristol HG and other Bristol lorries appeared in the 1988 book *Bristol Goods Vehicles*, written and published by Allen Janes and Phil Sposito. Here it is relevant just to give details of BBW's involvement. The platform bodies were 24 feet 6 inches long and 7 feet 4$^{1}/_{2}$ inches wide. They featured light alloy section bearers and one-piece alloy side raves. There was an alloy headboard, to fit behind the cab, 2 feet 6 inches high. BRS stipulated that the floor of the platform was to be made of wood. BBW devised the classification HGP1 for the platform bodies and they were built on the last 49 chassis of the first HG6L sanction (chassis numbers 88.152-200). The completed lorries entered service between January and June 1955. During the same period, BBW was building its last double-deck and single-deck bus bodies.

It is interesting to note that the cabs built by the other concerns had been ordered through BBW and they were built to Bristol's specification. Following construction, they were actually mounted on the HG6L chassis at BBW – in effect, the Brislington works were going out in almost exactly the same way that they came in, by their involvement in mounting other makers' structures; in 1900, of course, it was trams that were being built.

With the coming of the second sanction of HG chassis, numbers 96.001-121, BBW also had the job of building many of the cabs themselves. A prototype was constructed in May 1954, while a production run was completed during 1955 on a further 94 chassis, while 101 chassis received BBW platform bodies. The cabs built on 88th sanction HGs by concerns including ECW, Burlingham and Metro-Cammell – all of whom were primarily involved in bus bodybuilding – had featured a rounded front dash, which proudly carried a grille to the familiar Bristol outline and similar to that on the new Bristol Lodekka bus. The windscreens fitted were very large compared to many a lorry of the time and these had either a sloping or curved base-line. The BBW cabs also featured the bulbous dash and large windscreens, but were easily identified by two main features. The grille was a little shallower and was squarer in outline – indeed, hardly complying to the traditional Bristol shape! – while the base-line of the windscreens was almost horizontal. The outcome, unfortunately, was less attractive than the products of the other builders.

The BBW cab was principally constructed from aluminium, but all the curved panels used new technology in being moulded in glass reinforced plastic, otherwise known as glass-fibre. The roof was moulded in one piece, with aluminium stiffeners, and an area at the front of the roof was finished flat, for carrying the fleetname British Road Services. The materials used in BBW cabs reduced the net weight of a completed HG6L by $^{3}/_{4}$ of a ton compared with the earliest examples, allowing an increase in the payload to over 15 tons.

In 1954, the MCW developed a second option of goods vehicle for BRS. This was a four-wheel tractor-unit, for articulated trailer operation. Britain until then had been somewhat wedded to the idea that heavy haulage should mean the use of multiple-axle rigid lorries; the advantages of articulated lorries were only just beginning to be realised, with their greater manoeuvrability and the ability to uncouple and quickly recouple to another semi-trailer. Bristol's articulated goods model was again powered by the Leyland engine and was designated HA6L. A 24-foot-long semi-trailer was designed under the designation of ST, to be supplied with the HA (although capable of being coupled to any tractor unit).

For the HA, and for any further HGs, a new style of all-glass-fibre cab, on a steel base, was designed by BBW and coded TC1 (Tractor Cab 1). The platform body for the Bristol ST was designated TP1 (Trailer Platform 1).

The prototype HA and ST combination was bodied, after lengthy road-testing, at Easter 1955. The TC1 cab looked very different from that on the 96th sanction HGs. It had a smooth, gently-curved front profile, with a shallow Bristol grille and a sloping base-line to the windscreens. The radiator filler-cap was relocated to the nearside rear corner of the cab, to enhance the smooth front profile further. The whole effect was very attractive. The first HAs comprised ten chassis

(112.001-010), with TC1 cabs, and all were delivered by late 1955. Concurrently, work started on the first 20 ST chassis (114.001-020), with TP1 platform bodies.

As an aside, it is interesting to note that not only have we seen the repetition of simple alphabetical code letters between BBW and the MCW for their various models, but even the more random pairing of letters 'HA' happened to be duplicated – BBW had built HA-Type *bodies* on 4-Tonner chassis in the early 1920s, as described in Chapter 2!

Following the completion of the TC1 cabs for the ten HA chassis, the Bristol Tramways & Carriage Company's Body Building Works were closed down. This had been planned for some time as there was insufficient work coming through to support the plant. The idea of rebodying earlier bus chassis to extend the vehicles' lives had run its course, as most buses with worn-out coachwork had either been treated (by BBW, ECW and others) or were being retired from service. The likelihood of new chassis being directed through BBW was out of the question, because requirements for new buses were dropping and both the MCW and ECW were finding they were unable to reach the production levels to which they had been accustomed. There were two reasons for this state. Firstly, operators had succeeded in eliminating the backlog, caused by the war years, in the replacement of worn-out stock; secondly, passenger loadings, having reached an all-time peak around the end of the 1940s, were now declining steadily, as ownership of private cars was beginning to increase, while a new home-entertainment medium – television – kept people from travelling during the evenings.

BBW's premises at the end of Brislington depot were cleared and certain stores items disposed of to Bristol Tramways and Thames Valley. Some pieces of equipment were passed to the MCW which, since 1955, incidentally, had adopted the new name of Bristol Commercial Vehicles Ltd. It had been agreed that the bulk of the BBW premises would be taken over by British Railways, for the housing and maintenance of road vehicles, a division that in later years functioned separately as the National Freight Corporation. The bays at the side next to the area used as a bus depot were equipped subsequently as a chassis finishing shop. It was here that chassis that had been produced on the nearby Chatsworth Road production line were sent, after being road-tested, for final adjustments to be made, before being despatched to the coach-builders' works.

Of the staff who remained at BBW to the end, all but eight men were found other jobs with BCV or Bristol Tramways. One foreman, however, together with BBW's last Works Manager, Mr H W Smith, expressed a desire to be transferred to the Railways.

The only work in which BBW was finally involved was the building of cabs and bodies for British Road Services' Bristol goods vehicles. A new order was placed with BCV and a meeting held in January 1956 to study the possibility of re-opening BBW! The meeting was attended by members of BRS, ECW and BCV, but the outcome was that BBW should not reopen. Instead, an alternative arrangement was made, in that the building of cabs and bodies would be undertaken in future by Longwell Green Coachworks. Thus the close working relationship between the two concerns, that had existed for the past decade, was to ensure that Longwell Green could enjoy steady if low-key activity for several more years to come, amid the conventional coach-building in which they were still involved. The moulds for the manufacture of the glass-fibre parts, together with the expertise in the handling of the material, plus the machines and tools, were transferred from south-east Bristol to east Bristol. The cabs made by Longwell Green were coded FGC/1 (Fibre Glass Cab/1) and differed from the BBW TC1 in that the radiator filler was located in the conventional position, above the Bristol grille. Therefore, the BBW cab could be recognised by the apparent lack of a filler.

**290.** When Bristol's MCW became involved in plans to build eight-wheel lorries for British Road Services, BBW was drawn in by having the capacity to build the platform bodies for these HG6L chassis. In 1955, they gained a much greater involvement by also building many of the cabs. This head-on view shows an unpainted BBW-cabbed HG6L – probably the first produced, on chassis 96.002 – posed at Arno's Castle, across the road from the Brislington works. The significance of the cab was that all the bulbous front panelling, together with the roof, was moulded from glass-reinforced plastic, or glass-fibre, a tough lightweight material that was gaining a lot of interest from automotive manufacturers. Strangely, the shape of the radiator-grille was barely of traditional Bristol outline, being too square-shouldered, whereas the grille on the cabs built by ECW and others had a much more convincing shape. Furthermore, the windscreens in BBW cabs, unlike those from other builders, had almost horizontal lower edges and did not follow the curve to the top of the dash panels.

**291**. Posed on The Portway, alongside the River Avon in Bristol, is a newly completed 96th Sanction HG6L, with BBW cab and platform body. The cab was painted red and the door carried the BTC's lion-and-wheel emblem, as also found on British Railways locomotives, as well as on the chassis/bodybuilders' plate on the platform of Bristol Lodekkas! Glass-fibre, as used extensively in cladding the framework of the BBW cab, could be moulded to any reasonable shape and the roof was designed to have an upright face, on which was applied the British Road Services fleetname. This name on the unpainted cab in Plate 290 is clearly carried by a specially prepared temporary board.

**292**. A BBW-cabbed HG6L is shown here outside the body shops in Brislington depot, all ready for delivery to the north-east of England for entry into service in June 1955. It had been allocated the fleet-number 1D577 and had received the Newcastle-upon-Tyne registration number WBB 870.

**293**. Late in 1955, the second of Bristol's new articulated lorries for BRS was completed and taken to The Downs for photography, as shown here. The tractor-unit was an HA6L, which carried an entirely new design of cab, coded **TC1-Type**. The whole cab was moulded in glass-fibre, on a steel base-plate. It was fabricated in two sections, the roof and the tops of the pillars forming one part. The cab front formed a smooth curve and to enhance this further, the radiator filler-cap was relocated to the rear of the cab, on the left hand side. The production of 10 TC1 cabs, and 20 **TP1-Type** platform bodies for the Bristol ST semi-trailers, as also depicted here, marked the final act of bodywork production at BBW, where the plant was closed towards the end of 1955. The BBW designs, moulds and know-how for the production of glass-fibre cabs were transferred to Longwell Green Coachworks, but their version reverted to a conventional front-mounted radiator filler. This lorry entered service early in 1956 as number 43A644, being registered in London as SLD 95.

Even after BBW had closed, their products continued to appear in advertisements through 1956. A specialist firm involved in the manufacture of the raw glass-fibre material, Fibreglass Ltd, carried an advertisement showing a 96th sanction HG6L with a BBW cab, while BIC Chemicals of Oldbury, near Birmingham, advertised their Beetle Polyester Resin for use in making glass-reinforced plastic and showed a TC1 cab for an HA tractor-unit, together with the moulded roof section for such as cab.

So the BBW shops were vacated finally in 1956 – 56 years after the first tram bodies had been assembled in the then-new buildings and 49 years after the first motor vehicle bodywork had been constructed, to Charles Challenger's designs, on Thornycroft chassis.

# Chapter 16

The nature of this chapter is to summarise the afterlife which some BBW bodies enjoyed. Most bus bodies were built with the intention of remaining with the chassis on which they were mounted for the entire useful life of the complete vehicle. After so many years' service, the vehicle usually would be sold off complete, for scrapping, as neither chassis nor body had any further value in a world of passenger transport that was continually being modernised.

Inevitably, there were exceptions to this state of affairs. In Chapter 2 we saw how the slow manufacture of new coachwork in the early 1920s resulted in bodies built as far back as 1907 being re-used to clothe new chassis, until the body shops had caught up with the backlog – see Plates 41 & 42. The caption to the same plates also mentions an afterlife that was to be fairly common for old bus bodies. This was their conversion to living accommodation – either as seaside holiday huts or, just as likely, for use on farms as hen-houses.

101 further uses for old bodies could probably be enumerated, but of more concern is the transfer of old bodies to other chassis, for continued use in public service as buses or coaches. In the days before the Great War, it was expected that bodies would be swapped around to meet traffic needs; for example to provide more char-à-bancs in summer or more saloon buses in winter. Records are sketchy and, besides, body movements were too numerous to detail. The destruction of bodies during the war years was sometimes met with the transfer of bodies from chassis which themselves had been damaged during blackout conditions by, for example, running into debris or falling into bomb craters. The years from the late 1940s to the late 1950s, however, produced a different set of circumstances that resulted in several movements of BBW bodies.

By 1949, bus manufacturers were unable to meet the huge demand for new stock and an effort was made to curb the desire of operators to increase their fleets to cater for the flow of trade. An order was issued proclaiming that new chassis would only be delivered providing the operator could prove that an equal number of old buses had been replaced. Bristol built some L-Type chassis in 1949 for this purpose and the chassis numbers received a suffix letter R to distinguish them (e.g. 73.133R to 73.200R). They were supplied to three operators who showed they had replaced earlier stock in various ways, such as the transfer of the bodies from the old chassis to the new L-Types. In the case of the BT&CC fleet, 12 L5G chassis were supplied and

on to the new chassis BT&CC mounted wartime, utility, S14-Type bodies, which had been built by Bence at Longwell Green. The move involved almost half of the S14 bodies that had been built, on B-Type chassis, and to prove further that the B-Types had, indeed, been taken out of service, the 1930/31 registration numbers were transferred with the bodies – not so much a case of 'cherished' registrations, which are popular nowadays, but a repeat of the practice frequently carried out in the early years of the century.

It hardly needs to be said that the B-Type chassis and the L-Type chassis of 20 years later had little in common, other than accepting half-cab bodywork. The S14 bodies needed to be lengthened to fit the Ls, as well as being remodelled around the front end. At the same time, the structure was rebuilt to prolong the bodies' life.

By 1951, the oldest un-rebodied double-deckers in BT&CC's fleet were 1938/39 K5Gs. These started to be taken out of service from this time, but rather than the chassis being regarded as fit for further use, it was some of the BBW bodies that were re-used. These bodies were actually in fine condition, as they had been rebuilt in the late 1940s, either by BT&CC themselves or by coachbuilders such as ECW, Longwell Green and Portsmouth Aviation. It was decided to transfer these 1938/39 bodies to *newer* chassis, but ones that had been supplied with wartime utility bodywork. Two bodies replaced utility Bristol bodies on Unfrozen K5G chassis, another displaced a Park Royal body from a similar chassis, but the outcome of a further eight transfers caused some raised eyebrows and, indeed, not a little consternation in the offices of another chassis maker. The reason is that these bodies were placed on wartime Guy Arab I chassis, all but two of which were also fitted with Bristol PV2 radiators!

By the middle of the 1950s, BT&CC had displaced from service most examples of their large fleet of pre-war L-Types that retained their original bodies – the S4-Types, the S6 class, and so on. The time then came to review the state of the rebodied J-Types, most of which had received post-war Tilling Standard coachwork. Most operators regarded a rebodying exercise as a means of prolonging a vehicle's life for maybe as little as seven years, no matter what condition the new body might be in at the end of that spell. In fact, the timber-framed bodies built in the 1946-1949 period had been constructed using wood that was unavoidably of lower durability than desired and, consequently, they were showing signs of weakening by the mid-1950s. Therefore, BT&CC started to withdraw and sell J-Types with 1947- to 1949-Style bodies from 1956.

Structural defects were not a problem, though, with the metal-framed BBW bodies of the 1950- and 1951-Styles (nor with the ECW metal-framed bodies mounted on other Js around 1949). A different approach was made to these. It was decided to re-mount these bodies on L-Type chassis, especially early post-war examples whose original ECW bodywork was also suffering from deteriorating timber. Other subjects were the twelve 1949 L5Gs which had entered service carrying the lengthened wartime Bence-built bodies, as described in an earlier paragraph in this chapter. Withdrawals of the J-Types concerned, to commence the programme of body moves, started as early as 1954. Of the 23 1950-Style bodies and 26 1951-Style – 49 BBW bodies altogether – only nine were not remounted on L-Types, being instead sold in the late 1950s, still on the J-Type chassis.

In fact, there were not as many early post-war Ls needing to have their coachwork replaced as there were BBW and ECW metal-framed bodies, so BT&CC made the surprising decision to rebody some late-model pre-war Ls. Five of the chosen vehicles had already received PV2 radiators and new BBW bodies in 1949, so in 1956/57, the 1949 bodies were replaced either by 1949 ECW bodies, or by 1950/51 BBW bodies! The material for the framework of the respective bodies made all the difference! Additionally, some 1941/42 L-Types still carrying their original high radiators and BBW S6-family bodies were chosen to received low radiators and to be rebodied – despite the fact that some sister buses had already been withdrawn and sold!

Further changes overcame seven of the 1950/51-Style BBW bodies upon being moved to the L-Type chassis. This was a result of the re-introduction of 'one-man-operation'; to try to balance the loss of passenger traffic against rising costs, as well as countering staff shortages, it was agreed in 1957 that drivers of single-deckers on more lightly-trafficked routes could also take the fares, thereby dispensing with the services of a conductor. The rear-entrance bodies therefore needed to be rebuilt with a door at the front instead, while having an aperture made in the bulkhead, through which cash and tickets could be passed – a system very like that employed on BBW L2 bodies 30 years before!

The foregoing paragraphs give the impression that the 1949-Style BBW bodies were not particularly sound by the mid-1950s. It will be recalled from Chapter 10 that Red & White had received two 1949-Style single-deckers, mounted on 1937/38 Albion Valkyrie chassis. Evidently, the structure of these bodies caused Red & White no great concern, because in 1957, both were transferred to members of their fleet of 1947 Valkyries, these being two of the few that had escaped being rebodied with new BBW S23 bodies in 1951-53.

Very few BBW-bodied buses were sold for further passenger work with major operators elsewhere in the country. A few disposals deserve to be mentioned, though. In 1955, the Isle of Wight's main operator, Southern Vectis, was faced with a major increase in demand for its buses as the railways on the island were closed down. A request, doubtless channelled through the BTC, for suitable second-hand double-deckers was met with the supply of 14 pre-war-model K5Gs from the Bristol Tramways fleet, eight of which had BBW bodies. They served Southern Vectis for another two to three years. In the meantime, since 1951-53, four other pre-war Bristol-bodied K5Gs had been working BT&CC's Weston-super-Mare sea-front service during the summer as open-toppers, giving holidaymakers a special way of enjoying the sea air and scenery. The Ks were replaced by new Lodekkas in 1961, but two of the four were sold for further sea-side work, ironically with Southern Vectis. Eastern Counties were in the market for suitable used double-deckers in the late 1950s and among the K5Gs acquired were three of BT&CC's 1939 examples bearing 1949-Style BBW bodies. They ran in Eastern Counties' red livery from 1959 to 1961.

The only BBW-bodied L5Gs to be sold for further service with a major operator were three of BT&CC's 1941 batch of City buses. These passed in 1952 to a well-known Bristol operator, Pontypridd Urban District Council. They ran there for a further five years, with the front doors of their two-doorway bodies locked or panelled over.

After the Gosport & Fareham Omnibus Company (known as 'Provincial') had acquired a former Red & White Guy Arab with a 1951 BBW DD18 body in 1965, they bought two of the DD21 rebodied examples direct from Red & White the following year. All three worked for Provincial until 1970. On 1st January 1970, Provincial became a member of the latest manifestation of State-controlled bus ownership, in succession to the British Transport Commission, namely the National Bus Company; therefore, these three Guy Arabs had the distinction of being the only BBW bodied buses to serve the NBC! In 1967, incidentally, the company had bought a bare Guy Arab III chassis from a scrap dealer, for modernising and rebodying in their ongoing programme; as it happened, the bus had previously been United Welsh 1201, one of the pair that had carried BBW DD19 bodies.

A small number of BBW-bodied single-deckers was exported after Bristol Tramways had finished with them. A few with wartime Bence-built bodies found their way to Cyprus, some with 1951-Style bodies to Southern Rhodesia, but the furthest travelled was a 1939 L-Type, CFH 608. This bus took a product of BBW half way round the world in 1954, to Japan, with the Women's Voluntary Service (WVS). They were giving aid to that country, still struggling to recover from its devastation by the atom bombs which had been dropped in 1945.

Bringing the story up to the 1990s, bus enthusiasts are nowadays keen to preserve old buses and are remarkably able to restore them to their former glory. Happily, some BBW bodies are among these even if the choice of coachwork was more by chance than design. A list of BBW bodies that survive in 1999 appears among the Appendices.

**294**. It was mentioned in Plate 235 that Longwell Green built five new lowbridge bodies in 1946 for mounting on 1936 GO5G chassis. The bodies displaced from these chassis were all-metal products. Doubtless, they were still structurally sound and it was decided to use them to replace a miscellany of early-1930s bodies on the five oldest G-Types in the fleet, C3000-4. This view shows C3000 (HY 3630), which had chassis G.101 built in 1931 and which originally carried the BBW piano-fronted body shown in Plate 152. In this late-1940s view, C3000 is carrying the 1936 **AM6-Type** body from 3040 (CHY 117). In 1950, the chassis was again to be rebodied, this time gaining a new structure by ECW. *(Mike Mogridge)*

**295**. In 1949, as described in the text at the start of this chapter, BT&CC was permitted to receive 12 new L5G chassis, provided it could be proved that an equal number of old buses had been scrapped. In order to do this, the 12 new L5Gs received bodies that were transferred from 1930/31 B-Type chassis. These bodies were wartime utility **S14-Type** bodies that had been built by Bence and as seen in Plate 233. To fit the new L5Gs, the S14s had to be lengthened and rebuilt at the front. Lengthening was achieved by the insertion of a short bay amidships – this was 12 years before a similar but much more widely publicised arrangement was used to obtain extra length on London Transport Routemasters! It was not only the bodies that were transferred from the B-Types, as the 1930/31 registration numbers came with the bodies; seen here outside Bath Abbey is Bath Services' 2297 (HW 9059). The body and registration came from 377, which had chassis number B.599. *(S.N.J.White, courtesy Roy Marshall)*

**296**. In 1950/51, a start was made at withdrawing from service BT&CC's pre-war K5Gs, other than those which had been given new 1949-Style bodies. The DD5/DD6 series of bodies on 11 of the earliest K5Gs to be withdrawn were then chosen to be transferred to wartime chassis, in place of utility bodies. The receiving chassis in most cases were Guy Arabs. Among them was one of several Arabs run by Cheltenham District Traction Company, a former Red & White subsidiary now under BT&CC administration. This picture of 54 (FAD 255), taken in April 1953, shows the combination of 1944 Guy Arab II chassis and 1938 BBW body, painted in CDTC's dark-red livery. In fact, Cheltenham's 54 was one of only two Guys that did not receive a Bristol PV2 radiator at the time of rebodying. *(R F Mack)*

**297**. All but nine of BBW's 49 metal-framed 1950- and 1951-Style bodies were chosen to be transferred, in the mid-1950s, from their J-Type chassis to later L-Types. Most replaced early post-war ECW bodies, whose wooden framework was showing signs of deterioration. The **1950-Style** body shown here can be seen, by the extra beading along the side, to have been built as one of the ten coaches as shown

in Plate 255. All ten were re-equipped by late 1954 with 35 bus seats and repainted in bus livery, the polished beading being overpainted. This body was originally on JO6A 2205 (DHY 657) – see Plate 256. In November 1958, the body was transferred to 2382 (KHY 383), a 1948 L6B whose original ECW body, by chance, had also been built as an Express-service coach and had also undergone the demotion to bus duties. With this 1950 BBW body, 2382 remained in service until 1965 (sister vehicles that were not rebodied were sold in 1960/61). This bus and 2381 (KHY 382), which had received a 1951-Style body, became the last BBW-bodied buses to remain in service in the Bristol fleet! Happily, 2382 then passed into preservation and, interestingly, carries its original coach-style livery again. *(Allan Macfarlane)*

**298**. A Bristol chassis, a Bristol engine, a Bristol registration and a Bristol coat-of-arms on the side of its Bristol body ... yet the bus was photographed in Swindon! 2384 (LHT 902) was a 1948 L6B that, like the bus in the plate above, was built with an ECW Express-service body. The **1950-Style** BBW bus body was built on a 1937 JO5G chassis (2065: EHT 99) and was transferred to the L6B in November 1958. It was pictured in September 1962, with a year of service still ahead of it, yet the 1948 Ls that retained their original timber-framed ECW bodies had been withdrawn in 1960. *(Allan Macfarlane)*

**299**. Seven of the 1950/51-Style BBW bodies, and one of the 1949 ECW examples, were rebuilt during or soon after mounting on the L-Type chassis, to enable the buses to work under 'one-man-operation', with the driver taking the fares. Seen here is a **1951-Style** body, transferred from 1934 J-Type 2359 (AHU 807) to 1948 L-Type 2385 (LHT 903). The body had been rebuilt by eliminating the rear doorway, providing a new entrance at the front, complete with folding doors across the foot of the steps, cutting away the front bulkhead behind the cab and installing an angled window between the bulkhead and the cab nearside window, to facilitate the driver's collection of fares. The seating capacity remained at 35. Note the neat installation of a narrow window between the doorway and the first main side window and the removal of the Autovac fuel-feed tank from the bulkhead, as a conventional fuel pump had been fitted. 2385 is shown at Weston-super-Mare Station on service 93, the company's first route to be converted to one-man working. *(M.J.Tozer)*

**300**. Among the bodies chosen to be replaced by the metal-framed bodies exemplified in the previous three plates were five of the **1949-Style** BBW bodies on 1938/39 L-Type chassis. This picture was taken in April 1956 at BT&CC's Lawrence Hill depot and shows the seven-year-old dual-doorway body from 2122 (FHT 257) dumped on the J-Type chassis frame of 2376 (CHT 333), after it had been displaced by the latter's ECW body of exactly the same age, but benefiting from metal framework. Alongside is the 1941 BBW **S6-Type** body from 2162 (HAE 12), placed on the frame of JO6A 2204 (DHY 656), whose 1950-Style former-coach-seated body had gone on to a modernised 2162. Unexpectedly, the combination of the engineless chassis with the 1949-Style body did

see further use after sale, as it became a site hut at the Chittening Industrial Estate near Avonmouth, being placed just too far from the guarded gateway to be clearly identified by one young enthusiast; a return trip with binoculars did the trick! Note this body had a side destination box – at least one 1951 body was also built with this redundant item! *(B.V.B.G.)*

**301**. The two **1949-Style** bodies built for Red & White, as shown in Plate 252, were regarded as being of better quality than the 1947 Pickering bodies on two more of their Albion Valkyrie CX13 chassis. So, in 1957, the two were transferred from S1437 and S3838 to S20/1747 (FWO 652/49). The body illustrated previously is therefore seen again here, after transfer. Compared to the insert picture in Plate 258, this view shows the slightly raised wind-screen, the longer cab leading side window and revised shape to the cab door, due to the Albion chassis configuration. *(R.H.G.Simpson)*

**302**. The acquisition by major operators of second-hand BBW-bodied buses for further use was uncommon. When BT&CC withdrew their 1941 batch of dual-doorway City-fleet L5Gs in 1952, three of them were bought by Pontypridd Urban District Council, where the Bristol/BBW combination was already well known. Seen here is 66 (HAE 20, formerly C2709). Pontypridd did not require to use the front doorways, so these were sealed shut. Note the sign 'No Entry' on the front door – a sliding unit that had been fitted in 1946. The three L5Gs remained in Pontypridd's service until 1957. *(Roy Gingell/B.V.B.G.)*

**303**. The Southern Vectis Omnibus Company was faced with providing considerably enhanced services when railways on the Isle of Wight were closed down from 1952. Late in 1955, 14 pre-war K5Gs were bought from Bristol Tramways to cater for the biggest conversion; most were BBW-bodied. Southern Vectis 775 (FHT 811, formerly C3245) had a **DD6-Type** body and is seen here at Alum Bay. BT&CC and Southern Vectis both used Tilling-green livery. The device below the destination box is a small route-number holder. *(Allan Macfarlane Collection)*

**304**. Eastern Counties experienced a vehicle shortage in 1959 and bought three K5Gs from Bristol Omnibus Company (as BT&CC had become in 1958). The chassis were from the same batch as the Southern Vectis bus in the plate above, but these three carried **1949-Style** bodies. They were used on Norwich city services, where they were the first BBW-bodied buses to run since Eastern Counties had sent their ex-Norwich Electric Tramways B-Types with L1 bodies (Plate 94) to be rebodied by ECW in 1937. Eastern Counties LKH26 (FHT 806, formerly C3240 and also shown in Plate 247) is shown here. *(Dave Withers/B.V.B.G.)*

**305**. Happily, a small number of BBW-bodied buses has survived in preservation. The best known is the deep-blue and white 1940 Bristol Tramways K5G, C3336 (GHT 154). It has the sole surviving **DD6-Type** body (see also Plates 215 & 216). It was meticulously reconstructed by The Bristol Vintage Bus Group, taking up several years of the members' spare time ... not to mention several hundred pounds of their money! Preservation is immensely time-consuming and costly, but when the results turn out like this, there is the certainty of tremendous admiration at Rally sites each summer. *(Allan Macfarlane)*

**306**. Four of BT&CC's 1950-Style BBW metal-framed single-deckers are still around (two originally having been coaches, as mentioned in Plate 297) and one of these graces the cover. Only in 1998, though, did the Bristol Vintage Bus Group complete many more years of labour in restoring a **1947-Style S15** body. This bus, which was BT&CC's 2355 (AHU 803) and is mounted on a 1934 Bristol J-Type chassis, is shown here and can be compared with Plate 238. Another single-decker preserved is the S25-Type depicted in Plates 280 & 281. *(B.V.B.G.)*

**307**. Other than the B.V.B.G.'s DD6 shown in Plate 305, only one BBW double-decker is known to survive. Fittingly, it is an example of the large number of bodies built for Red & White. Of interest, however, it is one of only five **DD18-Types** to be built. Originally Red & White L442 (EWO 467), it was one of several of their Guys to be sold in later life for further service with Provincial, the Gosport & Fareham Omnibus Company. In preservation, the bus was restored to carry the emerald-green Provincial livery, as number 77. *(Allan Macfarlane)*

**308**. This photograph, which was taken in July 1991, illustrates the oldest BBW body known to survive, as well as giving an idea of the extent of the work required to bring a long-neglected specimen back to pristine condition. West Riding placed 142 (HL 1803) in service in 1924, with **HA-Type** 32-seat front-entrance bodywork built at the Bristol Aeroplane Company's plant in Filton. The body was found languishing and overgrown in a yard in West Yorkshire in the 1980s and is being worked upon as time permits. *(Ian Hunter)*

# Listings of BBW Body Production

In the following lists, the code entered under the heading 'Layout' is that adopted throughout the bus-enthusiast world to describe the configuration and seating capacity of a body. In the code, the initial letter means the following:-

B     single-deck Bus, for stage carriage work.
C     Coach, with high-backed seats for long-distance or tourist work.
Ch    Char-à-banc, for outings, with continuous seating across the width of the vehicle and no central gangway.
FB    Fully-fronted Bus, where there is a full-width cab when the chassis design also caters for a half-cab.
H     Highbridge double-decker, with central gangways on both decks.
L     Lowbridge double-decker, with a sunken, offside upperdeck gangway and lowered roof-line.
UB    Utility specification Bus, built while World War II restrictions applied.
UH    Utility Highbridge double-decker, also built to Wartime specification.

The numerical part of the code indicates the seating capacity. In double-deck bodies, the capacity of the upper saloon is shown 'over' that for the lower saloon, e.g. 30/26 means 30 seats upstairs, 26 down. The final letter or letters relate to the entrance position:-

F     Front entrance, either close behind the engine and front wheel or, after 1950, ahead of a set-back front axle.
R     Rear entrance.
C     Central entrance.
D     Dual doorways (front and rear).
RO    Rear entrance on a double-decker featuring an exposed 'Outside' staircase.
RD    Rear entrance double-decker with doors added to the rear platform.
8     An eight-foot-wide body on an earlier chassis built for 7ft 6in wide bodywork.

## Initial Production, 1907-1915

Note: All but one were built for BT&CC. Only passenger bodywork is listed.

A great deal of research has been undertaken over many years into the vehicles listed in this section, from photographs and surviving records. A small number of vehicles have eluded positive identification, but the list here is believed to be reasonably accurate.

| BODY NAME or Description | LAYOUT | CHASSIS TYPE | DATES | REGISTRATIONS | NOTES | GRAND TOTAL |
|---|---|---|---|---|---|---|
| Char-à-banc | B27R, convertible to Ch32 | 1906 Thornycroft Type 80 | 3 & 4/07 | AE 727, 729 and ? | *1* | 3 |
| All-Seasons Char-à-banc | "    "    " | "    "    " | 8 & 10/07 | AE 725 & ?729 | *1* | 2 |
| Small Bus | B16F | Type C40 | 5-7/08 | AE 770-775 (second issue) | | 6 |
| Large Closed Saloon | B28R | 1906 Thornycroft 80 | 7/09-6/10 | AE 726/30-3/6? | | 6 |
| Small Bus | B16F | Type C40 | 4-11/11 | AE 779/80 (2nd issue), AE 1155/9 | 2 | 4 |
| Char-à-banc | Ch22 | Type C40 | 6/11 | AE 1156-1158 | | 3 |
| Open Touring | B27F, convertible to Ch32 | Type C60 | 1 (&3?)/12 | AE 2551 (& AE 2780?) | | |
| | | | 8/12 | Y 1589/90 | | |
| | | | 3-5/13 | Y 1887, AE 3187/9/93 | | ?8 |
| Large Bus | B28R | Type C60 | 1/12 | AE 2550/2/4 (?2555/6) | | |
| | | | 4/13 | AE 3188 | | ?6 |
| Small Bus | B16F | Type C40 | 4/12 | AE 2781 | | |
| | | Type C45 | 9/12 | AE 770 (3rd issue) | | |
| | | Type C40 | /13 | AE 3186 | | 3 |
| Composite | B20F (conv to 22) | Type C45 | 8/12 | Y 1584 | | |
| | | "    " | 11/12 | AE 3163 | | |
| | | "    " | 3/13 | AE 3191 | | |

| BODY NAME or Description | LAYOUT | CHASSIS TYPE | DATES | REGISTRATIONS | NOTES | GRAND TOTAL |
|---|---|---|---|---|---|---|
| Composite (cont.) | B18F (conv to 20?) | Type C45 | 10/13 | AE 2784 | | |
| | unconfirmed | " " | 9-10/13 | AE 2785/6/8/9 | | 8 |
| Torpedo | Ch22 | Type C45 | 8-9/12 | AE 2773, AD 2571 | | |
| | | Type C60 | 1/13 | AE 3195 | | |
| | | Type C45 | 4 & 5/13 | FH 629 & AD 2788 | | |
| | | " " | 5-7/13 | AE 3180-3185, 2793-2799, Y 1990 | | 19 |
| *At Leek Lane:-* | | | | | | |
| Torpedo | Ch14 | Dennis 18hp | -/12 | Y 1583 | | |
| Hotel Bus | B14F | Dennis 30cwt | -/12 | AE 2424 (Lansdown Hotel, Bath) | | |
| | B8F | Lacre 1-Ton | -/12 | AE 2774 (Grand Hotel, Bristol) | | |
| | B10F | Dennis 15cwt | -/13 | AE 2787 (York House Hotel, Bath) | | |
| | B12R? | Lacre 30cwt | -/13 | AE 3178 (Royal Hotel, Bristol) | | |
| | B8F | Lacre 1-Ton | -/13 | AD 2789 (hotels in Cheltenham) | | 6 |
| *At Tram Depot (continued):-* | | | | | | |
| Motor Workshop | Aircraft repair van | Type MWS | 10/13 | French registration 8723-Z | *3* | 1 |
| Medium Closed Bus | B20F | Type C45 | 11/13 | AE 2782 | | 1 |
| Large Closed Bus | B28R | Type C65 | 12/13-1/14 | AE 3194/8/9 | | |
| | | Type C50 | 2-5/14 | AE 3196/7, 3781-3787 | | 12 |
| Torpedo | Ch28 | Type C50 | 5/14 | Imperial Tramways DC 495 | *4* | |
| | | | 5-8/14 | Y 2519-2522, FH 630, AD 2787, FB 041/2, AE 3788-3792 | *5* | 14 |
| Open Touring | B??F | Type C50 | 8-9/14 | AE 3793-3798 | *6* | 6 |
| Composite | B20F conv to 22 | Type C50 | 9-10/14 | Y 2523, FH 631, AE 3799, 3800, AE 4971/2 | | 6 |
| Unknown | B29R | Type W | 3/15 | AE 4973 | *7* | 1 |

Approximate total of BBW bodies built on new chassis in this period = 115
In addition, several chassis received new bodies at quite an early stage and several new chassis received second-hand bodies.

NOTES:

1 The term 'Char-à-banc' was applied by the company. The vehicles had fixed roofs and, in the case of the All-Seasons Char-à-banc, windows all round. When used on stage services, 27 seats were available, while extra seats could be fitted in the central gangway for outings, bringing the capacity to 32. Some 1907 bodies were remounted on new Bristol 4-tonner chassis in 1920.

2 The second issue of registrations AE 779/80 may have occured in 1909 and the chassis originally may have had cut-down double-deck bodies. AE 779 received a new B17F body in 1912.

3 The MWS was fully equipped as a mobile repair wagon for the British & Colonial Aeroplane Company's 'Bristol' military aircraft. The vehicle was driven without fault to Paris in December 1913 for exhibition at the Paris Salon, making the return journey in very snowy conditions.

4 The Imperial Tramways Torpedo was the first Bristol passenger vehicle to be supplied new to an operator other than the Bristol Tramways & Carriage Company itself.

5 Three other 28-seat Torpedos were built, in July/August 1914, and described as being in grey, but they were never registered. Their acquisition by the military authorities cannot be ruled out.

6 At least AE 3793/4 very quickly received second-hand Large Closed Bus B28R bodies.

7 The body from the Type W was transferred in 1920 to a new 4-Tonner chassis, registered HT 1516.

For a while, in 1914, body numbers were issued, in a series parallel to that used for chassis or stock numbers, but not in the same sequence.

# 4-Tonner chassis

| BODY CODE | LAYOUT | CHASSIS No. RANGE | DATES | CUSTOMER | REGISTRATIONS | NOTES | SUB-TOTAL | GRAND TOTAL |
|---|---|---|---|---|---|---|---|---|
| A | Ch28 | 1209-1385 | 1920-22 | BT&CC | HT 10xx through to HT 48xx, plus some FB, FH and YA | | 62 | 62 |
| B | B29R | 1249-1268 | 1920/21 | BT&CC | HT 20xx, plus FH and AD | | 12 | 12 |
| BAC-built B | B29R | 1217-1446 | 1920/21 | BT&CC | HT 15xx to HT 45xx, plus AD & FH | | 100 | |
| | | | 1921 | Bath Tramways 27 & 28 | FB 2558 and 2627 | | 2 | |
| | | | " | Middlesbrough Corpn. 86/7 | DC 2363/4 | | 2 | |
| | | | " | Devon Motor Transport | TA 1962/3, 2230/1 | | 4 | |
| | | | " | Powell & Gough, Ludlow | NT 546 | | 1 | 109 |
| BAC-built C | B30D | 1360, 1403-1549, + 1581-7/9-93 | 1922-24 | BT&CC | HT 53xx to HT 63xx | | 49 | |
| | | | | BT&CC | HT 15xx to HT 26xx | 8 | 12 | |
| | | | | West Riding 101-119 | HL 1320-5/73-82, 1430-32 | | 19 | |
| | | | | Devon Motor Transport | TA 4311/2, 5392/3, 5609-12, AF 8918/80/1, CO 6741/2 | | 13 | |
| | | | | Jersey Motor Transport 1-7 | J 958 through to J 2111 | | 7 | |
| | | | | Doncaster Corpn. 1-13 | WY 56xx to 88xx, WT 1519, 2834-6 | | 13 | |
| | | | | Corris Railway | FF 1445/6 | | 2 | |
| | | | | Rhondda 14 | NY 3450 | | 1 | |
| | | | | Graham, Kirkintilloch | SN 2646 | | 1 | |
| | | | | Demonstrator | HU 21 | | 1 | |
| | | | | Sunderland District 50, 51 | PT 2955/6 | | 2 | 120 |
| BAC-built HA | Various | 1534/60-80/ 94-1645 | 1924/25 | The Astley | NR 3534 | | 1 | |
| | | | | West Riding 139-150 | HL 1800-1811 | | 12 | |
| | | | | Manchester Corporation | ND 6234-7, 8183, 8201 | | 6 | |
| | | | | Chesterfield Corp. 45-47 | NU 3644-6 | | 3 | |
| | | | | Devon Motor Transport | AF & CO, other than those above | | 18 | |
| | | | | BT&CC | HU 11xx & HU 1968 | | 6 | 46 |
| BAC-built HA | C31F | 1556 & 1641 | 1924 | BT&CC | HU 881-889 & 984 | | 10 | 10 |
| | Various | 1655 & 1744 | 1925/26 | BT&CC | HU 1969 through to HU 6611 | | 22 | |
| | | | | Chesterfield Corp. 52-4,64-74 | NU 6423 through to NU 8108 | | 14 | |
| | | | | Rhondda 29-31 | NY 8869-8871 | | 3 | |
| | | | | Doncaster Corp. 20 | WU 2851 | | 1 | |
| | | | | West Riding 201-212 | HL 2657-2668 | | 12 | |
| | | | | Aberdare U.D.C. 37 & 36 | NY 9631 & 9777 | | 2 | |
| | | | | West Hartlepool Corp. 2, 3 | EF 3252/3 | | 2 | 56 |
| J | B29D | 1745-9/63/4/95-9 | 1926/27 | BT&CC | HU 6628 through to HU 8153 | | 12 | 12 |

Total number of BBW/BAC bodies built on 4-Tonner chassis = 427

NOTES:

8    These twelve bodies were mounted on 1920 chassis which had originally carried 1907-1915 bodies.

# 2-Tonner chassis

| BODY CODE | LAYOUT | CHASSIS No. RANGE | DATES | CUSTOMER | REGISTRATIONS | NOTES | SUB-TOTAL | GRAND TOTAL |
|---|---|---|---|---|---|---|---|---|
| Unknown | Ch20 | 0101 | 1923 | Demonstrator | HT 6520 | | 1 | 1 |
| FB | FB24F | 0102 (lwb) | 1923 | Demonstrator | HT 6524 | | 1 | 1 |
| BAC-built FB | FB20F | 0106 & 0227 | 1923/24 | Doncaster Corp. 21/2 | WT 982/1 | | 2 | |
| | | | | Devon Motor Transport | TA 8114-8119 | | 6 | |
| | | | | West Riding 151-200 | HL 1776-9, 1812-9, 2006-43 | 9 | 50 | |
| | | | | BT&CC | HT 9967-70/2 | | 5 | |
| | | | | Lancashire United 71/2 | TC 9786 & 9812 | | 2 | 65 |
| " | FB24F | 0108 (lwb) | 1923 | St Helens Corporation 51 | DJ 1871 | | 1 | |
| " | " | 0124 (lwb) | 1923 | BT&CC | HT 8171 | | 1 | 2 |
| FB | " | 0238/44/6/53(lwb) | 1925 | West Hartlepool Corpn. 7-10 | EF 2807-10 | | 4 | |
| " | " | 0251/2 (lwb) | 1925 | BT&CC | HU 3515/6 | | 2 | 6 |
| " | FB20F | 0241, 0291 & 0302/3 | 1925/26 | BT&CC | HU 2121 through to HU 6623, & YB 2170/1, 2963 | | 18 | 18 |
| " | FB16F | 0287 | 1926 | BT&CC/Grand Hotel | HU 6124 | | 1 | 1 |
| BAC-built | FC20F | 0122/32-77 | 1923/24 | BT&CC | HT 9745 through to HU 16 | | 47 | 47 |
| BB | B20F | 0297 & 0314 | 1927 | BT&CC | HU 8170 through to HW 7 | | 11 | 11 |
| CB | B20F | 0343 & 0353 | 1929 | BT&CC | HW 5640-3, 6038/9 | | 6 | 6 |
| Unknown | C20F | 0315/44 & 0355 | 1928/9 | BT&CC | HW1630, 5638/9/50, 6031/46/7 | | 7 | 7 |
| AM2 | B20F | 0356-0366 | 1932 | BT&CC | HY 7641-7651 | | 11 | 11 |

Total number of BBW/BAC bodies built on 2-Tonner chassis = 176

NOTES:

9      The total includes the second body on chassis 0101, which became HL 1778.

**309**. At the 1925 Commercial Show, Bristol exhibited a 2-Tonner complete with **FB-Type** bodywork, among other products. The bus is seen here, with Bristol registration HU 4327, after painting in the colours of Bangor Blue Motors Ltd of Bangor, Caernarvonshire. It was placed on hire to this operator from December 1925 to March 1926. The low winter sunlight shows up the arrangement of the front doorway.

# A-Type chassis

| BODY CODE | LAYOUT | CHASSIS No. RANGE | DATES | CUSTOMER | REGISTRATIONS | NOTES | GRAND TOTAL |
|---|---|---|---|---|---|---|---|
| Unknown | FB32D | A.101 | 1925 | BT&CC | HU 4325 | | 1 |
| Unknown | H26/26RO | A.109-114 | 1927 | Manchester Corporation | NF 4078-80, 4143-5 | | 6 |
| Unknown | B36R | A.115/22/3 | 1927/28 | Bath Tramways | FB 5890, 6700/1 | | 3 |

Total number of BBW bodies built on A-Type chassis = 10

# B-Type chassis

with 'square-edged' bodies

| BODY CODE | LAYOUT | CHASSIS No. RANGE | DATES | CUSTOMER | REGISTRATIONS | NOTES | SUB-TOTAL | GRAND TOTAL |
|---|---|---|---|---|---|---|---|---|
| AB | B30D | B.101 | 1926 | BT&CC | HU 9991 | 10 | 1 | 1 |
| Unknown | C26D | B.146/7/9-157 | 1927 | BT&CC | HU 9646, HW 8-10, 151-3/7-60 | | 11 | |
| | | B.148 | 1928 | Baxter, Clapham Common, 3 | YV 3659 | | 1 | 12 |
| L1 | B30D | B.198 & B.415 | 1927-30 | BT&CC | HW 641 through to HW 8361-3 | | 42 | |
| | | B.208/15/25 | 1927 | Rhondda 47, 49 & 48 | TX 4436/4/2 | 11 | 3 | |
| | | B.241/3 | 1928 | Bradford Corporation 338/7 | KW 3577/6 | | 2 | |
| | | B.242/52/3, B.352 | 1928/29 | Wigan Corporation 31, 35-37 | EK 6282, 6323/4, 6409 | 12 | 4 | |
| | | B.244 | 1928 | Doncaster Corporation 33 | DT 799 | | 1 | |
| | | B.245/56/7 | 1928 | Jersey Motor Transport 16-18 | J 4326/47/53 | | 3 | |
| | | B.277/81 | 1928 | Norwich Electric T'ways 15, 16 | VG 378/9 | | 2 | |
| | | B.307-10/13 | 1928 | Rhondda 51-55 | TX 6379/81/3/5/7 | | 5 | |
| | | B.373 | 1929 | Merseyside Touring Co 72 | EM 2303 | | 1 | 63 |
| L2 | B30D | B.158/61/2, 332, 406 | 1927-29 | Aberdare UDC 40, 32/9/4/5 | TX 4105/9/7, 5854, 7998 | | 5 | |
| | | B.311 | 1928 | Demonstrator | HW 3107 | 13 | 1 | 6 |
| L3 | B32F | B.283/4 | 1928 | St Helens Corporation 17, 18 | DJ 3648/9 | | 2 | |
| | | B.392-403 | 1929 | West Riding 256-267 | HL 4131-4142 | | 12 | |
| | | B.550 & 575 | 1929 | BT&CC | HW 62xx through to HW 68xx | | 23 | |
| | | B.553 | 1929 | Demonstrator | HW 6638 | 14 | 1 | 38 |
| EB | B32R | B.181-195 | 1927 | Manchester Corporation | NF 7810 through to NF 8709 | | 15 | 15 |
| EB4 | B30C | B.238 | 1928 | Chesterfield Corporation 84 | RA 4279 | | 1 | 1 |
| M | B32R | B.287-91/7-303 | 1928 | Manchester Corporation | VM 1965 through to VM 3256 | | 12 | 12 |
| MA | B34R | B.315-326 | 1928 | Bradford Corporation 341-352 | KW 4360-4371 | | 12 | |
| | B32R | B.404/5 | 1929 | Merthyr Tydfil Corpn. 20, 21 | HB 3474/5 | | 2 | 14 |
| Unknown | C26D | B.305/14/55 | 1929 | BT&CC | HW 6032/3/5 | | 3 | |
| | | B.407 | 1929 | Baxter, Clapham Common, 1 | UU 3129 | | 1 | 4 |
| N | C26F | B.334 & B.343 | 1929 | Greyhound, Bristol | HW 3642-50 | | 9 | |
| | | B.338 | 1929 | Demonstrator | HW 3864 | 15 | 1 | |
| | C32F | B.333/44 | 1929 | West Riding 268 & 269 | HL 4218/9 | | 2 | 12 |
| L8 | B30D | B.378 | 1930 | BT&CC | HW 8366 | | 1 | 1 |
| L9 | B31D | B.596/8/9, 603/4 | 1930 | BT&CC | HW 8369/70, 9058/9/63 | | 5 | 5 |
| P1 | B26C | B.638-641 | 1930 | Pontypridd UDC 1-4 | TX 9539/41/3/5 | | 4 | 4 |

Total number of BBW bodied B-Type chassis in this section = 188

NOTES:

10    The AB body was transferred in April 1930 from B.101 to D.101, which, in July 1930, was re-engined and renumbered B.777 (HY 1969).

11    Rhondda TX 4432/4/6 have not been verified as L1 and have also been quoted as seating B32R.

12    Wigan Corporation's EK 6323/4 were delivered in primer, for final painting to be undertaken at Wigan.

13    Demonstrator HW 3107 was sold to Aberdare UDC 33 in December 1928.

14    Demonstrator HW 6638 was sold to Merseyside Touring Company 74 in January 1930.

15    Demonstrator HW 3864 was sold to Merseyside Touring Company 34 in June 1929.

# B-Type and D-Type chassis

with 'rounded' bodies

| BODY CODE | LAYOUT | CHASSIS No. RANGE | DATES | CUSTOMER | REGISTRATIONS | NOTES | SUB-TOTAL | GRAND TOTAL |
|---|---|---|---|---|---|---|---|---|
| L4 | B30F | B.580-594 | 1930 | West Riding 293-307 | HL 4536-4550 | | 15 | |
| | B26F | B.595/7 | 1930 | Stockton-on-Tees Corpn. 9 & 10 | UP 3712/3 | | 2 | 17 |
| L5 | B32D | B.600 | 1929 | Demonstrator | | 16 | 1 | |
| | | B.601/2/6 | 1930 | Merthyr Tydfil Corpn. 22-24 | HB 3589/90, 3649 | | 3 | |
| | | B.628/34 | 1930 | Aberdare U.D.C. 38 & 37 | TX 9957 & 9392 | | 2 | 6 |
| L10 | B31D | B.611 & B.700 | 1930/31 | BT&CC | HW 9065 through to HY 1968 | | 26 | |
| | | B.652/4/5, B.703 | 1930 | Greyhound, Bristol | HY 340, 731-3 | | 4 | |
| | | B.715 | 1930 | Demonstrator | HY 734 | 17 | 1 | |
| | | B.698 | 1930 | Bence, Hanham | DG 1432 | 18 | 1 | |
| | | B.615 | 1930 | The Astley, Broughton Astley, 9 | UT 7300 | | 1 | |
| | | D.101/2/4 | 1930 | Demonstrators | HY 747, HY 20 & HY 1284 | 19 | 3 | |
| | | B.774, B.815 | 1931/32 | Aberdare U.D.C. 30 & 29 | TG 2175, 4356 | | 2 | |
| | | B.866/7 | 1933 | "       "       27 & 28 | TG 5569/8 | | 2 | 40 |
| Q | C30F | B.633/51 | 1930 | Graham, Kirkintilloch 4 & 6 | SN 5014/62 | | 2 | |
| | | D.118 | 1931 | "       "       20 | SN 5304 | | 1 | 3 |
| L7 | B30D | B.384 | 1930 | BT&CC | HY 325 | | 1 | 1 |
| L10-1 | B31D | B.101 & B.385 | 1930 | BT&CC | HU 9991 & HY 335 | 20 | 2 | 2 |
| L6-1 | B32F | B.561 | 1931 | BT&CC | HY 1961 | 21 | 1 | |
| | | B.612 & B.773 | 1931 | BT&CC | HY 1953 through to HY 3453 | | 22 | |
| | | B.702/13/25 | 1931 | Bence, Hanham | DG 2208-10 | 18 | 3 | |
| | | B.704/19 | 1931 | Coast Line, Musselburgh | SY 4506/7 | | 2 | |
| | | B.712 | 1931 | Demonstrator | HY 2396 | 22 | 1 | |
| | B30F | B.737-748 | 1931 | West Riding 326-337 | HL 4861-4872 | | 12 | |
| | | B.790 | 1931 | Doncaster Corporation 39 | DT 3296 | 23 | 1 | 42 |
| L6-2 | B30F | D.106 & D.136 | 1931 | BT&CC | HY 3442 through to HY 4237 | | 14 | |
| | | D.107-9/12-4 | 1931 | Rhondda 72 to 77 | TG 1780/2/4, 1844-6 | | 6 | |
| | | D.115 | 1931 | Greyhound, Bristol | HY 2399 | | 1 | 21 |
| Q1 | C26F | D.103/5 | 1931 | Demonstrators | HY 1952 & HY 6227 | 24 | 2 | |
| | | B.764/6-70 | 1931 | Greyhound, Bristol | HY 2701-4/8/9 | | 6 | 8 |
| XB | B32F | D.110 | 1931 | BT&CC | HY 3449 | | 1 | 1 |
| Q2 | C26F | D.119 & D.142 | 1932 | BT&CC | HY 2714 through to HY 6229 | | 11 | |
| | | D.140 | 1932 | Greyhound, Bristol | HY 6197 | | 1 | 12 |
| AM1 | B30D | B.705 & B.876 | 1932-34 | BT&CC | HY 6029 through to AHU 960 | 23 | 93 | |
| | B30D | D.111/43-50 | 1932 | BT&CC | HY 7423-7431 | | 9 | |
| | B31D | B.816/7 | 1933 | Coast Line, Musselburgh | SY 4730/1 | | 2 | |
| | B28D? | B.226 | 1935 | BT&CC | BHU 635 | 25 | 1 | 105 |

Total number of BBW bodied B- and D-Type chassis in this section = 258
Combined total of BBW bodies on B-Type chassis = 397
Total number of BBW bodies on D-Type chassis = 49

NOTES:

16     Demonstrator B.600 was sold to Merthyr Tydfil Corporation 25 in January 1930 and registered HB 3569.

17     Demonstrator HY 734 was sold to BT&CC later in 1930.

18     The buses for Bence, Hanham, were delivered in primer for final painting by Bence. Bence had become a subsidiary of BT&CC in 1930.

19     Demonstrators HY 747, 20 & 1284 were sold to BT&CC in 1931/32.

20     The L10-1 body on B.101 replaced its original AB body, after the latter had been moved to D.101 – see Note 10.

21     Chassis B.561 was built in 1929 and supplied to Northern Counties for fitting with a coach body as their 1929 Show exhibit. This vehicle was returned to the MCW in May 1930, but the coach body was then transferred to chassis D.103. The latter was re-engined in July 1930 and renumbered B.778, passing to BT&CC for service as HY 4. B.561 then received a new L6-1 body in April 1931, for BT&CC.

22     B.712 demonstrated to Glasgow Corporation before being sold to BT&CC in August 1931.

23     The body on B.790 was originally mounted on B.705, which chassis was then used for development work, before receiving a new AM1 body (q.v.).

24     Demonstrators HY 1952 and HY 6227 were sold to BT&CC in May 1932.

25     B.226 was completed in November 1927 as an Instructional Chassis. It was brought up to service standards in 1935, when it received the AM1 body and was first registered.

# G-Type chassis

| BODY CODE | LAYOUT | CHASSIS No. RANGE | DATES | CUSTOMER | REGISTRATIONS | NOTES | SUB-TOTAL | GRAND TOTAL |
|---|---|---|---|---|---|---|---|---|
| Unknown | H24/24R | G.101 | 1932 | Demonstrator | HY 3630 | 26 | 1 | 1 |
| AM6 | H24/24R | G.104-109 | 1933-35 | BT&CC | AHW 74, BHT 530-534 | | 6 | |
| | H26/22R | GO5G.4 | 1934 | Demonstrator | AHY 418 | 27 | 1 | |
| | H28/24R | GO5G.28, 30 | 1935 | BT&CC | BHU 975, BHW 639 | | 2 | |
| | " | G.129-138 | 1935/36 | BT&CC | BHY 692-695, CAE 861-866 | | 10 | |
| | " | GO5G.62 & 127 | 1936 | BT&CC | CHU, CHW & CHY | | 24 | 43 |
| AM9 | H26/22R | GO5G.31-34 | 1935 | Exeter Corporation 45/8/7/6 | BFJ 155/8/7/6 | | 4 | 4 |
| DD1 | H24/24R | GO6G.1 | 1934 | Pontypridd U.D.C. 21 | TG 8256 | | 1 | |
| | " | GO6G.2 | 1934 | Aberdare U.D.C. 2 | TG 8389 | | 1 | |
| | H28/26R | GO6G.3 | 1934 | BT&CC | AHY 417 | | 1 | |
| | H26/26R | GO6G.5 | 1936 | Pontypridd U.D.C. 22 | BTX 88 | | 1 | 4 |
| DD2 | H26/28R | GO5G.128-137 | 1936 | BT&CC | DAE 369-378 | | 10 | |
| | H26/26R | GO5G.161-170 | 1937 | BT&CC C3059-C3068 batch | DHT 938-943, DHU 349-352 | | 10 | 20 |
| DD3 | H28/26R | GO5G.203-214 | 1937 | BT&CC 3070-3081 batch | EAE 281-289, 596-598 | | 12 | 12 |

Total number of BBW bodied G-Type chassis = 84

NOTES:

26    Demonstrator HY 3630 was sold to Greyhound, Bristol, in December 1932.

27    Demonstrator AHY 418 was sold to Doncaster Corporation 50 in May 1935.

**310**. To the order of Pontypridd Urban District Council, BBW built its fourth and final **DD1-Type** body in December 1936, on the last of only five GO6G chassis (GO6G.4 had received a Northern Counties body for Red & White of Chepstow). Although very similar to the 1934 DD1 shown in Plate 165, there was a revision to the layout of opening windows in the lower-deck and the farings to the canopy and platform were not so distinctive. The paintwork characteristic below the D-shaped upper-deck window was repeated, however. The seating capacity was increased by two (to 26) in each saloon and the lower-deck revision can be detected by the reduction in the length of the inward-facing seats over the rear wheel arches. These now accommodated three instead of four, to permit an extra pair of forward-facing seats to be installed on each side. This bus carried fleet number 22 and it was registered BTX 88.

# H-Type and J-Type chassis

and non-Bristol chassis sent for rebodying

| BODY CODE | LAYOUT | CHASSIS No. RANGE | DATES | CUSTOMER | REGISTRATIONS | NOTES | SUB-TOTAL | GRAND TOTAL |
|---|---|---|---|---|---|---|---|---|
| L11 | B31R? | J.101 | 1932 | Demonstrator | HY 6504 | 28 | 1 | 1 |
| AM3 | B36R | H.102 | 1933 | Demonstrator | HY 7537 | 29 | 1 | |
| | " | H.101 | 1933 | Development vehicle | AHW 393 | 30 | 1 | |
| | " | H.103-111 | 1933 | Western National 100-108 | FJ 8930-8938 | | 9 | |
| | B34D | J.112-121 | 1933 | BT&CC | HY 8251-8260 | | 10 | |
| | B36R | J.122 | 1933 | Demonstrator | HY 8339 | 31 | 1 | |
| | " | H.162/3 | 1934 | BT&CC | AHT 658/9 | | 2 | |
| | B34D | J.147-155/7/8 | 1934 | BT&CC | AHT 968-974, AHU 26, 503-505 | | 11 | 35 |
| AM5 | C26F | J.110/1/23-6 | 1933 | Greyhound, Bristol | HY 9377-9382 | | 6 | |
| | | J.129-146 | 1934 | BT&CC | AHU 801-811, AHW 534-540 | | 18 | 24 |
| AM8 | B31F | J.MW.1 | 1934 | Doncaster Corporation 44 | DT 4793 | | 1 | 1 |
| Q3 | C32F | JO5G.2 | 1934 | Graham, Kirkintilloch, 28 | SN 6309 | | 1 | 1 |
| Q4 | C32R | JO4D.1 | 1935 | BT&CC | BHU 294 | | 1 | |
| | | J.156 & J.JW.186 | 1935 | BT&CC | BHU 295, 388, 636-652 | | 19 | 20 |
| Unknown | C32R | 1928/29 Tilling-Stevens B10A2 | 1935/36 | Western/Southern National | DB 51xx/52xx, UF 3069, 3597 | | 40 | 40 |
| AM7 | B34D | J.NW.54-66/8/71 | 1935 | BT&CC | BHU 963-71/6-81 | | 15 | |
| | B32F | J.AX.1 | 1935 | BT&CC | BHW 429 | | 1 | |
| | | J.NW.67,69,70,72 | 1935 | BT&CC | BHW 430-433 | | 4 | |
| | B34D | JO6A.1 | 1936 | BT&CC | CAE 955 | | 1 | |
| | | J.NW.88, 89, 92 | 1936 | BT&CC | CHT 332/3/6 | | 3 | |
| | B32F | JO6A.2 | 1936 | BT&CC | CHU 413 | | 1 | |
| | B34D | J.NW.96/7 | 1936 | BT&CC | CHU 561/2 | | 2 | |
| | | J.JW.217-225 | 1936 | BT&CC | CHU 563-571 | | 9 | |
| | | J.NW.85 | 1936 | BT&CC | CHW 50 | | 1 | 37 |
| S1 | B34D | JO5G.15 | 1935 | Demonstrator | BHY 691 | 32 | 1 | |
| | | J.NW.90/1/3 | 1936 | BT&CC | CHT 334/5/7 | | 3 | |
| | | J.NW.94/5 | 1936 | BT&CC | CHU 559/60 | | 2 | |
| | | J.PW.1 | 1936 | BT&CC | CHW 49 | | 1 | |
| | | J.NW.86/7 | 1936 | BT&CC | CHW 51/2 | | 2 | 9 |
| L12 | B36F | J.NW.52/3 | 1935 | West Hartlepool Corpn. 14 & 16 | EF 5634/6 | | 2 | 2 |
| L13 | C28F | JO5G.41 | 1935 | Demonstrator | CAE 154 | 33 | 1 | 1 |
| Q5 | C26F | J.JW.226 | 1936 | BT&CC | CHW 567 | | 1 | 1 |
| S2 | B34R | JO5G.207 | 1936 | Demonstrator | CHY 821 | 34 | 1 | 1 |
| S3 | B34D | JO5G.289 & 522 | 1937 | BT&CC 2058-2081 batch | EHT 97-102, 536-553 | | 24 | |
| | | JO4D.2-7 | 1937 | BT&CC (Gloucester city) 1240-5 | BFH 502/3, 519/20, 504, 521 | | 6 | 30 |

Total number of BBW bodies on H-Type chassis = 13

Total number of BBW bodies on J-Type chassis = 150

Total number of BBW bodies on non-Bristol chassis = 40

NOTES:

28    Demonstrator HY 6504 was sold to BT&CC in June 1933.

29    Demonstrator HY 7537 was sold to BT&CC in February 1934.

30    Chassis H.101 was converted and renumbered as JO5G.1 before the bodied bus was displayed at the October 1933 Commercial Motor Show. It was sold to BT&CC in June 1934, when it was first registered.

31    Demonstrator HY 8339 was sold to BT&CC in May 1934.

32    Demonstrator BHY 691 was sold to BT&CC in November 1935.

33    CAE 154 was known as the Golden Demonstration Coach. It was later sold to BT&CC.

34    Demonstrator CHY 821 was later sold to BT&CC.

# K-Type chassis

pre-war-style production

| BODY CODE | LAYOUT | CHASSIS No. RANGE | DATES | CUSTOMER | REGISTRATIONS | NOTES | SUB-TOTAL | GRAND TOTAL |
|---|---|---|---|---|---|---|---|---|
| DD3? | H26/26R | K5G.42.1 | 1938 | BT&CC C3082 | EAE 280 | 35 | 1 | |
| | H28/26R | " " 12-23 | 1938 | BT&CC C3083-C3094 | EHU 218-229 | | 12 | 13 |
| DD4? | H30/26R | K5G.42.50/81-84 | 1938 | BT&CC C3095-C3099 | EHY 557-561 | | 5 | |
| | H28/28R | " " 85-101 | 1938 | BT&CC C3100-C3116 | EHY 562-578 | | 17 | |
| | H28/26R | " 45.23/4 | 1938 | Pontypridd U.D.C. 23 & 24 | DNY 684/5 | | 2 | 24 |
| DD5? | H28/28R | K5G.45.53 & 81 | 1938 | BT&CC C3145-9/56-61/8-73 | FHT 88-104 | | 17 | |
| | | " " 95 & 122 | 1938/39 | BT&CC C3174-C3201 batch | FHT 119-130, 241-256 | | 28 | 45 |
| Unknown | H30/26R | K5G.47.35-46 | 1939 | BT&CC C3216-C3227 | FHT 260-271 | | 12 | |
| | | " " 47-60 | 1939 | Bath Electric T'ways 3800-13 | GL 6601-6614 | | 14 | |
| | | GO5G.138-47/ 149-54 | 1939 | Bath Electric T'ways 3814-29 | DKN 31-46 | 36 | 16 | 42 |
| DD6 | H30/26R | K5G.47.94-100 | 1939 | BT&CC C3228-C3234 | FHT 794-800 | | 7 | |
| | | " 49.001-016 | 1939 | BT&CC C3235-C3250 | FHT 801-816 | | 16 | |
| | | " " 069-075 | 1939 | BT&CC C3251-C3257 | FHT 824-830 | | 7 | |
| | | " " 076 thro' to K5G.57.085 | 1939-42 | BT&CC C3258-92, 3604-09, C3317-53, 3620/1 | GAE 456-490, GHT 129-169, GHU 489/90, HHT 141/2 | | 80 | |
| | | K5G.53.044-046 | 1939 | Pontypridd U.D.C. 28-30 | ETG 138-140 | | 3 | 113 |

The following DD6 bodies were built in 1941/42 on earlier chassis whose original bodies had been damaged or destroyed by enemy action

| DD6 | H24/24R | G.105 | 1942 | BT&CC C3007 | BHT 530 | | 1 | |
|---|---|---|---|---|---|---|---|---|
| | H30/26R | GO5G.209/10 | 1941 | BT&CC 3076/7 | EAE 597, 286 | | 2 | |
| | | K5G.45.69, 72 | 1941 | BT&CC C3161/4 | FHT 98, 84 | | 2 | 5 |

Total number of BBW bodies built on new K-Type chassis in this period = 221

Total number of BBW bodies built on ex-M&D G-Type chassis = 16

Total number of BBW bodies for rebodying earlier chassis during the war = 5

NOTES:

35    To gain operational experience, chassis K5G.42.1 (EAE 280) entered service with the 1937 DD2 body from C3063 (DHT 942). This body was returned to DHT 942 in December 1937 and EAE 280 received its new body in 1938.

36    The GO5G chassis of DKN 31-46 were new in 1936 with bodies by Weymann for Maidstone & District and Chatham & District. The chassis were returned to BT&CC in 1938 in part-exchange for new K5Gs, which received the Weymann bodies, while the GO5G chassis received new BBW bodies for Bath Electric Tramways.

Around 1950, twelve of the DD5-DD6 bodies from BT&CC K5Gs were used to replace wartime Utility bodies, as follows:-

| | | | | | |
|---|---|---|---|---|---|
| Body from | C3156 (FHT 93) | in 6/51 | to 1944 Guy Arab II chassis of | Cheltenham District 54 (FAD 255) | |
| | C3157 (FHT 94) | in 9/51 | to 1943 Guy Arab I chassis of | 3641 (HHW 16) | |
| | C3170 (FHT 101) | in 7/51 | to 1943 " " " " | 3638 (HHW 13) | |
| | C3173 (FHT 104) | in 7/51 | to 1942 Unfrozen K5G chassis of | 3629 (HHU 890) | |
| | C3176 (FHT 121) | in 1/51 | to 1942 " " " | 3627 (HHT 148), displacing a BBW UH30/26R body | |
| | C3188 (FHT 245) | in 12/51 | to 1942 Guy Arab I chassis of | 3633 (HHU 355) | |
| | C3200 (FHT 255) | in 4/52 | to 1942 Unfrozen K5G chassis of | 3625 (HHT 146), displacing a BBW UH30/26R body | |
| | C3220 (FHT 264) | in 8/51 | to 1942 Guy Arab I chassis of | 3630 (HHU 352) | |
| | C3228 (FHT 794) | in 8/52 | to 1942 " " " " | 3636 (HHU 358) | |
| | C3230 (FHT 796) | in 7/52 | to 1943 " " " " | 3640 (HHW 15) | |
| | C3241 (FHT 807) | in 10/49 | to 1946 K6A chassis of | C3382 (JHT 21) | |
| | C3347 (GHT 165) | in 11/52 | to 1942 Guy Arab I chassis of | 3631 (HHU 353) | |

The body removed from C3241 in 1949 became available when the chassis was chosen to receive a new BBW '1949-Style' body (q.v.).

The Guy Arab chassis, while being prepared to receive the BBW bodies, were re-equipped with Bristol PV2 radiators, except for 3638 and Cheltenham District 54.

# L-Type chassis

pre-war-style production, plus non-Bristol chassis and chassis sent for rebodying

| BODY CODE | LAYOUT | CHASSIS No. RANGE | DATES | CUSTOMER | REGISTRATIONS | NOTES | SUB-TOTAL | GRAND TOTAL |
|---|---|---|---|---|---|---|---|---|
| Unknown | B31R | 1928/29 Tilling-Stevens B10A2 | 1937 | Keighley-West Yorkshire or York-West Yorkshire | WW 7102-7126 | | 25 | 25 |
| Unknown | B32R | 1929 AEC Reliance | 1937 | Southern National 2880/8/95 | DR 5112, YC 6651, TM 5265 | | 3 | |
| | | | | Western National 2879/81/7/91 | DF 7475, 7523, 7916/7 | | | |
| | | | | 3232/7-9/54 | DR 5386, 5697, 5580, 5623, 5527 | | | |
| | | | | 3253/75 | CV 420, 1320 | | 11 | |
| | | 1929 Leyland Tiger TS1 | 1937 | Southern National 3545/6 | DV 1072, DR 5476 | 37 | 2 | |
| | | 1929 Leyland Lion LT1 | 1937 | Western National 3434 | YC 6677 | | 1 | |
| | | 1930 Leyland Lion LT2 | 1937 | Western National 2938/9/41 | YC 8662/3, 8801 | | 3 | |
| | | | | Southern National 2971/4-8 | YC 8685, 8986/7, 9411-13 | | 6 | 26 |
| Unknown | B26F | Dennis Mace | 1937 | Western National 628-644 | CTA 521-537 | | 17 | 17 |
| S4 | B32D | L5G.43.1, 3, 64-68 | 1938 | BT&CC 2082-2088 | FAE 56-62 | | 7 | |
| | | " 44.66-75 | 1938 | Bath T'ways Mtr Co. 2237-46 | GL 6027-6036 | | 10 | |
| | | L4G.44.76-82 | 1938 | BT&CC (Gloucester city) 1246-52 | CFH 19-25 | | 7 | |
| | | L5G.44.103-105 | 1938 | BT&CC 2122-2124 | FHT 257-259 | | 3 | 27 |
| S5 | B32D | Dennis Lancet 2 | 1938/39 | BT&CC 2089-2091 | FHT 77/8/6 | | 3 | 3 |
| S6 | B32F | L5G.46.123-140 | 1939 | BT&CC 2125-2142 | FHT 272-289 | | 18 | |
| | | " " 141-150 | 1939 | Bath T'ways Mtr Co. 2250-9 | GL 6615-6624 | | 10 | |
| | | " 50.072-076 | 1941 | BT&CC 2161-2165 | HAE 11-15 | | 5 | |
| | | " " 077/80/3/91 | 1941 | Bath T'ways Mtr Co. 2260-3 | GL 7809-7812 | | 4 | |
| | | " " 081/2/4 | 1941 | Doncaster Corporation 18-20 | BDT 979-981 | | 3 | |
| | | " " 086-088 | 1941 | BT&CC (Gloucester city) 1259-61 | DFH 449-451 | 38 | 3 | |
| | | " " 079 & 092/56 | 1942 | BT&CC 2166, 2168 | HHT 149, 151 | 38,39 | 2 | 45 |
| Unknown | B32D | L4G.48.058-063 | 1939 | BT&CC (Gloucester city) 1253-8 | CFH 603-608 | | 6 | |
| | | L5G.50.078/85/9 & 081/56, 082/56, 084/56 | 1941 | BT&CC C2705-C2710 | HAE 16-21 | 39 | 6 | 12 |
| Unknown | B35R | L5G.52.019-031 | 1940 | Western National 323-335 | DOD 508-520 | | 13 | |
| | | " " 032-036 | 1940 | Southern National 336-340 | DOD 525-529 | | 5 | |
| | | H.103-122/32-5/47-61 | 1940-43 | Western National 100-138 | FJ 8930-8968 | | 39 | |
| | | L5G.52.027 | 1942 | Western National 331 | DOD 516 | 40 | 1 | 58 |
| Unknown | B36R | L5G.54.100 | 1940 | Pontypridd U.D.C. 16 | ETX 322 | | 1 | 1 |

Total number of BBW bodies on new L-Type chassis in this period = 103

Total number of BBW bodies built on new Dennis chassis = 20

Total number of BBW bodies for rebodying earlier chassis = 91

NOTES:

37    In March 1946, the body from 3545 was transferred to the Leyland Tiger TS2 chassis of 2874 (UU 1894).

38    The bodies on DFH 449 and HHT 149 originally had seating for 34.

39    The chassis of HAE 19-21 and HHT 151 were built to replace 50th Sanction L5Gs diverted due to the war to Doncaster (BBW S6-bodied BDT 979-981, as shown) and Rotherham Corporations; they took their chassis numbers, but with a suffix '/56', as they were authorised by Sanction 56.

40    DOD 516 was new with a BBW body in 1940, but received a similar body in 1942 after the original was destroyed by enemy action.

# Wartime utility production

on 'Unfrozen' or recent chassis

| BODY CODE | LAYOUT | CHASSIS No. RANGE | | DATES | CUSTOMER | REGISTRATIONS | NOTES | SUB-TOTAL | GRAND TOTAL |
|---|---|---|---|---|---|---|---|---|---|
| Unknown | UB36F | L5G.56.006 | | 1942 | Edinburgh Corporation X15 | DSF 987 | | 1 | |
| | UB34F | " | " 007/8 | 1942 | Western National 365/6 | GTA 390/1 | | 2 | |
| | UB34F | " | 50.090/56 | 1942 | BT&CC 2167 | HHT 150 | 41 | 1 | |
| Unknown | UH30/26R | K5G.57.001/2 | | 1942 | Pontypridd U.D.C. 17 & 18 | ETX 763/4 | | 2 | |
| | | " | " 004-009 | 1942 | BT&CC 3622-3627 | HHT 143-148 | | 6 | |
| | | " | " 020-3/47 | 1942 | Maidstone & District DH13-17 | GKR 743-747 | | 5 | |
| | | " | " 045/6 | 1942 | Colchester Corporation 35 & 36 | JPU 581/2 | | 2 | |
| | | " | " 048/9/60 | 1942 | Chatham & District 907-909 | GKR 748-750 | | 3 | |
| | | " | " 062 | 1942 | BT&CC 3628 | HHU 351 | | 1 | |
| | | " | 51.041, 53.068 | 1942 | BT&CC C3277 & 3607 | GAE 475 & GHT 132 | 42 | 2 | 2 |

NOTES:

41    See Note 39 above for explanation of the chassis-number of HHT 150.

42    The bodies on GAE 475 and GHT 132 replaced their original DD6 bodies which had been destroyed by enemy action.

---

**NOTE: In the tables that follow all bodies were built for BT&CC and all displaced bodies were by BBW, unless otherwise stated.**

---

# Wartime utility production

by Bence Motor Bodies of Longwell Green, for rebodying earlier chassis

Note: In many cases, the registration numbers are NOT in sequence with the fleet-numbers in the same block of vehicles.

| BODY CODE | LAYOUT | CHASSIS TYPE | BODYWORK DISPLACED | DATES | FLEET-NUMBERS | REGISTRATIONS | NOTES | SUB-TOTAL | GRAND TOTAL |
|---|---|---|---|---|---|---|---|---|---|
| S13 | UB37R | JO5G | AM3/36 | 1943 | 2000 | AHW 393 | | 1 | |
| | | JO4D | Q4/32 | 1943 | 2001 | BHU 294 | | 1 | |
| | | J (5LW) | Q4/32 | 1943-45 | 2029-37/47-55 | BHU 295, 388, 636/8-652 | 43 | 18 | |
| | | L5G | S6/32 | 1943 | 2126 | FHT 273 | | 1 | |
| | | " | Duple C32R | 1944 | 2155/56 | FHT 792/3 | | 2 | |
| | | J (5LW) | AM7/34 | 1945 | C2700 | CHW 50 | 43, 44 | 1 | 24 |
| S14 | UB34F | B-Type | London Lorries C26F | 1943? | 579-591/3 | HW 60xx, 62xx and 66xx | 45 | 14 | |
| | | | L9 | 1943/44 | 376-378 | HW 8369/70, 9059 | | 3 | |
| | | | Northern Counties version of L10 | 1944 | 381-5/91/4 | HW 9070, 9493/4/7/9, 9501/76 | | 7 | |
| | | | L10 | 1943 | 426 | DG 1432 (ex-Bence, Hanham) | | 1 | |
| | | | " | c.1944 | 436 | HY 1967 | | 1 | |
| | | | L6-1 | c.1944 | 445/7/8/51/4/63 | HY 1953/6, 2394/6/8, 3443 | | 6 | 32 |

NOTES:

43    In post-war years, many or all of the BHU-registered vehicles, together with CHW 50, received low-level PV2 radiators and bonnets.

44    The body on C2700 (CHW 50) was rebuilt in 1951 to UB34D.

45    Several S14 bodies were built with only 29 seats, arranged around the perimeter of the saloon to facilitate maximum standing space. They were fitted with the normal arrangement of seating at the end of the war.

In 1949, the S14 bodies and the registration numbers of HW 8369/70, 9059, 9493/9, 9576, DG 1432, HY 1953/6 and 2394/6/8 were transferred to new L5G chassis, to form buses numbered 2296/8/7/9, 2421/2/0/4/3/6/7/5, respectively.

# Early post-war production

by Longwell Green Coachworks, for rebodying earlier chassis.
NOTE: All were built for BT&CC and the displaced BBW bodies were all transferred to older chassis, as shown.

| BODY CODE | LAYOUT | CHASSIS TYPE | BODYWORK DISPLACED | DATES | FLEET-NUMBERS | REGISTRATIONS | NOTES | GRAND TOTAL |
|---|---|---|---|---|---|---|---|---|
| Unknown | L27/28R | GO5G | AM6 | 1946 | 3038/40/5-7 | CHY 115/7, 440-442 | *46* | 5 |

*The displaced 1936 AM6 bodies were transferred to the earliest G-Type chassis in the fleet, as follows:-*

| BODY FROM | RECEIVING CHASSIS | FLEET-NUMBERS | REGISTRATIONS | BODYWORK DISPLACED |
|---|---|---|---|---|
| 3038 | G.116 (5LW) | C3004 | HY 6896 | Beadle H52R |
| 3040 | G.101 (5LW) | C3000 | HY 3630 | BBW H48R |
| 3045 | G.114 (5LW) | C3003 | HY 6605 | Cowieson H51R |
| 3046 | G.103 (5LW) | C3001 | HY 3629 | Brush H48R |
| 3047 | G.119 (5LW) | C3002 | HY 6198 | Beadle H52R |

NOTES:
46    In October 1948, 3038/40/5-7 were transferred to Gloucester City Services and were renumbered L1515-9. The chassis were then fitted with low-level PV2 radiators and bonnets. In March 1951, the buses were transferred to Bath Tramway Motor Company and they were renumbered L3906-10. They were then fitted with AEC 7.7-litre engines. In August to October 1952, they were transferred back to BT&CC's Country Services fleet, but with new numbers L4151/0/2-4.

# Tilling Standard bodies – '1947-Style'

| BODY CODE | LAYOUT | CHASSIS Year & Type | BODYWORK DISPLACED | DATES | FLEET-NUMBERS | REGISTRATIONS | NOTES | GRAND TOTAL |
|---|---|---|---|---|---|---|---|---|
| S15 | B35R | 1933 J (5LW) | second-hand | 12/46 | 2371/3 | HY 9380/2 | *47* | |
| | | 1934 " | " " | " | 2353/65 | AHU 801, AHW 538 | | |
| | | 1933 " | AM3/34 | " | 2011/3 | HY 8254/6 | | |
| | | 1934 " | " | " | 2018/9 | AHT 968, AHU 26 | | |
| | | " " | second-hand | 1/47 | 2350/64 | AHW 540 & 537 | | |
| | | 1933 " | " | 5/47 | 2369 | HY 9378 | | |
| | | 1934 " | " | 6/47 | 2355 | AHU 803 | | |
| | | " " | " | 7/47 | 2356/60 | AHU 804/9 | | |
| | | " " | " | 11/47 | 2362 | AHW 535 | | |
| | | " " | " | 1/48 | 2354 | AHU 802 | | 16 |

Summary of buses rebodied with the '1947-Style' single-decker:
(in fleet-number order) 2011/3/8/9, 2350/3-6/60/2/4/5/9/71/3
(in registration-number order) HY 8254/6, 9378/80/2, AHT 968, AHU 26, 801-4/9, AHW 535/7/8/40

| BODY CODE | LAYOUT | CHASSIS Year & Type | BODYWORK DISPLACED | DATES | FLEET-NUMBERS | REGISTRATIONS | NOTES | GRAND TOTAL |
|---|---|---|---|---|---|---|---|---|
| Unknown | H30/26R | new Leyland Titan PD1 | | 8/47-1/48 | C4000-C4011 | KHW 241-250, 621/2 | *47* | 12 |

NOTES:
47    Several of the 1947-Style bodies were built or completed by Longwell Green Coachworks. The Bristol J-Type chassis were fitted with PV2 radiators in the late 1940s/early 1950s.

# Tilling Standard bodies – '1948-Style'

| BODY CODE | LAYOUT | CHASSIS Year & Type | BODYWORK DISPLACED | DATES | FLEET-NUMBERS | REGISTRATIONS | NOTES | GRAND TOTAL |
|---|---|---|---|---|---|---|---|---|
| Unknown | B35R | 1934 J (5LW) | AM3/34 | 3/48 | 2020/2 | AHT 969 & 971 | *48* | |
| | | 1935 " | AM7/34 | " | 2111 | BHU 967 | | |
| | | 1933 " | AM3/34 | 5/48 | 2012 | HY 8255 | | |
| | | 1934 " | " | " | 2027/8 | AHT 974, AHU 505 | | |
| | | 1933 " | " | 6/48 | 2014 | HY 8257 | | |
| | | 1935 " | AM7/34 | " | 2117 & 2193 | BHU 965 & 980 | | |
| | | " " | " | 7/48 | 2115 | BHU 963 | | |
| | | 1934 " | AM3/34 | " | 2021 | AHT 970 | | |
| | | 1933 " | " | 8/48 | 2015 | HY 8258 | | |
| | | 1934 " | second-hand | " | 2351 | AHW 534 | | |
| | | " " | AM3/34 | 9/48 | 2026 | AHT 973 | | |
| | | 1933 " | AM3/36 | 10/48 | 2007 | HY 8338 | | |
| | | " " | AM3/34 | " | 2009 | HY 8252 | | |
| | | 1934 " | " | " | 2025 | AHU 504 | | |
| | | 1935 " | AM7/34 | " | 2114 | BHU 977 | | |
| | | 1933 " | AM3/34 | 11/48 | 2010/6 | HY 8253/9 | | |
| | | 1936 " | AM7/34 | 12/48 | 2045 | CHU 570 | | |
| | | 1935 " | " | " | 2113/6/8 | BHU 976/64/8 | | |
| | | 1934 H (5LW) | AM3/36 | 1/49 | 2157 | AHT 659 | *48* | |
| | | 1935 J (5LW) | AM7/34 | 2/49 | 2112 | BHU 970 | | |
| | | " " | AM7/32 | " | 2119 | BHW 433 | | |
| | | 1933 " | AM3/34 | " | 2017 | HY 8260 | | |
| | | 1934 " | " | " | 2024 | AHU 503 | | |
| | | 1935 " | AM7/34 | 3/49 | 2110 | BHU 966 | | 3( |

Summary of buses rebodied with the '1948-Style' single-decker:
(in fleet-number order) 2007/9/10/2/4-7/20-2/4-8/45, 2110-9/57/93, 2351
(in registration-number order) HY 8252/3/5/7-60, 8338, AHT 659, 969-71/3/4, AHU 503-5, AHW 534, BHU 963-8/70/6/7/80, BHW 433, CHU 570

| BODY CODE | LAYOUT | CHASSIS Year & Type | BODYWORK DISPLACED | DATES | FLEET-NUMBERS | REGISTRATIONS | NOTES | GRAND TOTAL |
|---|---|---|---|---|---|---|---|---|
| Unknown | H30/26R | new Leyland Titan PD1 | | 1/48-10/48 | C4022-5/7-9/31 C4033/40/1/7/8 | KHY 391-4/6-8, 400 LAE 2, 9, 10, 16, 17 | | |
| Unknown | H30/26R | 1936 GO5G | DD2 | 7/48 | C3051/2/5 | DAE 376/5/2 | *48* | |
| | | 1932 G (5LW) | AM6 | 8/48 | C3003 | HY 6605 | *49* | |
| | | 1937 GO5G | DD2 | 9/48 | C3060 | DHU 351 | | 1( |

NOTES:
48     The G-Type, H-Type and J-Type chassis were fitted with PV2 radiators in the late 1940s/early 1950s.
49     The AM6 body was built in 1936 and was transferred to C3003 from 3045 (CHY 440) in 1946 – see 'Early post-war production', above.

# Tilling Standard bodies – '1949-Style' single-deckers

| BODY CODE | LAYOUT | CHASSIS Year & Type | BODYWORK DISPLACED | DATES | FLEET-NUMBERS | REGISTRATIONS | NOTES | GRAND TOTAL | REPLACEMENT BODY & DATE |
|---|---|---|---|---|---|---|---|---|---|
| S18 | B33D | 1938 L5G | S4/32 | 4/49 | 2082 | FAE 56 | *50* | | 1951-Style BBW B35R, 6/57 |
| " | " | " " | " | " | 2084 | " 58 | *50* | | |
| | | " " | " | 5/49 | 2122 | FHT 257 | | | 1949 ECW B35R, 4/56 |
| | | " " | " | " | 2123 | " 258 | | | 1950-Style BBW ex-coach B35R, 5/56 |
| | | " " | S6/32 | " | 2133 | " 280 | | | 1950-Style BBW B35R, 5/57 |
| u/k | B35R | 1939 L4G | code u/k | " | 1254 | CFH 604 | | | 1950-Style BBW ex-coach B35R, 2/57 |
| | | " " | " | " | 1255 | " 605 | | | |
| | | 1936 J (5LW) | AM7/34 | 6/49 | 2041 | CHU 566 | | | |
| | | " " | " | " | 2043 | " 568 | | | |
| | | 1937 JO5G | S3/34 | " | 2063 | EHT 547 | | | |
| | | " JO4G | " | 8/49 | 1243 | BFH 520 | | | |
| | | 1939 L4G | code u/k | " | 1253 | CFH 603 | | | |
| | | 1937 JO4G | S3/34 | " | 1244 | BFH 504 | | | |
| | | " " | " | 9/49 | 1245 | " 521 | | | |
| S18 | B33D | 1933 J (5LW) | AM3/34 | 1/50 | 2008 | HY 8251 | | | |
| | | 1936 " | AM7/34 | 2/50 | C2704 | CHU 562 | | | |
| | | 1932 " | second-hand | " | 2057 | HY 6504 | | | |
| | | 1936 " | S1/34 | " | C2702 | CHW 52 | | | |
| | | " " | " | 3/50 | C2701 | " 51 | | | |
| | | " " | AM7/34 | " | C2703 | CHU 561 | | | |
| | | " " | S1/34 | 4/50 | C2731 | " 560 | | 21 | |
| u/k | B35R | 1937 Albion | | | | Red & White | | | |
| | | Valkyrie | u/k | 3/50 | 331 | BAX 331 | *51* | | |
| | | 1938 " | " | 10/50 | 736 | EXF 263 | *51* | 2 | |

NOTES:

50   The bodies on 2082/4 featured side windows of the '1948-Style'.

51   In the 1951 Red & White fleet renumbering scheme, 331 and 736 became S1437 and S3838, respectively. In 3 & 6/57, the bodies were transferred to 1947 Albion Valkyries S20/1747 (FWO 652/49), respectively.

# Tilling Standard bodies – '1949-Style' double-deckers

| BODY CODE | LAYOUT | CHASSIS Year & Type | BODYWORK DISPLACED | DATES | FLEET-NUMBERS | REGISTRATIONS | NOTES | GRAND TOTAL |
|---|---|---|---|---|---|---|---|---|
| Unknown | H30/26R | 1938 K5G | DD3? | 12/48 | C3087/91 | EHU 222/6 | | |
| | | " | " | 1/49 | C3084/92 | " 219/27 | | |
| | | " | DD4? | " | C3097 | EHY 559 | | |
| | | " | DD3? | 2/49 | C3083/5/90 | EHU 218/20/5 | | |
| | | " | " | 3/49 | C3086/8/9 | " 221/3/4 | | |
| | | " | " | 4/49 | C3093 | " 228 | | |
| | | " | DD4? | 6/49 | C3095 | EHY 557 | | |
| | | " | DD3? | 7/49 | C3082 | EAE 280 | | |
| | | " | DD4? | " | C3107/9 | EHY 569/71 | | |
| | | " | " | 8/49 | C3104/8 | " 566/70 | | |
| | | " | DD3? | 9/49 | C3094 | EHU 229 | | |
| | | " | DD4? | " | C3111 | EHY 573 | | |
| | | " | " | 10/49 | C3103/12-4 | " 565/74-6 | | |
| | | " | " | 11/49 | C3105 | " 567 | | |
| | | 1939 K5G | DD6 | " | C3241 | FHT 806 | | |
| | | 1938 K5G | DD4? | 12/49 | C3110/5 | EHY 572/7 | | |
| | | 1939 K5G | DD6 | " | C3235/8/9 | FHT 801/4/5 | | |
| | | 1938 K5G | DD4? | 1/50 | C3099, C3116 | EHY 561/78 | | |
| | | " " | " | 2/50 | C3100/6 | " 562/8 | | |
| | | 1939 K5G | DD6 | " | C3237/40 | FHT 803/6 | | |
| | | " " | " | 3/50 | C3242 | " 808 | | 38 |

Summary of buses rebodied with the '1949-Style' double-decker:
C3082 (EAE 280), C3083-94 (EHU 218-229), C3095/7/9, C3100/3-16 (EHY 557/9/61/2/5-78), C3235/7-42 (FHT 801/3-8).

# Tilling Standard bodies – '1950-Style' single-deckers

| BODY CODE | LAYOUT | CHASSIS Year & Date | BODY DISPLACED | DATE | FLEET NOS. | REG. | NOTES | GRAND TOTAL | FURTHER USE FOR BODY & DATE | BODY DISPLACED | NOTES |
|---|---|---|---|---|---|---|---|---|---|---|---|
| u/k | C31R | 1937 JO6A | Duple C32R | 5/50 | 2202 | DHY 654 | 52 | | 1941 L5G 2171 (DFH 450), 2/56 | S6/32 | |
| " | " | " " | " | " | 2205 | " 657 | | | 1948 L6B 2382 (KHY 383), 11/58 | ECW | |
| | | " JO5G | " | " | 2207 | " 659 | | | | | |
| | " | " " | " | " | 2209 | " 661 | | | 1941 L5G 1259 (DFH 449), 2/57 | S6/32 | |
| | " | " " | S3/34 | " | 2060 | EHT 98 | | | 1947 L5G 2188 (JHT 843), 2/59 | ECW | 53 |
| | " | " JO6A | Duple C32R | 6/50 | 2201 | DHY 653 | | | | | |
| | " | " " | " | " | 2203 | " 655 | | | 1941 L5G 2161 (HAE 11), 2/56 | S6/32 | |
| | " | " " | " | " | 2204 | " 656 | | | 1941 L5G 2162 (HAE 12), 2/56 | S6/32 | |
| | " | " " | " | " | 2206 | " 658 | | | 1938 L5G 2123 (FHT 258), 5/56 | 1949-Style | |
| | " | " JO5G | " | " | 2208 | " 660 | | 10 | 1939 L5G 1254 (CFH 604), 2/57 | 1949-Style | |
| S20 | B35R | " " | S3/34 | 7/50 | 2067 | EHT 101 | | | 1939 L5G 2133 (FHT 280), 5/57 | 1949-Style | |
| | | 1934 J (5LW) | second-hand | 8/50 | 2358 | AHU 806 | | | 1947 L5G 2186 (JHT 841), 9/57 | ECW | 54 |
| | | 1937 JO5G | S3/34 | " | 2072 | EHT 552 | | | 1948 L6B 2378 (KHW 643), 11/58 | " | |
| | | " " | " | " | 2078 | " 540 | | | 1949 L5G 2424 (HY 1953), 6/57 | S14/34 | |
| | | " " | " | " | 1240 | BFH 502 | | | 1947 L5G 2183 (JHT 836), 2/59 | ECW | |
| | | " " | " | 9/50 | 2068 | EHT 102 | | | 1948 L5G 2383 (LHT 905), 4/57 | " | |
| | | 1934 J (5LW) | second-hand | 10/50 | 2366 | AHW 539 | | | 1947 L5G 2190 (JHT 845), 3/57 | " | |
| | | 1937 JO5G | S3/34 | " | 2059 | EHT 97 | | | 1947 L5G 2184 (JHT 837), 11/58 | " | |
| | | " " | " | " | 2065 | " 99 | | | 1948 L6B 2384 (LHT 902), 11/58 | " | |
| | | " " | " | " | 2069 | " 549 | | | 1946 L5G 2174 (JHT 827), 4/57 | " | |
| | | " " | second-hand | " | 2074 | " 536 | | | 1948 L5G 2388 (LHT 911), 10/58 | " | |
| | | " " | S3/34 | " | 2080 | " 542 | | | 1948 L5G 2393 (LHT 919), 10/58 | " | |
| | | " " | " | 11/50 | 2264 | " 551 | | 13 | | | |

NOTES:

52    The 1950 Express-service coach bodies were repainted in 1953 or 1954 into bus livery and all were reseated by October 1954 to B35R

53    The 1950 former coach body from 2060 was rebuilt at the time of mounting on to 2188 to B35F for one-man-operation. In the course of repanelling, the bodyside trim was removed, leaving only that at the rear.

54    The 1950 body from 2358 that was transferred to 2186 was rebuilt in March 1958 to B35F for one-man-operation.

# Tilling Standard bodies – '1951-Style' single-deckers

| BODY CODE | LAYOUT | CHASSIS Year & Date | BODY DISPLACED | DATE | FLEET NOS. | REG. | NOTES | GRAND TOTAL | FURTHER USE FOR BODY & DATE | BODY DISPLACED | NOTES |
|---|---|---|---|---|---|---|---|---|---|---|---|
| u/k | B35R | 1934 J (5LW) | second-hand | 11/50 | 2352 | AHU 811 | | | | | |
| | | 1937 JO5G | S3/34 | " | 2058 | EHT 544 | | | 1948 L5G 2272 (LHT 916), 11/58 | ECW | |
| | | " " | " | " | 2062 | " 546 | | | 1938 L5G 2082 (FAE 56), 6/57 | 1949-Style | 55 |
| | | " " | " | " | 2077 | " 539 | | | 1949 L5G 2422 (HW 9576), 8/57 | S14/34 | 56 |
| | | " " | " | " | 1242 | BFH 519 | | | 1948 L5G 2268 (LHT 907), 1/59 | ECW | |
| | | 1933 J (5LW) | second-hand | 12/50 | 2368 | HY 9377 | | | 1948 L5G 2391 (LHT 914), 11/57 | " | 56 |
| | | " " | " | " | 2372 | " 9381 | | | 1947 L5G 2185 (JHT 838), 2/58 | " | |
| | | " " | " | 1/51 | 2370 | " 9379 | | | 1949 L5G 2283 (LHW 922), 2/59 | " | |
| | | 1934 " | " | " | 2359 | AHU 807 | | | 1948 L5G 2385 (LHT 903), 9/57 | " | 56 |
| | | " " | " | " | 2361 | " 810 | | | 1949 L5G 2425 (HY 2398), 10/56 | S14/34 | |
| | | 1936 " | S1/34 | " | 2120 | CHT 335 | | | 1948 L6B 2381 (KHY 382), 2/59 | ECW | |
| | | 1937 JO5G | S3/34 | " | 2066 | EHT 100 | | | 1948 L5G 2270 (LHT 909), 11/57 | " | 56 |
| | | " " | Duple C32R | 2/51 | 2210 | DHY 662 | | | 1947 L5G 2189 (JHT 844), 4/57 | " | |
| | | " " | " | " | 2212 | " 664 | | | 1946 L5G 2180 (JHT 833), 6/57 | " | |
| | | " " | " | 3/51 | 2211 | " 663 | | | | | 57 |
| | | " " | " | " | 2213 | " 665 | | | 1948 L5G 2389 (LHT 912), 6/57 | ECW | |
| | | " " | S3/34 | " | 2265 | EHT 553 | | | | | |
| | | " " | " | " | 2266 | " 543 | | | | | |
| | | " " | " | " | 1241 | BFH 503 | | | 1947 L5G 2187 (JHT 842), 7/59 | ECW | |
| | | " " | second-hand | 4/51 | 2061 | EHT 545 | | | | | |
| | | " " | S3/34 | " | 2070 | " 550 | | | | | |
| | | 1934 J (5LW) | second-hand | 5/51 | 2357 | AHU 805 | | | 1949 L5G 2423 (HY 1956), 7/54 | S14/34 | |
| | | 1935 JO5G | L13 | " | 2006 | CAE 154 | | | 1947 L5G 2181 (JHT 834), 8/58 | ECW | |
| | | 1937 " | S3/34 | " | 2075 | EHT 537 | | | 1948 L6B 2377 (KHW 642), 2/59 | " | |
| | | " " | " | 6/51 | 2076 | " 538 | | | | | |
| | | 1936 JO6A | AM7/34 | " | 2003 | CAE 955 | | 26 | 1948 L6B 2269 (LHT 908), 2/57 | ECW | |

NOTES:

55    The 1951-Style body from 2062 that was transferred to 2082 was rebuilt in October 1957 to B35F for one-man-operation.

56    The 1951-Style bodies from 2066/77, 2359/68 were rebuilt at the time of mounting on to 2270, 2422, 2385/91 to B35F for one-man-operation.

57    After withdrawal from service, the 1951-Style body on 2211 was converted to a van with tail-lift, in 6/59, for company use; the vehicle was renumbered W94 in the 'Works Vehicle' series. In 3/60, the BBW van body was transferred to the 1949 L5G chassis of 2284 (LHW 907), to form vehicle number W96.

# Tilling Standard bodies – '1949-Style' double-deckers

for Red & White and United Welsh

| BODY CODE | LAYOUT | CHASSIS Date & Type | DATES | CUSTOMER | REGISTRATIONS | NOTES | GRAND TOTAL |
|---|---|---|---|---|---|---|---|
| unknown | L27/28R | 1942 Guy Arab I | Early 1951 | Red & White L142 | EAX 644 | | |
| | | 1943 " Arab II | " " | " " L1043 | EWO 491 | | |
| | | 1944 " " | 1 & 2/51 | " " L6/744 | EU 7696, 7840 | 58 | 4 |
| DD14 | H30/26R | 1940 Albion Venturer | 1950-10/51 | United Welsh 653-655 | DWN 157-159 | | 3 |
| DD17 | " | 1943 Guy Arab II | 3/51 | United Welsh 687 | EWO 497 | 59 | |
| | | 1944 " " | 11/51 | " " 678 | DWN 380 | | 2 |
| DD19 | " | new Guy Arab III | 5/51 | United Welsh 1200/1 | HCY 295/6 | | 2 |

NOTES:

58      Red & White L6/744 (EU 7696 & 7840) had been acquired from the related fleet of Griffin Motor Company, Brynmawr.

59      United Welsh 687 (EWO 497) had previously been transferred from Red & White.

# Tilling Standard bodies for Red & White and United Welsh, 1951-1954

| BODY CODE | LAYOUT | CHASSIS Date & Type | DATES | CUSTOMER | REGISTRATIONS | NOTES | GRAND TOTAL |
|---|---|---|---|---|---|---|---|
| DD18 | L27/28RD | 1942 Guy Arab I | 7-8/51 | Red & White L2/442 | EAX 645, EWO 467 | | |
| | | 1943 " Arab II | " | " " L11/1243 | EWO 493/4 | | |
| | | " " " 1 | 2/51 | " " L1643 | EDG 973 | 60 | 5 |
| S23 | B35R | 1946 Albion Valkyrie | 9/51- /52 | Red & White S1-946 | FAX 305-313 | | |
| | | " " " | 10/51- 1/53 | " " S10-2646 | EWO 759-775 | | |
| | | " " " | 11/51- /52 | " " S27-3046 | FAX 301-304 | | |
| | | 1947 " " | 11/51-11/53 | " " S1-1547 | FWO 635-9/55/6/40-7 | | 45 |
| DD20 | H30/26R | 1943 Guy Arab II | 1952 | United Welsh 666/7 | DWN 327/8 | | |
| | | 1944 " " | " | " " 677/81 | " 379 & 431 | | |
| | | 1943/44 " " | " | " " 690-2 | EWO 500, 753/4 | 61 | |
| | | 1944 " " | " | " " 693-5 | FAD 831/4/5 | 62 | 10 |
| DD21 | L27/28RD | 1942 Guy Arab I | late 1952 | Red & White L342 | EAX 646 | | |
| | | 1943 " Arab II | 6/54, 11/53 | " " L9/1343 | EWO 469/95 | | |
| | | " " " | 5/52- 6/54 | " " L14/5/7-2043 | EDG 968/71/2/6/5/4 | 60 | |
| | | 1944 " " | 4/52- 2/54 | " " L1-544 | EWO 752/5/7/6/8 | 63 | 14 |
| S24 | B35R | 1947 Leyland Tiger PS1/1 | late 52/early 53 | Red & White S24/5/747 | EU 8390, 8437 & 8540 | 64 | 3 |

NOTES:

60      Red & White L14-2043 (EDG 968/71/3/2/6/5/4) had previously been transferred from Cheltenham District.

61      United Welsh 690-2 (EWO 500, 753/4) had previously been transferred from Red & White.

62      United Welsh 693-5 (FAD 831/4/5) had been intended for Cheltenham District.

63      Red & White L544 (EWO 758) later received a windscreen from a Duple-bodied Guy Arab III.

64      Red & White S24/5/747 (EU 8390, 8437 & 8540) had been in the related fleet of Griffin Motor Company of Brynmawr. The S24 bodies were built by Longwell Green Coach Works.

# Bodies of Lydney Coachworks origin

finished or constructed by BBW after March 1952

| BODY CODE | LAYOUT | CHASSIS Date & Type | DATES | CUSTOMER | REGISTRATIONS | NOTES | GRAND TOTAL |
|---|---|---|---|---|---|---|---|
| None | C41F | new Leyland Royal Tiger PSU1/13 | by 8/52 | Red & White UC17-2251 | JWO 543-548 | | |
| | | " " " | " | United Welsh 999, 1000 | GWN 863/4 | 65 | 8 |
| UF1 | B45F | " " " | 11/52-7/53 | Red & White U6-3751 | JWO 221-242 & 549-558 | 66 | 32 |
| UF2 | C41C | new Guy Arab UF | 3-5/53 | South Midland 86-89 | SFC 501-504 | 67 | 4 |

NOTES

65      The bodies on Red & White UC17-2251 (JWO 543-548) and United Welsh 999 and 1000 (GWN 863/4) were Lydney bodies that were finished off by BBW.

66      The UF1 bodies on Red & White U6-3751 (JWO 221-242, 549-558) were built by BBW to Lydney design, from parts obtained from Lydney Coachworks.

67      The UF2 bodies on South Midland 86-89 (SFC 501-504) were built by BBW from parts obtained from Lydney Coachworks and were based on a Leyland design. South Midland was now a subsidiary of Thames Valley.

# Tilling Standard bodies – final production, 1954/55

| BODY CODE | LAYOUT | CHASSIS<br>Date & Type | DATES | CUSTOMER | REGISTRATIONS | NOTES | GRAND<br>TOTAL |
|---|---|---|---|---|---|---|---|
| S25 | B39R | lengthened 1942 L5G | 3/54 | Western National 366 | GTA 391 | 68 | |
| | | "      "      " | 2-3/54 | Southern National 372/3 | "   394/5 | | |
| | | "    1948 L6A | 2/54 | "      " 1236 | HOD 99 | 69 | |
| DD22 | L27/28R | 1939 K5G | 5/54 | Western National 285 | DDV 19 | | |
| | | 1941 " | 3-4/54 | Southern National 357-359 | FTA 640-642 | | |
| | | 1942 " | 5/54 | Western National 348/9 | GTA 392/3 | | |
| DD23 | L27/28R8 | 1942 K5G | 7/54 | United Counties 703/4 | BRP 232/3 | 70 | |
| | | 1944 " | " | "      " 707-709 | CBD 762-764 | | |
| DD24 | L27/26R | 1946 AEC Regal I | 7/54 | Western SMT C284/8/92, 300 | BAG 82/6, 90, 104 | | |
| | | "   "   " | 11/54 | "   " C275/6 | "   73/4 | | |
| | | "   "   " | 1/55 | "   " C280/90, 303/6 | "   78, 88, 107/10 | | |
| | | "   "   " | 3/55 | "   " C308/9 | "   112/3 | | 1 |
| S26 | B43R | lengthened 1938 L5G | 7/55 | Southern National 374-376 | CVF 843/4/8 | 71 | |

NOTES:

68   Western National 366 (GTA 391) had originally carried a BBW UB34F utility body.
69   Southern National 1236 (HOD 99) had previously been a Beadle-bodied Royal Blue coach, but its original body was destroyed by fire in 1951.
70   The DD23 bodies for United Counties were the only eight-foot-wide bodies built by BBW, other than those of Lydney origin.
71   Southern National 374-6 (CVF 843/4/8) had been purchased from Eastern Counties in 3/54.

---

## Grand total of BBW passenger bodies constructed between 1907 and 1955 = 2,343

These figures include the bodies built by the Bristol Aeroplane Company, Bence Motor Bodies and Longwell Green Coachworks on behalf of BBW, but do not include the eight Lydney bodies finished by BBW.

---

# List of BBW bodies known to survive in 1999

This list has been prepared with the kind assistance of Alan Neale.

| BODY CODE | LAYOUT | DATE | CHASSIS | CUSTOMER | REG'N | PRESENT OWNER | NOTES |
|---|---|---|---|---|---|---|---|
| HA | B32F | 1924 | 4-Tonner | West Riding 142 | HL 1803 | Graham Donaldson, Dewsbury | |
| DD6 | H30/26R | 1940 | K5G | BT&CC C3336 | GHT 154 | B.V.B.G., Bristol | |
| Unknown | B35R | 1942 | 1933 H (5LW) | Western National 137 | FJ 8967 | Colin Billington, Maidenhead | Undergoing restoration from a Showman's van. |
| S15 | B35R | 1947 | 1934 J (5LW) | BT&CC 2355 | AHU 803 | B.V.B.G., Bristol | Restoration completed in 1998. |
| Unknown | B35R | 1950 | 1948 L6B | BT&CC 2382 | KHY 383 | Mr Swineard; kept at Dover Transport Mus. | Restored to its original coach livery. |
| Unknown | B(35)R | 1950 | 1939 L5G | BT&CC 1254 | CFH 604 | Carter's Steam Fair, Maidenhead | Used as living accommodation, but exterior maintained in good condition. |
| S20 | B35R | 1950 | 1946 L5G | BT&CC 2174 | JHT 827 | K M Pearce, Claverham, nr. Bristol | Owned by Pearce family since 1962. |
| S20 | B35R | 1950 | 1948 L5G | BT&CC 2388 | LHT 911 | Kelvin Amos, Nailsea, near Bristol | |
| Unknown | B35R | 1951 | 1946 L5G | BT&CC 2180 | JHT 833 | | In Zimbabwe, having been exported in 1961. Until 1991 it was an outside museum in Mutare. |
| DD18 | L27/28RD | 1951 | 1942 Guy Arab I | Red & White L442 | EWO 467 | D & J Allen, Ross-on-Wye | Preserved in livery of Provincial 77. |
| S25 | B39R | 1954 | 1942 L5G | Southern National 373 | GTA 395 | R Cook, Honiton | Kept at West of England Transport Museum, Winkleigh. |